PHYSICAL ACTIVITY AND LEARNING AFTER SCHOOL

Also Available

The Psychology of Reading: Theory and Applications
Paula J. Schwanenflugel and Nancy Flanagan Knapp

Physical Activity and Learning After School

The PAL Program

edited by
Paula J. Schwanenflugel
Phillip D. Tomporowski

THE GUILFORD PRESS
New York   London

Library of Congress Cataloging-in-Publication data is available from the publisher.

ISBN 978-1-4625-3267-4 (paperback)
ISBN 978-1-4625-3268-1 (hardcover)

To the memory of Dr. Martha "Marty" Carr,
who inspired us to bring research-based
educational practices to after-school programming

To Dr. Clifton A. "Cliff" Bale,
who inspired us to translate research
on the physiology and biochemistry
of obesity into after-school activities for children

Both of these scholars provided models
for conducting important interdisciplinary research.

About the Editors

Paula J. Schwanenflugel, PhD, is Professor of Educational Psychology at the University of Georgia. Dr. Schwanenflugel is author or coauthor of several books and numerous book chapters and journal articles on the development of reading fluency and vocabulary learning in young children. She is a codirector of the Physical Activity and Learning (PAL) Program, a project involving faculty from multiple disciplines at the University of Georgia. Dr. Schwanenflugel oversees the PAL reading enrichment program.

Phillip D. Tomporowski, PhD, is Professor of Kinesiology at the University of Georgia. Dr. Tomporowski is author or coauthor of several books and numerous book chapters and journal articles on the role of exercise in improving cognitive functioning in children and older adults. He is the principal investigator and director of the PAL Program.

Contributors

Megan P. Brock, MS, Department of Educational Psychology, College of Education, University of Georgia, Athens, Georgia

Martha M. Carr, PhD (deceased), Department of Educational Psychology, College of Education, University of Georgia, Athens, Georgia

Justin T. Dooly, MAT, Department of Educational Theory and Practice, College of Education, University of Georgia, Athens, Georgia

Jennifer L. Gay, PhD, College of Public Health, University of Georgia, Athens, Georgia

Yi-Jung Lee, MS, Department of Mathematics and Science Education, College of Education, University of Georgia, Athens, Georgia

E. Nicole McCluney, MS, Department of Kinesiology, College of Education, University of Georgia, Athens, Georgia

Bryan A. McCullick, PhD, Department of Kinesiology, College of Education, University of Georgia, Athens, Georgia

Paula J. Schwanenflugel, PhD, Department of Educational Psychology, College of Education, University of Georgia, Athens, Georgia

Phillip D. Tomporowski, PhD, Department of Kinesiology, College of Education, University of Georgia, Athens, Georgia

Katherine Wargo, MPH, Centers for Disease Control and Prevention, Atlanta, Georgia

Contents

1

The Physical Activity and Learning Program and the 21st Century Community Learning Centers Initiative

Bryan A. McCullick
Phillip D. Tomporowski

If you are reading this book, chances are that you have a significant interest in developing or are already involved in a nonschooltime program designed to benefit children. If that is the case, then welcome to the "club." The editors of this book and the authors of the chapters in it are also concerned with children's well-being and have embarked on a 5-year journey toward developing and implementing a program that can help children improve physically, academically, and socially.

The aim of this chapter is to provide you with background information about and a description of how the contributors to this book, a group of university faculty, graduate and undergraduate students, principals, and other partners, created a research-based after-school program (ASP) designed to improve children's physical, academic, and social performance. In addition to describing the process and the parties involved, we present an overview of the funding source through which the program is supported—the *21st Century Community Learning Centers* (CCLC) program.

Our reason for providing this background information and overview is to familiarize you with one way in which such an ASP was established and is operated. Our intent is not to imply that our way is the best or only way; we just suggest that the process we pursued, and the challenges and modest success we experienced, is one with which readers might empathize and from which they could learn. Recognizing that not all who seek to develop ASPs have the same objectives that we do, we believe that our experiences and an outline of the corresponding details about our program can provide some helpful guidance, regardless of the specific goals for any program.

Although we could write much about the minutiae we had to confront and the barriers we had to navigate, we do not want to communicate details that might only be pertinent to our own particular setting. You will, no doubt, encounter your own issues unique to your own settings. Instead, we present (1) a brief historical overview of why ASPs have become ubiquitous and how they contribute to today's schooling, (2) the development of our particular program from its birth in laboratory settings, (3) our implementation process through the 21st CCLC program, and, finally, (4) an overview of our Physical Activity and Learning (PAL) Program, its aims, components, and multiple outcomes.

20th- and 21st-Century Views of Schooling

Before walking you through the process of how we started the PAL Program, we believe that it is essential to locate it in the landscape of modern education. In order to do this, it helps to discuss American schooling in a historical context. This section provides a brief summary of the contrast between schooling in the 20th and 21st centuries, so that you can gain an understanding of why programs like ours are needed and valued.

Shifting Views of Education

Prior to the industrialization of North America in the early decades of the 20th century, families lived primarily in rural farming areas. In concert with the migration of workers and their families to large cities, public school systems that were designed to address industrial-age priorities emerged. One role of public schools was to accommodate the need for future workers in an industrialized society. Education focused on the identification of talented youth and on training that connected them to future jobs and careers. Public schools were viewed by policymakers as institutions that instilled individuals with a work ethic and the capacity to benefit from vocational training. They were designed to meet the needs of the period for disciplined, skilled individuals who could withstand the demands of labor required on the shop floor and the industrial assembly line (Lawson, 1993; Lawson, Tomporowski, & Pendleton, 2014).

The progressive education movement, which influenced educators from the late 1800s to the 1960s, stressed the selection of classroom instruction that focused on teaching useful skills (Tomporowski, 2003). Teachers in early 20th-century schools were trained to teach classes on specific topics, which were presented in a modular fashion. Teachers were also charged with establishing good citizenship attitudes and moral development in their students. Over the ensuing decades, children's in-school activities were often influenced by prevailing political and cultural attitudes and military needs (Lawson, 2009). Less emphasis was placed on children's education during periods prior to or following the school day. It was left to parents to address children's needs during nonschooltime. The rise of community programs (e.g., YMCA, YWCA, Boys and Girls Clubs) during the early 20th century, the promotion of sports clubs in the mid-20th century, and the growth of before- and after-school activity programs over the past few decades attested to the dichotomy between in-school and out-of-school education. ASPs for children, particularly those for children from low-income families, were the domain of charitable and religious groups, certainly not the public sector.

Early 20th-century American schools were quite successful in preparing individuals for future employment and giving them opportunities to advance both economically and socially. The impact of the American school system was particularly effective in providing instruction and guidance to children of immigrant families. In-school educators and out-of-school coaches often came to serve as surrogate parents and guardians for children and youth whose families were faced with assimilating into a new nation and culture (Lawson, 1993).

Social changes beginning in the 1960s, shifts toward industrial globalization, and federal legislation, such as the No Child Left Behind educational funding act, have led to debates about the focus of American education and its place in modern society. Some educators suggest a radical change in how children are educated (Lawson, 2009). Researchers who study educational policies suggest that modern schools need to change and adapt to the way that the world has changed. Predictions about the effects of globalization, population mobility, and changes in employment opportunities have led to recommendations concerning the role of schools and the preparation of students. Beyond introducing students to the skills that they will need in the workplace, public schools are seen as part of an ecological network that maximizes the interactive nature of multiple factors that determine an individual's physical, mental, and social well-being. The World Health Organization (WHO) adopted an ecological model of healthy development in the late 1990s that emphasized five interactive levels: (1) the individual, which reflects each person's unique personality traits and dispositions; (2) interpersonal relationships, which fulfill children's needs for care and support from parents, family, and friends; (3) social institutions, such as schools, in which teachers enhance both academic and social development; (4) the community groups, such as religious or social organizations that teach sets of rules and expectancies for developing children; and (5) policymakers, whose opinions strongly influence local, state, or federal regulations.

21st-Century Views of Education

This ecological model, with its focus on integration of input from multiple constituents, differs considerably from the early 20th-century educational approach. It champions a mutually beneficial relationship among schools, parents, community organizations, and policymakers. Furthermore, advocates of contemporary ecological approaches to education emphasize the importance of the "whole child," that is, one who is educated throughout each day at home, and before, during, and after school. The "Whole School, Whole Community, Whole Child (WSCC)" ecological model, for example, expands upon the WHO model and emphasizes the importance of the social and emotional climate and the physical environment. The developers of the WSCC model stressed the need for learning conditions that enrich each child's physical, mental, social, and affective development. The belief is that children who feel they are in safe and predictable environments, and who are challenged by mentally and physically engaging learning tasks, will develop the critical thinking skills they need throughout their lives. Proponents of the WSCC model stress the need for schools and communities to change from teaching specific content information to providing cross-disciplinary learning experiences.

The shift in the focus of children's educational experiences reflected the American family's economic needs. In the late 1990s there were more Americans working over 50 hours per week than in almost all other industrialized nations (Jacobs & Gerson, 1998). The percentage of women working outside the home shifted from 40% in 1976 to 55% in 1993 (Rones, Ilg, & Gardner, 1997). Coupled with welfare reform legislation in 1996 (the Personal Responsibility and Work Reconciliation Act; Giuliani, 1996), which reduced welfare entitlements, U.S. work patterns changed dramatically. These economic and social changes led policymakers to target out-of-school time for those children who were in greatest need of educational experiences—children who live in poverty.

More than 20 million of those living in poverty in the United States today are under the age of 18 years. Data showing that individuals living in communities of concentrated poverty (e.g., an income of less than $24,300 for a family of four) increased from 49.5 million people to 77.4 million between 2000 and 2010 are particularly troubling. Based on reports of recent census data (Afterschool Alliance, 2016), black and Hispanic children are at least two times as likely as white children to live in communities of concentrated poverty; 45% of black, 35% of Hispanic, and 12% of white children are in families living in communities of concentrated poverty.

The negative impact of poverty on children's development and on their ability to gain from educational experiences is well supported by research. Numerous studies have linked environmental conditions in communities of concentrated poverty with a wide range of biological, behavioral, and mental health outcomes. Children who live in concentrated poverty show a higher incidence of health problems,

higher levels of stress, and behavioral control issues than those not living in poverty. All of these factors have been purported to compromise children's learning
and academic achievement. Indeed, some of the conditions associated with childhood poverty, such as poorer academic skills and physical well-being, have been
targeted by elements of the ASP described in this book.

Policymakers have enacted a number of national and state programs that
enhance the development of children of families in lower-income tiers. The Head
Start program, for example, is a national, large-scale intervention study that began
in 1965. It was initiated to evaluate the impact of enhanced social and educational
services on preschool children who lived in low-income, multirisk communities.
Head Start reflected a change in the views of the educability of children. During
the first half of the 20th century, the consensus was that human intelligence was
essentially fixed by genetic factors, and that environmental conditions and educational methods contributed relatively little to adaptive intellectual function. In
the 1960s, a number of influential psychologists and social scientists promoted
the view that intelligence was mutable and could be affected either in a positive or
negative manner by environmental factors (Ramey & Ramey, 2004). The question
of how environmental enrichment may affect children's general intelligence has
been, and continues to be, debated vigorously (Zigler & Styfco, 2004). Indeed, the
assumption that environmental enrichment can enhance children's cognitive development is central to several recently conducted studies that examine the effects of
exercise training on children's mental performance (see Chapter 4, Tomporowski
& McCullick, this volume).

21st Century Community Learning Centers

More recently, policymakers and concerned organizations have focused directly on
the need for quality out-of-school enrichment programs. In 2000 the Afterschool
Alliance was created with the mission to increase public and private investment in
quality after-school initiatives at the national, state, and local levels (Afterschool
Alliance, 2016). As a public–private partnership, the alliance helped expand children's after-school experiences through the 21st CCLC ASP. The 21st CCLC program is the only federal funding source dedicated exclusively to ASPs. The national
program was authorized as part of the No Child Left Behind Act in 2002, and
then later transferred the administration of the grants from the U.S. Department
of Education to the state education agencies.

The 21st CCLC program was again reauthorized in 2015 in the Every Student
Succeeds Act (ESSA). Each state receives funds based on its share of Title I funding
for low-income students. Grants support ASPs that provide a wide array of services
to students attending high-poverty, low-performing schools. Funds can be used for
services including literacy education; integrated education, health, social service,

recreational, or cultural programs; summer and weekend school programs; and parenting skills programs.

Entities eligible to apply for funding include local educational agencies (LEAs), cities, counties, community-based agencies, other public or private entities (which may include faith-based organizations), or a consortium of two or more such agencies, organizations, or entities. Applicants are required to plan their programs through a collaborative process that includes parents, youth, representatives of participating schools or local educational agencies, governmental agencies (e.g., cities, counties, parks and recreation departments), community organizations, and the private sector.

As we explained at the outset, the focus of this chapter is to describe the history of the development of the PAL Program, funded by a 21st CCLC grant administered by the Georgia Department of Education. After telling the story of how the PAL Program developed, we present a general overview of the goals and structure of an ASP that combines the expertise of six University of Georgia faculty to provide theory-based interventions that enhance children's health, academic performance, socialization, and well-being. We then introduce the topics described in the remaining chapters of the book. Each chapter was developed as a collaboration between each University of Georgia faculty member and his or her graduate and undergraduate students.

Development of the PAL Program

The PAL Program was designed as a translational research intervention. The goal of translational research is the uptake, implementation, and sustainability of research findings in real-world conditions (Estabrooks & Glasgow, 2006). Much of the basic science research conducted worldwide is performed in university and national laboratories. However, the tripartite mission of the University of Georgia is to serve the needs of the state and the nation via teaching, research, and service. By developing after-school programming in our community around research-based practices, we were putting into practice an interdisciplinary effort targeted at all of these missions. Our early work was motivated by our research experiences and the desire to improve the lives of children in our community.

Our translational research approach was designed to determine whether exercise interventions conducted under laboratory conditions would show similar beneficial effects in authentic ASPs. Our methods were guided by a general RE-AIM model of translational research developed by Glasgow and colleagues (Gaglio, Shoup, & Glasgow, 2013; Glasgow, Klesges, Dzewaltowski, Bull, & Eastbrooks, 2004). The model consists of five components:

Reach: The number of children and parents expected to participate.
Effectiveness: The impact of the intervention on participants' quality of life.

    Adoption: The success of the program based on the number of schools that
       adopt it.
    Implementation: How consistently the program is delivered and the time and
       cost of the intervention.
    Maintenance: The degree to which the program maintains participants' adher-
       ence and becomes institutionalized.

The themes of the RE-AIM model are reflected in the following chapters of this
book.

Formative Laboratory-Based Research

Our understanding of the relationship among exercise, brain function, and cognition advanced considerably in the early 2000s. Initial experiments conducted
with older adults revealed that systematic aerobic exercise produced changes in
the structure and functioning of the central nervous system and corresponding
changes in executive functions, which are central to information processing and
decision making (Kramer et al., 1999). During this period, parallel research conducted with animals revealed that exercise training improved neural integrity via
brain plasticity and learning. The consensus of these researchers was that exercise
training held the potential for long-term changes in the way that individuals think
and learn (Kempermann, 2008; Kempermann et al., 2010).

These early findings influenced researchers interested in children's mental
development. The rationale for targeting children was expressed in terms of the
cognitive reserve hypothesis, which proposed that the benefits of aerobic exercise
would be greatest for children and older adults because they had more to gain from
enrichment interventions than young and middle-age adults, who were at the peak
of their physical and mental abilities (Etnier & Chang, 2009).

A number of studies have demonstrated a positive relationship between children's level of physical fitness and physical activity levels and cognitive and academic performance. As Chapter 4 describes in greater detail, reviews of the literature conclude that exercise interventions have a small-to-moderate effect-size
benefit on children's cognition (Donnelly et al., 2016; Fedewa & Ahn, 2011);
however, the strength of the relationship appears to differ according to the type
of intervention, and even small benefits can accumulate over time if they are systematic. Beginning in the mid-2010s, we began to consider the effects of different
types of exercise and physical activities on children's cognitive function and academic achievement.

Exercise Intervention

Early research funded by the National Institutes of Health (NIH) conducted at
Augusta University (formerly known as Augusta University) focused on the health

benefits of aerobic exercise on children's health. An initial program called FIT-KID trial was an ASP conducted as a field-based study at 18 elementary schools in the Augusta, Georgia, area. Children who participated in 80-minute sessions of vigorous game activities improved in fitness and lost weight during the school months (Gutin, Barbeau, & Yin, 2004). As a follow-up, a laboratory-based experiment called the PLAY trial tested dose–response effects of exercise on health risk factors and mental function of 222 healthy, overweight children ages 7–11. A dose–response effect for exercise on children's performance on standardized tests of cognition and academic achievement was observed, as were improvements in children's social behavior (Davis et al., 2007; Davis et al., 2011). Similar laboratory research conducted over several decades by multiple researchers illustrates that the benefits children derive from exercise will impact not only their physical development, but also their mental development, cognitive function, and academic achievement (Donnelly et al., 2016). Working in concert with like-minded researchers and teacher educators, we created a theory-based approach to *physical activity games* (PAGs), which were field tested in a community elementary school in 2011–2013 and later described in a book, *Enhancing Children's Cognition with Physical Activities Games* (Tomporowski, McCullick, & Pesce, 2015).

Physical Activity Games

Our PAGs are designed to challenge children's decision-making and strategy skills. Games are played at moderate-to-vigorous levels of aerobic activity and require children to make rapid decisions concerning when, where, and how to move. When conducted properly, alterations and variations in the way games are played give children the opportunity to learn and practice decision-making skills and strategies. During transitions between games, children have opportunities to describe how and why they selected ways to achieve the goals of the games. Through student–teacher discussions, children consider alternative ways to play games and interact with their peers. Together the PAGs are assumed to create the conditions required to enhance the cognitive and metacognitive processes that underlie children's self-control and self-awareness (see McCluney, Chapter 5, this volume).

The physical activity component of the PAL Program reflects information gleaned from over 20 years of after-school interventions conducted by researchers at the Georgia Prevention Institute (GPI) of Augusta University and the University of Georgia (UGA). Over the past 4 years, our goal has been to modify the exercise intervention used in prior laboratory-based research for application in traditional school settings. Modifications have been based on recent advances in educational theory and evidence that bouts of physical activity prepare children to succeed in STEM (science, technology, engineering, and mathematics) classes. In 2010, support from the Georgia Board of Regents led to the development of an instructional manual for the PAG portion of this intervention. Our work enabled us to receive other financial support to conduct two successful pilot after-school physical activity programs at one of the current PAL Program sites in 2011 and 2013.

A number of group-participation games chosen for the PAL Program are derived from the book *Enhancing Children's Cognition with Physical Activity Games* (Tomporowski et al., 2015). The PAL Program games are used each day to afford children the opportunity to engage in physical activity at the intensity and the duration needed to reap real health benefits. The activities capitalize on developmentally linked motor behaviors and games designed to motivate children to be physically active. The instructional model is innovative, as it engages children in developmentally appropriate games, as opposed to simply leading repetitive aerobic exercise programs in which children quickly lose interest. Engagement is characterized by relatively high amounts of attention, interest, effort, and enjoyment that occur during the process of learning. Furthermore, the games are structured so that children from ages 7–11 can safely and appropriately play together, which is paramount in ASP settings that serve children from a wide age range.

Children in the PAL Program benefit from the games in three important ways. The games (1) provide children the opportunity to meet established national physical activity guidelines (Physical Activity Guidelines Advisory Committee, 2008), (2) promote the motor skill development necessary to engage in recreation and games across the lifespan, and (3) develop problem-solving skills that strengthen the development of fundamental cognitive abilities, such as inhibition and planning, which underlie math, reading, and science. These predictions are based on over two decades of basic research. The structure of the PAL Program differs from the traditional ASP organizational structure in that children engage in PAGs before beginning academic enrichment. Recent research demonstrates that a brief period of mentally engaging physical activity prepares children to attend and learn, which counters the long-held belief that physical arousal interferes with academic learning. In fact, several studies reveal the opposite to be true (Donnelly et al., 2016). The PAL Program schedule is designed to use physical activity to optimize gains from math and reading programs that follow physical activity programming.

Pilot Studies

If we could provide one caution to readers, who are considering the development of an ASP with goals similar to ours, we would suggest experimenting with several ideas before putting together a proposal. While 2014 was the first year of the PAL Program, the idea for the program was born well before then, and our ideas were supported by laboratory research that had to be tested in the "real world." Without this step, it is doubtful we would have been able to make a case for our program to school administrators and funding agencies. Internal funding from the UGA provided support to conduct a pilot study to assess the implementation of the PAG intervention as part of an ongoing ASP in a community elementary school. With the assistance of school administers and staff, children in grades 2–5 were recruited to participate in a 60-minute intervention, which was delivered by trained university students. The interventions were conducted during over a 2-year period (2011–2013) and generated the quantitative and qualitative data needed to refine PAG parameters and the teacher-training and implementation methods. The results of the interventions provided the basis for the application to the 21st CCLC funding initiative.

During these interventions, the PAGs that had been created and modified were taught to children in an existing ASP. Beyond providing the ASP with a structured physical activity that the program would not ordinarily have, it allowed us to see how well the PAGs would work for children of varying ages at different developmental, skill, and cognitive levels. Additional problems were noted, and the games were modified as necessary, with a few games being altered significantly because they were too complex; however, an overwhelming majority were modified only modestly or not changed at all.

In addition to refining the PAGs, another intervention sought to determine whether a teacher training program could help an inexperienced ASP proctor learn to teach PAGs that engaged children physically and cognitively at rates akin to a high-quality physical education class. Using modeling, individualized instructional supervision, and a gradual assignment of instructional responsibilities, we were able to train an adult to teach PAGs that resulted in high rates of student engagement both physically (64%) and cognitively (34%). While the results of this intervention provided data on only one ASP proctor who was able to provide specialized and targeted training, the findings did hold promise for the idea that we might be able to help other ASP proctors who were not trained to teach physical activity do so in a way that benefited children (McCullick & Tomporowski, 2014). The results of these interventions provided the basis for the PAL Program and the impetus to seek funding for it.

The 21st CCLC Application Process

Once we thought we had implemented an effective PAL Program, it was time to expand it and inquire about introducing it to local schools. As previously mentioned, the 21st CCLC program was an obvious fit as a funding source, but an application to this program became a major undertaking. Thus, we began a process that warranted that we simultaneously: (1) seek school-district and individual school partners, (2) conduct needs assessments, and (3) find partners with expertise in other facets of a comprehensive ASP to join us. At this point, we feel that a description of the PAL Program development would be incomplete if we were not able to share the not-so-easy road we traveled to implementation. Not only would it be incomplete, it would be unfair, because it might suggest that all one needs to do start a program is to find a funding source. So this section of the chapter is intended to outline the major issues we confronted as we tried to bring the PAL Program to fruition. A review of potential funding sources revealed the unique characteristics of the 21st CCLC.

School Administration and Environment

The principals of two elementary schools in a local school district agreed to collaborate with the authors. We met with the district's deputy superintendent and other administrative personnel to discuss the collaborative nature of the project, the selection of elementary schools, and the strategies for gathering needs-assessment data. Discussions were directed toward incorporating a specialized PAGs learning experience, a specialized mathematics enrichment program, and a specialized reading enrichment program for children with academic and social needs. The particular arrangement of the proposed enrichment activities to be offered was discussed in detail, and the responsibilities and commitments of both sets of partners were agreed upon. The superintendent granted access to the county student database for the identification and recruitment of children. UGA faculty described the recruitment parameters required by the 21st CCLC program to members of each of the schools' councils, which included parents, teachers, and community members. The primary purpose of these meetings was to address methods to best identify students who might benefit from the proposed ASP. A focus-group approach was used to gather information.

Both schools were nearly identical in terms of the number of students, but there were differences that needed to be closely considered (see Table 1.1). School A already had an ASP in place. However, the program required parents to pay a fee for both the activity and transportation, which made it financially prohibitive for many of the students' families, especially those who had multiple children needing after-school services. In terms of recruitment, this meant that we had to be very clear that we were distinct from the existing ASP and that cost and transportation would be covered for all children. The information gathered from our meetings sent a clear message to us that these two obstacles made it nearly impossible for some families to send their children to ASPs. Logistically, this required careful organization of resources (gymnasium and classroom space), and cooperation between the PAL Program and the existing ASP had to be negotiated and established.

At School B, there was no existing ASP even though there appeared to be a demand for one. The principal made it clear that parents wanted an ASP, but not necessarily for the reasons we were offering ours—they merely needed child care for their children after the school day ended. This might have seemed to provide an advantage for us in terms of recruiting students, but it created another small obstacle in that we had to communicate to parents that the program was only targeting children in grades 2–5 who were performing suboptimally in both math and reading achievement.

Further, we had to consider the issues inherent with ASPs, such as the differences in children's developmental levels. Unlike during the school day when children are grouped in classes by age (e.g., 8-year-olds in second grade), an ASP can only segregate the children so much by age, something that needed to be considered given the range of skills and sizes of the children involved. Because we only had 30 spaces available for distribution among four grade levels, it was nearly impossible for us to operate the PAL Program without intermingling children of different ages, developmental levels, and size. We were able to group second and third graders separately from the fourth and fifth graders for reading and math enrichment sessions, but for the PAGs portion, all 30 students would be participating at once. This meant that our PAGs had to be designed so that children of varying skill and strength levels and physical sizes could participate safely and in a way that met their respective needs.

Community Demographics

The criteria established by the 21st CCLC program for the recruitment of students are factors that affect the educational outcomes of the identified students. These factors may include poverty rates in the communities to be served; literacy and math rates/scores; educational levels for the identified students and their families; grade retention data; short-term suspension/discipline rates; long-term suspensions or expulsion data; and attendance data. The children who were selected to attend resided in a high-poverty county in northeast Georgia, which, based on the 2010 Census, had a population of over 100,000 people spread among over 40,000 households. The ethnic makeup was diverse, with approximately 60% white, 25%

TABLE 1.1. Demographic Information for Schools
in the PAL Program

	August	
	School A	School B
Number of students	486	483
African American	34%	48%
Asian American	1%	0%
Hispanic American	8%	42%
Multiracial	4%	3%
European American	53%	6%

black or African American, 10% Hispanic, and approximately 5% Asian or Native American. Median family income was low, approximately a little over $30,000, with a per capita income of around $20,000. About one-third of the population had incomes below the poverty line. The county ranked among the high-poverty counties both in the state and nationally, establishing it as well within the top 10 high-poverty communities in the nation.

Establishing Intervention Goals

The purpose of the 21st CCLC program, as described in the federal statute, is to provide opportunities for communities to establish or expand activities that focus on improved academic achievement, on enrichment services that reinforce and complement the academic program, and on family literacy and related educational development services. In order to determine specific goals for the children in the schools we were targeting, we needed to drill down deeper into the data and consult multiple parties. A needs assessment revealed the necessity of providing enrichment activities that focused on improving the physical health, academic success, and the social climate for a number of children who attended the targeted elementary schools. Considerable research suggests that enrichment services that emphasize children's physical activity programs can favorably impact not only health but also many other dimensions of children's lives.

The *ecological family model* (Davidson, Jurkowski, & Lawson, 2013), which is central to the PAL Program, describes multiple factors that impact a child's development. The ecological family model is a specific variant of ecological systems theory of human development that concentrates on family functioning. The theory claims that "human behavior cannot be understood without taking into consideration the contexts in which it occurs" (p. 1862). When considering families, the view is that parenting and family functioning are best understood in terms of the broader impacts that encourage or discourage particular behaviors. These broader impacts include policies and the media, family demographics, community characteristics, organizational characteristics, such as schools and parental occupations, and child characteristics. The goal of the PAL Program was to embed the program within this larger ecological family context.

The children selected for the PAL Program were influenced by many factors that might affect their participation, for example, large family size, economic disadvantages, lack of sufficient mentorship and guidance, lack of access to game and play activities, and many others. No single factor was responsible for some of these children to find it difficult to meet and overcome the everyday academic and social challenges experienced in school settings.

A description of PAL Program goals, outcome measures, and related activities is provided in Table 1.2. The math and reading enrichment activities portions of the PAL Program were linked to the Georgia Performance Standards *(www.*

georgiastandards.org/Standards/Pages/BrowseStandards/BrowseGPS.aspx). The math enrichment activities targeted mathematics fluency and sense of number line at each grade level (see Lee, Chapter 7, this volume, for details). The reading enrichment activities directly targeted reading fluency and informational text literacy (see Brock & Schwanenflugel, Chapter 10, this volume, for details). The PAGs were aligned with the Georgia Performance Standards for physical education in grades 2–5. They targeted children's health-related physical fitness and motor movement skills (see McCluney, Chapter 5, this volume, for details). To promote family engagement, the project codirectors worked directly with school administrators and advisory councils to reach out to parents in ways that were aligned with existing school efforts.

Since the underlying assumption of the PAL Program is that a physically healthy child has more potential to succeed academically than a physically unhealthy child, one of our aims was to inform both children and families of the benefits of a physically active lifestyle. Children who live in concentrated poverty areas are affected by a multitude of factors that can alter their physical, social, and mental development (Jurkowski, Lawson, Green Mills, Wilner, & Davison, 2014). Children who gain knowledge through their physical movements and experience become more efficient in their thinking and problem solving (Thelen, 2004). Self-initiated actions are critical for learning and are particularly important for young children. Some researchers suggest that many children exhibit an *exercise deficit disorder*

TABLE 1.2. The Goals, Outcome Measures, and Related Activities for the PAL Program

Goals	Outcome measures	Activities
Meeting children's academic needs	a) AIMSweb benchmarking system for mathematics b) AIMSweb benchmarking system for reading c) Grade reports d) Georgia Milestones scores e) Classroom teacher survey f) Enrichment-specific assessments of progress	a) Grade-appropriate math enrichment activities focused on fluency AND mental representation b) Grade-appropriate reading enrichment activities focused on reading fluency AND information text comprehension c) Daily homework assistance
Meeting children's physical activity needs	a) FITNESSGRAM Test of aerobic fitness b) FITNESSGRAM Test of motor proficiency	a) PAGs
Meeting children's socialization needs through parent involvement and engagement	a) Parent attendance records; program agenda and sign-in sheets b) Parent Satisfaction Questionnaire	a) Parent engagement activities focused on family health b) Distribution and discussion of health information

(EDD) that leads to long-term negative consequences on physical and social habits (Faigenbaum, Stracciolini, & Myer, 2011). EDD is defined as "a pediatric medical condition characterized by reduced levels of moderate-to-vigorous physical activity (MVPA) that are below current recommendations and inconsistent with positive health outcomes" (Faigenbaum, Best, MacDonald, Myer, & Stracciolini, 2014, p. 297). The National Physical Activity Guidelines recommend that children be physically active 60 minutes per day to achieve long-term behavioral changes and health outcomes. Prevention efforts are known to be most successful if they are effectively established in early childhood. The impact of physical activity education on health is expected to be most effective if it is directed toward elementary school children and their parents or caregivers, with continued and repeated emphasis of these messages and initiatives through adolescence (Taras, 2005; Taras & Potts-Datema, 2005).

The physical activity component is the linchpin of the PAL Program. On a daily basis, bouts of physical activity are coupled with reading and math enrichment activities to promote fast rates of reading and math learning. Conducted on a regular basis, physical activity will promote improvements in both physical health and mental function—which together underlie children's behavior and learning.

Recruiting the Children Who Might Benefit Most

Recruitment included consulting school teachers, guidance counselors, and administrators to identify children who were (1) at risk of academic, physical fitness/health, and social–behavioral deficiencies; (2) from economically disadvantaged families; (3) not receiving academic enrichment services from any other program; and (4) not achieving adequate academic progress in mathematics and/or reading as measured by criterion-referenced competency test (CRCT) scores, which were the state assessments given in elementary school in grades 3 and 5. The relevant descriptive data for the children participating in the PAL Program are presented in Table 1.3. As of the writing of this book, 230 children in grades 2–5 have been served by the PAL Program.

Securing Cross-Disciplinary Partnerships and the Creation of the PAL Program

The PAL Program was developed and is being conducted under the leadership of six codirectors, each having a specific area of expertise. The intent of the partnership was to create a cross-disciplinary program that provided faculty an opportunity to serve as mentors for graduate and undergraduate students learning to provide theory-based interventions and to conduct research on building beneficial after-school environments for young children. Participating codirectors included faculty from the Department of Kinesiology (Phillip Tomporowski and Bryan McCullick); from the Department of Educational Psychology (Paula Schwanenflugel and

TABLE 1.3. Number and Characteristics of Children
Participating in the PAL Program 2014–2017

	Year 1	Year 2	Year 3
Number of children	89	77	64
Girls	31	37	31
Boys	58	40	33
African American	58	57	50
Asian American	0	0	0
Hispanic American	26	14	12
Multiracial	0	0	0
European American	5	6	1

Marty Carr); from the College of Education, Department of Health Promotion and Behavior (Jennifer Gay); from the College of Public Health, and Department of Human Development and Family Science and from the College of Family and Consumer Sciences (Emilie Smith). These faculty partners had a history of providing successful research-based interventions that had positively affected child outcomes in the context of schooling or public health.

The PAL Program application was submitted to the Georgia Department of Education, where it was reviewed and subsequently funded for a 5-year period beginning July 2014. The 21st CCLC program funding mechanism differs from typical academic research grants (e.g., NIH, National Science Foundation) in that the amount of funding is determined by the number of children provided services. In addition, funded programs are expected to develop sustainability to ensure that the intervention remains active following the end of the funding period.

Program Implementation

Overview of the Day

Programming began at 2:45 P.M. each day and ended at 5:30 P.M. Children enrolled in the PAL Program reported immediately to their designated space where program staff and volunteers awaited. The Georgia Afterschool & Youth Development Quality Standards (*http://georgiaasyd.org/quality-standards/*) indicate that ASPs should "incorporate academic support including homework assistance" (p. 8) and provide a "nutritious snack and/or meal options" if the program is of sufficient duration (p. 14). Toward this end, the PAL Program began each session with homework assistance from the program staff coupled with a healthy snack. While the children completed homework, staff and volunteers were available for assistance, mentoring, and maintaining an atmosphere conducive to completing the homework tasks (e.g., little to no distraction). Those students who may not have had homework were required to bring personal reading or other academic work and completed it during this 35-minute time period.

At approximately 3:20 P.M., children transitioned to the gymnasium along with the three PAL Program staff and any volunteers. For 45 minutes, the PAG teacher led a session of games, while other instructional staff and volunteers provided managerial support. At the conclusion of this period, children used the restroom, got water, and transitioned to one of two classrooms. For the remaining 45 minutes, children were given either math or reading enrichment activities before being transported home at 5:30 P.M. each day.

The Role of the University of Georgia

The vast majority of 21st CCLC grantees are nonprofit organizations, such as the Boys and Girls Clubs, YMCA, YWCA, and city organizations that partner with school districts. Nationwide, other universities and colleges also participate as grantees, but they are a minority. The PAL Program was an outgrowth the University of Georgia's land-grant mission and was a response to a specific university initiative—the University of Georgia Obesity Initiative.

As children mature into adolescence and young adulthood, their physical inactivity is linked to low levels of physical fitness and increases in overweight. Overweight children are more likely to become obese adults, and an overweight school-age child with an obese parent has a greater than 70% chance of being obese in young adulthood (Child Health Scorecard; How, 2011). These data are particularly important as The Commonwealth Fund's Child Health 2011 Scorecard ranked Georgia 43rd among the states and the District of Columbia for child health and 49th in the percentage of children who are overweight or obese. Overweight status among young children ages 2 to 5 years has increased 60% over the past decade and has reached epidemic proportions in Georgia. Another recent report indicated that 16.5% of Georgia children 10- to 17-years-old were obese (Levi, Segal, Rayburn, & Martin, 2015). Black students are more likely to be at risk of overweight than white students. FITNESSGRAM data collected in 2012 revealed that only 56.9% of elementary children in Georgia scored in the Healthy Fitness Zone for body mass index (BMI). FITNESSGRAM is a national health-related fitness assessment adopted by the Presidential Youth Fitness Program that measures children's fitness against a criterion for determining fitness that is related to good health and to a child's age and gender (Plowman & Meredith, 2013).

The increased prevalence of overweight and obese children in Georgia from 1984 to the present has affected all 19 of its health districts. The annual cost of obesity in Georgia is estimated at $2.1 billion, which includes direct health care costs and lost productivity from morbidity and mortality. A recent review of research shows clearly that childhood obesity negatively influences school performance and academic achievement (Smith, Hay, Campbell, & Trollor, 2011). While children who were overweight or obese were not targeted for recruitment, the PAL Program was designed for both prevention and remediation.

Graduate Training Model

To achieve the academic enrichment and the family engagement goals of the PAL Program, the faculty in this cross-disciplinary partnership volunteered to serve as codirectors, both to provide a service to the community and to train graduate students for applied settings. Funding from the 21st CCLC program was used to support graduate research assistants (GRAs) who received mentorship and training. The GRAs, however, provided direct instruction to children during after-school programming at two elementary schools. An organizational chart that describes the roles of school administrators, codirectors, and GRAs in the PAL Program is shown in Figure 1.1.

In the training model, programming began each day at 2:45 P.M., at the conclusion of the regular school day. Children enrolled in the PAL Program reported immediately to the designated location at each school where program staff and volunteers awaited. The program began each session with 35-minute period of homework and a nutritious snack in accordance with state standards. While children were completing homework, staff and volunteers were available for assistance, mentoring, and maintaining an atmosphere conducive to completing homework tasks. At 3:20 P.M., children transitioned to the gymnasium along with the three PAL Program staff and any volunteers. Volunteers were typically undergraduates who were receiving training in learning how to conduct research and programming in applied child settings. For 45 minutes, the PAG teacher led a session of games, while the other instructional staff and volunteers provided managerial support. At the conclusion of this period, children used the restroom, got water, and transitioned to one of two classrooms. For the remaining 45 minutes, children were given math or reading enrichment activities before being transported home at 5:30 P.M. each day. The PAL Program is currently in the third year of funding. Data gathering to measure the effectiveness of the program is ongoing.

Overview of the Chapters

The following chapters of the book provide readers both with general background information concerning ASPs and with specific information concerning the implementation of physical activity, math, and reading enrichment interventions. Paula J. Schwanenflugel, in Chapter 2, provides an overview of the quality and goals of contemporary ASPs. Methods of evaluating program quality are then addressed by

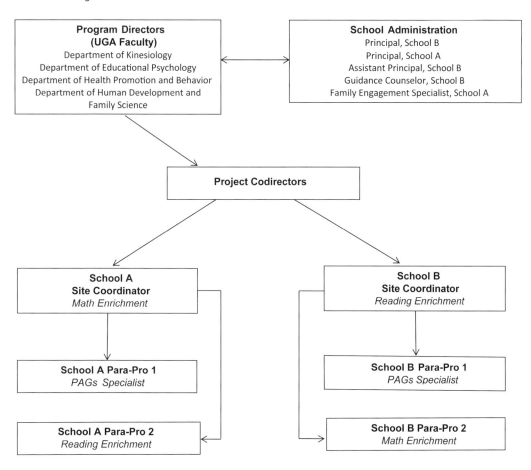

FIGURE 1.1. An organizational chart that describes the roles of school administrators, codirectors, and GRAs.

Katherine Wargo and Jennifer L. Gay in Chapter 3. These three chapters set the stage for describing three interactive theory-based interventions designed to promote children's engagement and learning. The theoretical and empirical rationale for the PAGs developed for the PAL Program is discussed by Phillip D. Tomporowski and Bryan A. McCullick in Chapter 4, and specific instructional methods for delivering these games are described by E. Nicole McCluney in Chapter 5. Theory-based approaches to teaching foundational skills related to mathematical number sense are discussed by Martha M. Carr in Chapter 6, and examples of pedagogical methods are described by Yi-Jung Lee in Chapter 7. Contemporary theories related to the development of children's reading fluency are described by Paula J. Schwanenflugel in Chapter 8, and research regarding elementary informational text literacy, with a particular attention to social studies literacy, is discussed by Justin T. Dooly in Chapter 9. Finally, instructional strategies for integrating reading fluency and informational text focus practices are detailed by Megan P. Brock and Paula J. Schwanenflugel in Chapter 10.

We hope to impress upon the readers of this book the full range of factors that can influence the development, implementation, and evaluation of translational research conducted in the after-school environment. University administrators often voice the need for closer "town and gown" relationships, particularly as they relate to education. Despite the mandate for universities to promote translational research, we have found that bridging the gap between the university institution and community organizations can be both challenging and incredibly rewarding. In this book, we provide an example of one translational intervention.

GLOSSARY

21st Century Community Learning Centers (21st CCLC)—ASPs supported by funds from the U.S. Department of Education's Office of Academic Improvement to provide academic enrichment opportunities during nonschool hours for children, particularly students attending high-poverty and low-performing schools. The programs are administered with oversight by state education agencies.

Ecological family model—A model of parenting and family functioning that claims that families are best understood in terms of the broader contextual factors that encourage or discourage particular family behaviors.

Exercise deficit disorder—A pediatric medical condition characterized by levels of moderate-to-vigorous physical activity below levels likely to lead to positive health outcomes.

Physical activity games—Games that require moderate-to-vigorous physical exercise and rapid decision making about how best to achieve the goals of the games.

References

Afterschool Alliance. (2016, August). *America after 3pm special report: Afterschool in communities of concentrated poverty*. Washington, DC: Author.

Davidson, K. K., Jurkowski, J. M., & Lawson, H. A. (2013). Reframing family-centered obesity prevention using the Family Ecological Model. *Public Health Nutrition, 16*(10), 1861–1869.

Davis, C. L., Tomporowski, P. D., Boyle, C. A., Waller, J. L., Miller, P. H., Naglieri, J. A., & Gregoski, M. (2007). Effects of aerobic exercise on overweight children's cognitive functioning: A randomized controlled trial. *Research Quarterly for Exercise and Sport, 78*(5), 510–519.

Davis, C. L., Tomporowski, P. D., McDowell, J. E., Austin, B. P., Yanasak, N. E., Allison, J. D., . . . Miller, P. H. (2011). Exercise improves executive function and achievement and alters brain activation in overweight children: A randomized, controlled trial. *Health Psychology, 30*(1), 91–98.

Donnelly, J. E., Hillman, C. H., Castelli, D., Etnier, J. L., Lee, S., Tomporowski, P.

D., . . . Szabo-Reed, N. (2016). Physical activity, cognitive function and academic achievement in children: American College of Sports Medicine Position Stand. *Medicine and Science in Sports and Exercise, 48*(6), 1197–1222.

Estabrooks, P. A., & Glasgow, R. E. (2006). Translating effective clinic-based physical activity interventions into practice. *American Journal of Preventive Medicine, 31*(4S), S45–S56.

Etnier, J. L., & Chang, Y.-K. (2009). The effect of physical activity on executive function: A brief commentary on definitions, measurement issues, and the current state of the literature. *Journal of Sport and Exercise Psychology, 31,* 469–483.

Faigenbaum, A. D., Best, T. M., MacDonald, J., Myer, G. D., & Stracciolini, A. (2014). Top 10 research questions related to exercise deficit disorder (EDD) in youth. *Research Quarterly for Exercise and Sport, 85*(3), 297–307.

Faigenbaum, A. D., Stracciolini, A., & Myer, G. D. (2011). Exercise deficit disorder in youth: A hidden truth. *Acta Paediatrica, 100*(11), 1423–1425.

Fedewa, A. L., & Ahn, S. (2011). The effects of physical activity and physical fitness on children's achievement and cognitive outcomes: A meta-analysis. *Research Quarterly for Exercise and Sport, 82*(3), 521–535.

Gaglio, B., Shoup, J. A., & Glasgow, R. E. (2013). The RE-AIM framework: A systematic review of use over time. *American Journal of Public Health, 103*(6), e38–e46.

Giuliani, R. W. (1996). Personal Responsibility and Work Opportunity Reconciliation Act of 1996. *Georgetown Journal on Fighting Poverty, 4,* 165.

Glasgow, R. E., Klesges, L. M., Dzewaltowski, D. A., Bull, S. S., & Eastbrooks, P. (2004). The future of health behavior change research: What is needed to improve translation of research into health practice? *Annals of Behavioral Medicine, 27*(1), 3–12.

Gutin, B., Barbeau, P., & Yin, Z. (2004). Exercise interventions for prevention of obesity and related disorders in youth. *Quest, 56,* 120–141.

How, S. K. (2011). *Securing a healthy future: Commonwealth Fund State Scorecard on Child Health System Performance, 2011.* New York: Commonwealth Fund.

Jacobs, J., & Gerson, K. (1998). Who are the over-worked Americans? *Review of Social Economy, 56*(4), 442–459.

Jurkowski, J. M., Lawson, H. A., Green Mills, L., Wilner, P., & Davison, K. K. (2014). The empowerment of low-income parents engaged in a childhood obesity intervention. *Family and Community Health, 37*(2), 104–118.

Kempermann, G. (2008). The neurogenic reserve hypothesis: What is adult hippocampal neurogenesis good for? *Trends in Neuroscience, 31*(4), 163–169.

Kempermann, G., Fabel, K., Ehninger, D., Babu, H., Leal-Galicia, P., Garthe, A., & Wolf, S. A. (2010). Why and how physical activity promotes experience-induced brain plasticity. *Frontiers in Neuroscience, 4,* 189.

Kramer, A. F., Hahn, S., Cohen, N. J., Banich, M. T., McAuley, E., Harrison, C. R., . . . Colcombe, A. (1999). Ageing, fitness and neurocognitive function. *Nature, 400,* 418–419.

Lawson, H. A. (1993). School reform, families, and health in the emergent national agenda for economic and social improvement: Implications. *Quest, 45*(3), 289–307.

Lawson, H. A. (2009). Paradigms, exemplars and social change. *Sport, Education, and Society, 14*(1), 97–119.

Lawson, H. A., Tomporowski, P. D., & Pendleton, D. M. (2014). New institutional designs to achieve better results for children. In R. Todaro (Ed.), *Physical education: Role of school programs, Children's attitudes, and health implications* (pp. 51–73). Hauppauge, NY: Nova Science.

Levi, J., Segal, L. M., Rayburn, J., & Martin, A. (2015). *State of obesity: Better policies for a healthier America: 2015.* Washington, DC: Trust for America's Health.

McCullick, B. A., & Tomporowski, P. D. (2014, February). *Teaching laypersons to "teach" physical activity games in after-school programs.* Paper presented at the Association Internationale des Ecoles Superieures d'Education Physique World Congress, Auckland, New Zealand.

Physical Activity Guidelines Advisory Committee. (2008). *Physical activity guidelines advisory committee report.* Washington, DC: U.S. Department of Health and Human Services.

Plowman, S. A., & Meredith, M. D. (2013). *FITNESSGRAM/ACTIVITYGRAM reference guide* (4th ed.). Dallas, TX: Cooper Institute.

Ramey, C. T., & Ramey, S. H. (2004). Early educational interventions and intelligence. In E. Zigler & S. J. Styfco (Eds.), *The Head Start debate* (pp. 3–17). Baltimore: Brookes.

Rones, P., Ilg, R., & Gardner, J. (1997). Trends in hours of work since the mid-1970s. *Monthly Labor Review, 120,* 3–14.

Smith, E., Hay, P., Campbell, L., & Trollor, J. N. (2011). A review of the association between obesity and cognitive function across the lifespan: Implications for novel approaches to prevention and treatment. *Obesity Reviews, 12,* 740.

Taras, H. (2005). Physical activity and student performance at school. *Journal of School Health, 75,* 214–218.

Taras, H., & Potts-Datema, W. (2005). Obesity and student performance at school. *Journal of School Health, 75*(8), 291–295.

Thelen, E. (2004). The central role of action in typical and atypical development: A dynamical systems perspective. In I. J. Stockman (Ed.), *Movement and action in learning and development: Clinical implications for pervasive developmental disorders* (pp. 49–74). New York: Elsevier.

Tomporowski, P. D. (2003). *Skill development: Integrating mind, body, and spirit.* Westport, CT: Praeger.

Tomporowski, P. D., McCullick, B., & Pesce, C. (2015). *Enhancing children's cognition with physical activity games.* Champaign, IL: Human Kinetics.

Zigler, E., & Styfco, S. J. (2004). *The Head Start debate.* Baltimore: Brookes.

2

Understanding After-School Programming for Elementary School Children

Paula J. Schwanenflugel

It is 2:50 P.M. and the school day has ended for the children at Lincoln Elementary. Outside, there is a seemingly endless line of cars carrying a sole occupant, often mothers, waiting for her children. As the cars cue up, Ms. Johnson and her assistant Ms. Jackson diligently check IDs, quickly dispatch children for home with their caretakers, and wave the cars on. Other teachers, such as Ms. Jordan, are leading long lines of children to yellow school buses that will take children home where an after-school caretaker (a parent, grandparent, or babysitter) awaits them. Some children in this line will have no one waiting for them, and they will use a key to get inside. These are the *latchkey kids,* a term popularized during World War II to describe children who had to care for themselves after school because their mothers, recently anointed the family breadwinner, had to remain at their workplace. Even today, we can expect that at least one child in every elementary school classroom, or approximately 800,000 elementary school children in the United States (Afterschool Alliance, 2014), is a latchkey kid. Until the workday is over, parents of these children will worry about their child's safety. Another teacher, Ms. Carson, walks a group of children to the cafeteria where the after-school program (ASP) is held at the school itself. Perhaps the parents of the latchkey children did not know that there were scholarships for the program. It can be hard to get the word out.

If you teach or do research in this field, you know that education policymakers often fail to recognize the importance of ASPs in our overall educational plan for our children. These programs only rarely figure into policy decisions regarding how well our educational system is functioning. The situation is beginning to change with the development of federal programs such as the 21st Century Community Learning Centers (CCLC) initiative, which competitively funds ASPs for children living in high-poverty neighborhoods. However, to a great extent, after-school programming in the United States has been a patched-together series of private, fee-based, public, and charitable initiatives of varying quality.

For parents especially, the availability of a high quality ASPs in their community can make all the difference in how productive they are at work. Approximately one-third of American working parents experience stress regarding after-school care issues (termed *parents' after-school stress* or PAS), which adds to their workplace stress in general (Gareis & Barnett, 2006). Worries regarding after-school time are part of the work–life balance problems that many American parents experience. Parents worry about the basic safety of their children and wonder whether their children are using their time after school in productive ways. They hope that the after-school arrangements they have made are reliable and of decent quality.

The purpose of this chapter is to provide a general overview of what we know, or think we know, about ASPs designed for elementary school children. I discuss the history of after-school programming and trace how our modern conceptualizations of after-school care can be found in the way our programs have been created historically. I discuss program availability and quality issues and obstacles to child participation, and describe the different goals that various ASPs have for children, and how these differences have influenced the way ASPs are structured. I will deal with whether ASPs have been found to have achieved these various goals. I will also point out unanswered questions and directions for future research.

What exactly is an ASP? Leos-Urbel (2015) provides a basic definition by noting that ASPs "meet regularly, with many operating every day, and offer a combination of activities including homework help or academic instruction as well as athletics or cultural enrichment" (p. 687). Durlack, Berger, and Celio (2009) offer a more expansive definition by defining ASPs as

> formal programs for school-age youth (ages 5–18) that operate outside of normal school hours for at least part of the year, are supervised or in some way monitored by adults, and that intentionally seek to promote young people's growth and development by focusing on one or more of the following areas: academic/cognitive, personal/social, cultural, artistic, or civic development. At the very least, after-school programs provide a safe, supportive alternative to a youth being on his or her own. (p. 44)

Note that each of these definitions mentions regularity in their availability, some kind of focus on academic skills, and child growth and enrichment. Child growth can take the form of physical fitness activities, too, and so this is often part of the definition. In this chapter, we focus solely on ASPs that are available outside the school day, not just during the summer, and on programs explicitly designed for elementary school children for whom self-care is a particularly problematic option.

Program Availability and Obstacles to Participation

One of the issues associated with after-school care is the mere availability of care. The Afterschool Alliance (2014), a consortium of foundation, business, and federal agencies dedicated to expanding the quantity and quality of after-school care, has probably sponsored the most research into the availability of programs and obstacles to after-school care in the United States. The Alliance and others report a lack of availability, particularly in high-poverty communities, as one of the major impediments. Many parents surveyed in these communities point out that there are no programs for their children (42%). Particularly, African American and Latino low-income parents indicate a general willingness to use such a program should one become available (greater than 70%). Indeed, when programs are available, children from low-income families are more likely to enroll than other children (Hynes & Sanders, 2011). Children of immigrant mothers are considerably less likely to be enrolled, regardless of income (Greenburg, 2013), and the reason for this is unclear. It might be that these parents may lack a cultural understanding of the place that ASPs might have in promoting achievement in young immigrant children. The availability of an ASP does seem to increase the likelihood that mothers will enter the workforce or look for work (Dynarski et al., 2004). Although the availability of programs has expanded greatly in the last two decades, there is still much more work to be done.

Current ASPs can found in a variety of settings. Many public schools themselves provide after-school care in place, such as the one at Lincoln Elementary mentioned at the beginning of this chapter, although 44% of schools have no afterschool programs at all. About 46% of these public school programs are fee based. Public schools located in central cities are more likely to host ASPs than rural schools are. Private schools in rural areas are the least likely to provide them (Hynes & Sanders, 2010). Some schools grant access to programs run by organizations such as the Boys and Girls Club, the YMCA, or faith-based groups, either by providing transportation to them or by hosting such programs at the school itself.

There are many obstacles to enrollment, which render the programs essentially unavailable (Parsad & Lewis, 2009). Some programs do not cover the specific hours that parents need for children to be cared for. That is, a substantial proportion (23%) of ASPs in public schools operate for fewer than 15 hours per week. Many of these low-hour programs are in low-income public schools and have a strictly remediation or tutoring focus (Hynes & Sanders, 2011). Other programs (25%) go out of their way to ensure proper coverage and endure well on into the evening, operating for more than 20 hours per week. The hours that most programs operate are somewhere in the middle, capturing the operation needs of most families.

The availability of transportation to and from programs can be a hindrance to participation. Fifty-one percent of parents assert that there is no transportation to available programs from their children's schools. The lack of transportation from the program site to the child's home is a hindrance for others. Fee-based programs, in particular, are unlikely to provide such transportation—only 4% do (Parsad & Lewis, 2009).

Of course, the availability of fee-based-only programs in many public schools continues to be a barrier for low-income families who cannot afford even modest fees (Afterschool Alliance, 2014). This is one reason that the latchkey kids may not attend an ASP held in their school building. Parents who pay for an ASP spend an average of $113 each week for their children to attend. This figure is clearly out of range for low-income families. There is an estimated 27% gap in ASP participation in the United States between low-income elementary school children and their non-low-income peers (Moore, Murphey, Bandy, & Cooper, 2014). Many low-income parents (68%) cite cost as a major barrier to having their child participate in these programs.

To sum up, availability, affordability, and transportation are the major impediments for children's participation in ASPs. Moreover, these obstacles affect some children more than others. These obstacles are unfortunate because studies show that the availability of formal ASPs can help parents keep their jobs (Afterschool Alliance, 2014). Indeed, 83% of parents indicated so when asked. Furthermore, 85% of them report that having their children in these programs gives them peace of mind, knowing that their children are safely taken care of after school. This peace of mind, no doubt, helps parents perform better in the workplace.

History of After-School Programming

At this point, you might be wondering about how we ended up with these gaps in after-school care. This situation can probably be traced to the way in which after-school care came about. Robert Halpern (2002) has conducted extensive archival research related to the history of after-school care in the United States, and much of our discussion is derived from his description of how ASPs emerged as a societal institution.

According to Halpern, ASPs emerged at the end of the 19th century when there was a general downturn in the need for child labor and compulsory education laws were enacted. There was a dramatic shift in school attendance at the turn of the 20th century, such that by 1928, 80% of children attended school. The majority of children now left schools, not once they had accomplished basic elementary school tasks, such as basic reading, writing, and arithmetic skills, but after eighth grade.

Schools in the late 19th and early 20th centuries were highly regimented places. However, after-school hours were virtually unstructured. Although some children found odd jobs that contributed to the family income during those times, others ran wild in the streets unmonitored, particularly working class boys and immigrant children who tended to have parents that both worked. The streets were unsafe, and the unsupervised time allowed for youth delinquency to flourish. The first after-school programs were developed in boys and boys' clubs, particularly in urban areas. The rationale was to provide wholesome activities that could compete as alternatives to the dangers of the street.

Early ASPs were charitable affairs run by middle-class adult volunteers, who were usually civically or religiously motivated. Occasionally, college students would receive practicum credits for participating. Activities were designed to introduce children to the tasks of adulthood: Girls were taught housekeeping, sewing, child rearing, and knitting, whereas boys received vocational training in skills, such as metal working, radio repair, and barbering. Sometimes, activities included the arts or basic hygiene. Children were sometimes given medical exams because they had no other access to medical care. Wilderness training and scout troops promoted the great outdoors and self-sufficiency as an alternative to hawking in the streets. New immigrants were introduced to American customs. By 1910, homework help, physical fitness, and sports began to be emphasized. During World War II, children in many programs helped with the war effort by making bandages, knitting clothing, collecting scrap metal, and planting Victory gardens. The goals for ASPs were child growth and development and learning useful skills children would not learn in school.

The programs were conducted in an unregimented way to attract children, in contrast to school itself. Children could come and go as they pleased, and little was required of them other than that they behaved. There was a lot of emphasis on learning by doing and playing rather than on learning through memorization and recitation.

Given its modest beginnings, the concept of after-school programming was successful. By 1959, there were approximately 550 clubs, mostly Boys Clubs. African American children or girls, when they were included, were taught housekeeping, although they were eventually included during the 1960s and 70s. African American children needed an alternative model to the negative identity that they found in the streets. People became increasingly aware that girls were a vulnerable population and, given modern conveniences and changes in attitudes, parents no longer expected girls to take on the lion's share of housework duties after school.

The number of ASPs exploded in the 1980s when mothers, particularly low-income mothers, joined the workforce in large numbers. Welfare reform in the 1990s also pushed welfare recipients into the workforce (Phillips, 2010), creating a growing danger for children in high-poverty families and putting them at increased risk in the after-school hours. By the mid-1990s, federal funds were finally made available for after-school care in low-income neighborhoods through the 21st Century Community Learning Centers Act (S. 1990, 1994a; H.R. 3734, 1994b) (21st CCLC). Although the initial investment in after-school programming was small, by the end of the 1990s the program was greatly expanded.

Today mothers of school-age children of all ethnicities and income levels can be found in the workplace. In the latest report, 69.9% of all mothers of school-age children work, and 60.6% of families have parents that both work, according to the U.S. Bureau of Labor Statistics (2016). The prevalence of after-school care has expanded societally. ASPs have emerged in child care centers, libraries, public housing projects, and public schools themselves. New sponsors have entered the field.

The 21st CCLC program is currently administered as a block grant to state departments of education, but there have been a number of legislative efforts from all sides to eliminate, reduce, or expand the federal role in after-school care (Phillips, 2010). Current appropriation in 2016 is approximately half of what it was in 2007, and future funding is uncertain.

Increasingly, ASPs have been entrusted to provide opportunities to extend the curriculum in ways that the public schools have not been able to do. There has been an increasing emphasis on fitness, health, arts, academic skill remediation, and extending the curriculum in interesting ways to promote children's growth. Many of these traditional school functions have been eclipsed during the school day because of modern schooling's emphasis on testing. ASPs have now been asked to be an important player in helping to narrow the achievement gap among children of different income levels and ethnicities. As the number of programs and the skills needed to support these new initiatives have grown over the 20th and into the 21st century, a professional staff has been added to provide program stability, coordination, and direction to child care workers and volunteers. However, these coordinators and instructors are still poorly paid relative to their skills, especially now that most have bachelors' or masters' degrees.

If you are familiar with ASPs, you can see that to a great extent many of the current practices that we see in modern ASPs can be traced to earlier programs. The Boys and Girls Clubs in our own area have a mix of full- and part-time professional staff and volunteers from the nearby universities to help out. Our own program employs education graduate students working part-time for coordinating and instructing, and we have a full-time director and faculty member overseeing the administration of funds to ensure adherence to 21st CCLC rules. A group of undergraduates and graduate students work for practicum credit or modest pay. We offer physical fitness and healthy snacks, homework help, and various types of academic enrichment. Homework help and physical activities have become a fixture in ASPs, in general. Our program endeavors to be research-based and effective. The emphases of modern ASPs are on helping schools accomplish tasks that have been eclipsed during the school day. Indeed, the Every Student Succeeds Act (Public Law 114–95; *www.congress.gov/114/plaws/publ95/PLAW-114publ95.pdf*) requires ASPs to supplement but not supplant regular school-day requirements, acknowledging the challenge to resist having federally funded ASPs become just another part of the school day. The goal of ASPs remains that of nurturing a more well-rounded, fully functioning child who is taken care of in a safe environment.

Goals of ASPs and Program Variety

Getting to the generally agreed-upon goal of promoting the development of a well-rounded child takes a variety of forms in ASPs. Importantly, having clear and specific program goals is vital for effective ASPs. The CRESST Afterschool Program Model (Huang & Dietel, 2011) includes program goals as one of the five components that are common to successful ASPs. According to Huang and Dietel (2011), goals should be "clear, rigorous, and supported across the program in structure and content" (p. 2). The goals should be codified in a written plan. Program funding and practices should be aligned with those goals, and evaluations should align with the goals.

What kinds of goals can ASPs have? ASPs have many different goals, ranging from just making sure that children are safe and get their homework done to programs aimed at enhancing children's social and emotional well-being, academic skills, general health and fitness, and appreciation for and participation in the arts. The goals for ASPs can be as different as the particular penchants of the people and organizations involved. Beyond the goals we describe in the following pages, there are also programs whose goal is to improve social–emotional growth and behavior issues in at-risk children. These programs have been reviewed extensively by Durlak, Weissberg, and Pachan (2010), and we recommend this source to readers who are interested in the effects of those programs. Next we discuss some of the more common goals for ASPs (see Box 2.1 for an overview) and what we think we know about their effects.

Child Safety Goals

Ensuring safety for children in the after-school hours is an implicit, unwritten, and, unfortunately, mostly unmeasured goal for all programs. This is probably a main goal of ASPs for parents and one that is strangely ignored in most ASP evaluations. It seems to be a goal that most evaluators take for granted. Indeed, when

---
BOX 2.1. COMMON GOALS FOR ASPs

- **Child safety goals.** The goal is for children to feel comfortable and safe, both physically and psychologically, and to have the opportunity to thrive under attentive, positive, and supportive adult care.
- **Homework goals.** The goal is to have children complete homework assigned by the school day teacher, in a supportive environment, and to learn best practices for completing homework.
- **Academic goals.** The goal is for children to improve, enrich, or expand on their knowledge of academic skills taught during the school day.
- **STEM goals.** The goal is to increase children's interest in and knowledge of topics related to science, technology, engineering, and math by learning from knowledgeable instructors.
- **Arts participation goals.** The goal is to increase children's interest in and knowledge of literary, visual, or performing arts using skilled professionals and authentic materials.
- **Fitness goals.** The goal is to increase children's knowledge of and activities related to living a physically fit and healthy life.

---

asked directly, both parents and children report an increased sense of safety in the after-school hours because of ASPs. Parents say that having their children in ASPs gives them peace of mind (Afterschool Alliance, 2014). Children report feeling safer and less likely to spend long hours in self-care, which can be dangerous (James-Burdumy, Dynarski, & Deke, 2007).

Most legitimate ASPs pay close attention to safety issues. ASP staff are usually vetted by being fingerprinted and evaluated for criminal records at the local, state, and federal levels. To work in the ASPs, staff need to have basic first aid and CPR training to address any health and safety issues that may occur. Staff monitor that children are not behaving in dangerous ways that imperil themselves and others. Thus, to a great extent, most ASPs would seem to have accomplished the goal of keeping children safe in the hours after school.

Homework Goals

Some programs have the goal of increasing the likelihood that children will complete their homework. *Homework* has been defined as "academic work assigned in school that is designed to extend the practice of academic skills into other environments during non-school hours" (Olympia, Sheridan, & Jenson, 1994). Homework is important for practicing or elaborating on skills acquired during the school day. In the upper grades, in particular, failing to complete homework can serve as an impediment to obtaining good grades. Going to school with homework completed can give children increased confidence about school, since lacking it is often a source of tension with teachers. ASPs are often considered by teachers to provide one solution to the homework completion problem.

However, homework is one facet of parental involvement with schools, and it is the issue around which parents and teachers are most likely to communicate. Homework serves to communicate the school curriculum to parents. Children's ability to complete homework without extensive help gives parents a normative sense as to whether their own children have the skills to complete what other children have presumably been able to carry out on their own. It allows parents to communicate achievement-related goals to their children.

Homework can also be a source of stress between parents and schools because not every family can provide high-quality support for it. Sometimes parents can be controlling and intrusive in managing their children's homework, and confuse children when they try to help. Their ways of helping can set a negative emotional tone around schooling (Patall, Cooper, & Robinson, 2008). Some homes do not have a proper space for children to concentrate while doing their homework. Not every child has a quiet room of his or her own where it can be completed in peace, and the child needs to jostle for homework space among all the other activities in the home. These issues will lead some children to avoid their homework altogether (Dumont, Trautwein, Nagy, & Nagengast, 2014).

So, there is a tension between having homework completed in the ASP and the possibility that parents will lack an understanding of what children are learning in school. Still, children can at least get a good, solid start on their daily homework in ASPs. They can provide the time, setting, and support for children to do their homework (Beck, 1999). Effective programs set aside approximately 45 minutes for homework (Huang & Dietel, 2011). They provide a quiet, structured setting that allows children to concentrate. They have a knowledgeable staff that can offer effective homework help. They can coach children in best practices associated with completing homework, including setting homework priorities, such as doing the most difficult homework first (Reisner, White, Russell, & Birmingham, 2004).

There are a number of challenges ASP staff face when trying to help with homework. Like parents, the staff need to have the knowledge and skills to be able to help with homework, which requires a knowledge of the modern curriculum that not all staff members have. In our own PAL Program, we notice this issue in the area of mathematics, where instructional approaches have undergone dramatic changes in recent years. Moreover, ASP staff need to be in the loop with teachers as to exactly what each child's homework is. Not knowing encourages children to deceive the staff about how much homework they might actually have. Our experience and research supports the idea that, when there are basic school-wide standards about the characteristics of and policies surrounding homework, communication between the teachers and ASP staff is greatly improved (Cosden, Morrison, Gutierrez, & Brown, 2004). If, for example, it is the school policy that each child read a book for 20 minutes each day and solve approximately 20 math problems, ASP instructors can quickly discern whether children have completed their homework or not.

Unfortunately, this communication is often lacking. Evaluations of 21st CCLC programs have indicated that enrollment in ASPs do not influence homework completion, primarily because the staff did not have effective ways to determine that the work was actually done (James-Burdumy et al., 2007). Indeed, even homework assistance programs with strict attendance policies that are designed explicitly to support homework completion have had minimal effects on the homework completion rates reported by teachers. The most noticeable effect of such programs appears to be protecting elementary school children with limited English proficiency from experiencing the academic decline usually found in this group as they proceed through school (Cosden et al., 2001). Presumably, these families often have very minimal resources for supporting homework.

Academic Goals

Many programs have academic achievement-focused goals that aim to improve children's academic standing or skills. This goal can be rather general (i.e., general improvement in academic functioning in some foundational skills such as general reading skills), or it can target specific cognitive skills.

General programs sometimes use packages expressly designed for ASPs, such as the reading program developed by the Success for All Foundation called *Adventure Island* that was focused around the five components of instruction (vocabulary, comprehension, fluency, oral-language development, and written expression) identified by the National Reading Panel as important for improving children's reading skills, or *Mathletics,* designed by Harcourt School Publishers for building mathematics skills after school. Often general programs hire certified teachers or highly trained professionals to implement them. These programs tend to be rather structured compared to other programs, as are these two examples. Further, in most of the general academic programs, both the curricula and evaluations are tailored toward determining if children are making progress academically. They are evaluated by looking for general skill improvements, such as what might be found on mandated state assessments of reading or mathematics or on standardized assessments of these academic topics.

General, as opposed to specific, programs would seem more likely to produce accelerated growth in children attending ASPs, but that is not always the case. For example, a large federal randomized field study evaluating the *Adventure Island* program found that the program did not improve children's skills compared to children merely receiving homework help (Black, Somers, Doolittle, Unterman, & Grossman, 2009). But sometimes these general programs, such as the *Mathletics* program, do instigate a general improvement in skills (Black, Doolittle, Zhu, Unterman, & Grossman, 2008). It is difficult to discern exactly why some general academic programs are successful and why others are not.

Specific programs, by contrast, target some key skill or skills relevant to an academic topic, such as scientific reasoning. The PAL Program academic enrichment strategies are examples of programs with specific skill goals. Our reading enrichment goal was to improve children's fluency in the reading of informational text. Our math enrichment goal was for children to develop a more highly elaborated and fluent concept of number. We set these goals because a deficit in both underlying skills had been shown in prior research to serve as major obstacles to academic achievement in mathematics and reading (See Chapters 6, 8, and 9, this volume, for further details). Specific skill programs, such as our own, look for more specific kinds of improvements. In our case, we looked for improvement in children's reading fluency or mathematical number sense as a result of the program because these were considered foundational for growth in these areas. Our academic enrichment programs did appear to improve children's skills in these areas, but in all fairness, ours was a smaller, more tightly controlled experimental program administered by researchers in their respective areas, which might not be practical everywhere.

Programs developed with the goal of improving children's academic skills exist in a variety of forms as well, and we next discuss some specific types of these programs.

Tutoring Programs Targeting Academic Goals

In recent decades, extensive use of after-school tutoring programs came about because of the requirement of the No Child Left Behind Act (NCLB) that schools not making sufficient annual yearly progress 3 years running needed to offer tutoring to children who need to improve their skills. Usually these tutoring programs were designed to improve children's reading or math skills.

Studies evaluating the benefits of tutoring programs have been mixed. One study evaluating the impact of after-school tutoring carried out as part of the 21st CCLC program by Dynarski and colleagues (2004) found no benefits from after-school tutoring. Similarly, Deke, Dragoset, Bogen, and Gill (2012) found that children who made the cut-off for receiving tutoring did not show better growth in academic skills compared to the ones barely missing it. Zimmer, Hamilton, and Christina (2010) indicated that effects, when they do occur, are larger for math than for reading. These outcomes have been very disappointing to the ASP community.

A number of problems that tutoring programs experience limits our ability to determine their effectiveness. Families generally self-select into these programs in the first place, so it is hard to know whether positive effects occur (when they do) because of the programs themselves or because children from such families might be simply more concerned about academic achievement. So children in these programs might achieve at a somewhat higher rate because of specific family characteristics, not because they received tutoring.

Second, attendance is a problem at tutoring programs. Children may need 30–40 hours of tutoring to improve their skills (Heinrich et al., 2014). If children do not attend regularly, they may not accumulate enough hours to show any improvement.

Third, some of the tutoring programs more or less duplicate what children already receive as instruction during the school day. The idea that more of the same is better is probably not true (Black et al., 2008). Programs that target the needs of specific learners, such as those designed explicitly for the needs of children with dyslexia, may have a greater impact (Katzir, Goldberg, Ben Aryeh, Donnelley, & Wolf, 2013).

Finally, matching instruction to needed skills can be a problem for private tutors who often do not receive any information from the school about the child's specific learning needs (Heinrich et al., 2014), leaving tutors to guess at what needs to be taught. Communication between the schools and the tutors would seem to be a basic part of ensuring that the tutoring has the potential to be effective. Note that often the schools that have been provided money for tutoring services have already been designated dysfunctional according to NCLB standards for not making annual yearly progress goals for 3 consecutive years. They may have spotty records or testing systems that would help tutors to know what the specific learning needs of children are. However, such schools are sometimes unwilling or unable to cooperate with tutoring services.

Programs Targeting STEM Motivation and Skills

After-school STEM programs target interests and skills related to science, technology, engineering, and math. They are often designed with the dual goals of both improving children's understanding of science and scientific reasoning and motivating students to pursue science careers. Increasingly, research has shown that children form the basic kernel of the desire to pursue a STEM career later somewhere between late elementary school and the end of middle school. Elementary school children start off having an interest in science, but this quickly gives way to disinterest over time, such that, by age 14, these negative attitudes about STEM have consolidated (Osborne, Simon, & Collins, 2003). Early interests in STEM begin affecting performance in coursework in middle school, and it determines how they concentrate their academic energies (Dabney et al., 2012; Newell, Zientek, Tharp, Vogt, & Moreno, 2015). Choices in coursework can open or close doors to a future science career.

ASPs can theoretically play a major role in encouraging STEM interests. Surveys of adults working in STEM fields have shown that having had positive experiences with science outside of school prior to age 14 was highly influential in their decision to pursue STEM careers (Dewitt et al., 2011). Because ASPs have more poor, Latino, and African American children than children from other groups, they may be one vehicle for bringing underrepresented groups into STEM fields (Krishnamurthi, Ballard, & Noam, 2014).

ASPs devoted to science have the latitude to allow children to intensely pursue larger projects centered around a single topic. Such projects might be difficult to pursue during the school day, where a more generalist focus is directed by the curriculum. The National Research Council (2009) proposes that these informal science contexts, such as the ones found in ASPs, might even be preferable to school day learning. That is, by providing enhanced opportunities to practice scientific reasoning and reflections around science and to engage in actual science practices, children can begin to identify with the scientific enterprise. ASPs often take the form of science clubs, after-school robotics clubs, science fairs, as well as science and math Olympiads, among others (Sahin, Ayar, & Adiguzel, 2014).

Indeed, students participating in STEM-related ASPs do have a greater likelihood of pursuing a career in the sciences later compared to their peers who did not participate in one (Dabney et al., 2012). Children participating in STEM programs have shown an increased interest in and knowledge base around science (Newell et al., 2015), and they have a better understanding of scientific reasoning when the programs are carried out well (Lundh, House, Means, & Harris, 2013). Unfortunately, like many of the studies showing a benefit of ASPs, children have self-selected (or their parents have selected them) into these STEM programs. Determining that the ASPs themselves are the root cause of these new interests and skills is difficult.

Some problems remain for ASPs that are considering an expansion of their STEM offerings. First, general ASPs may have difficulty broadening their STEM offerings so that they can be offered on a frequent enough basis to make a difference (Lundh et al., 2013). As with most offerings associated with after-school effectiveness, dosage is key. Second, most ASP staff do not themselves have the science background to meet children's growing science needs beyond the most basic levels. Observations of a number of after-school STEM programs suggest that the instruction offered often does not help children to engage in the kinds of reflections about science and scientific reasoning that might be necessary to spark a long-term interest in the subject (Lundh et al., 2013). Finally, expanded science activities may require additional instructional resources and financial support for materials that resource-poor ASPs simply cannot afford. Expansion might be most likely where there are university or business partners that can bring in talent and resources to support the program. Our impression is that these outside partners tend to want to work with older children who are further along in their knowledge development and skills, and most of the STEM programs we have identified seem to be targeted at older children, not elementary school children.

Arts Participation Goals

The goal of many ASPs is increasing children's participation in or appreciation of the arts by providing high-quality arts experiences. Some of these programs take an interdisciplinary approach by integrating academic subjects within the arts. In this era of high-stakes testing, the arts have been neglected during the school day, and after-school program are seen as the vehicle for filling in the gaps in the current curricula. Like STEM programs, however, fully arts-focused ASPs tend to be targeted at children beyond the elementary school level. Regardless, most people would agree that participation in the arts creates a more well-rounded child.

Unfortunately, experimental research examining the added value of elementary arts-focused ASPs is practically nonexistent. One small study by Mason and Chuang (2001) evaluated the social–emotional impacts of attending an arts program housed in the children's community called Kuumba Kids. The Kuumba Kids program was created to be a culturally responsive dance and drama program for African American children run by African American artists who engaged children in drama and dance activities. According to the program, its goals were not to improve arts appreciation but to improve children's social–emotional functioning: "to assist in the development of self-esteem, non-competitive creativity, and creative problem solving" (Mason & Chuang, 2001, p. 47). Children were randomly assigned to experimental and business-as-usual conditions. Unlike the other programs discussed here, it was a relatively short after-school intervention—a weekly program of 2-hour sessions carried out over 16 weeks. Outcomes were determined using an adapted version of the Behavior Assessment System for Children (BASC; Sandoval & Echandia, 1994), measuring leadership, attention, social skills and self-esteem, withdrawal, and self-reliance and adaptability based on ratings from teachers, parents, and children. There was statistically significant evidence for general increases in children's leadership competencies, in girls' self-esteem, and in boys' social skills, although not uniformly across all types of raters. Assuming that the program did have the positive effects indicated, these improved social–emotional skills can serve as protective factors as children proceed through school.

It is difficult to evaluate the effects of the impact of participating in arts-focused programs. It is well established that children who participate in the arts generally do better in school, but such children tend to be from the demographics that already do better in school. Deciding to participate in and maintain a connection to arts-focused ASPs is generally a personal decision among older children, so participation is highly self-selected as well. At the elementary level, arts-focused parents might be more likely to enroll their children in arts programs, too, so there are family factors to consider. Even if the goals of the program are more about children developing an appreciation for the arts rather than improving academic skills per se, deciding whether arts-focused ASPs support this rather direct goal is problematic. Disentangling the effects of arts-focused ASPs from preexisting differences based on demographic, familial, and personal factors is difficult, if not impossible.

Several researchers assert that participation in the arts may have some specific impacts on children's cognitive skills that help them do better in school. For example, Catterall (2012) suggested that music training instills the same spatial temporal reasoning skills required by mathematics and science, through practice in using abstract forms of notation, appreciating relative tonal distances between notes, and recognizing and manipulating patterns. Moritz, Yampolsky, Papadelis, Thomson, and Wolf (2013) have theorized that music training can help students practice sound and rhythm skills that supports the phonological and fluency skills needed for reading. Certainly, enacting plays within reading classrooms (a practice called *Readers' Theater*) has already been shown to be a good way to give children extra reading fluency practice and exposure to vocabulary that can support good reading comprehension (Young & Rasinski, 2009).

Montgomery, Rogouin, and Persaud (2013) recently reviewed some design principles that affected participation in and quality of arts-focused ASPs among youth from low-income, ethnic minority neighborhoods, according to interviews of middle and high school students participating in these programs. Youth claimed to want warm, sympathetic instructors who are working professionals in the area. They wanted programs that immediately immersed them in the practices of the art form, rather than just participating in lectures about it. They wanted the ASP to take place in authentic, comfortable settings and to learn the craft using authentic equipment. They wanted the ASP learnings to lead to some sort of public presentation or performance of the art. They hoped to make friends with other children having similar interests. These ideas would seem to apply to successful arts-focused programs directed at elementary school students too.

Fitness Goals

Obesity prevention and fitness goals have received greater attention from ASPs because of our increased societal awareness and attention to the issue. One goal for ASPs is to contribute meaningfully to increased physical fitness and decreased "fatness" of children.

Current national guidelines call for children to participate in at least 60 minutes of moderate-to-vigorous physical activity (MVPA) per day (Dentro et al., 2014). According to the Centers for Disease Control and Prevention, *vigorous physical activity* is exercise that raises children's heart rate and degree of sweating considerably, while increasing their level of breathing to the extent that it is difficult to hold a conversation. Vigorous activities include those such as hiking or bicycling briskly uphill, running, skipping, and jumping rope. *Moderate physical activity* is exercise that raises the heart rate a bit and increases the amount of breathing and sweating, but children can still hold a conversation while doing it. It includes activities such as walking or bicycling at a moderate pace on a flat terrain, playing on the school playground equipment, playing hopscotch or badminton, baton twirling or drumming. *Light physical activity* includes activities that do not cause sweating or shortness of breath, and generally children should be able to sing or carry on a conversation while doing the activity. Examples include standing around, bowling, slow bicycling, or walking a small dog around the neighborhood. They include more or less any activity that involves full-body movement and activities that are not sedentary. While the emphasis of this goal generally is increasing the MVPA children take part in, even increases in light physical activity have been shown to result in positive changes in waist circumference, blood pressure, and HDL cholesterol in children (Carson et al., 2013). Less than half of all elementary school children meet the 60-minute MVPA guidelines, and this number gets even worse as children get older, decreasing to approximately one-quarter of teens (Dentro et al., 2014). These trends have long-term, dilatory consequences for health if maintained over a lifetime.

Clearly, the elementary school years are the time to establish the exercise habit but, quite possibly, children may not even have the opportunity to exercise the way they should (Troiano et al., 2008). Certainly, trends such as increased television watching and videogame playing at home are part of the problem, but the changes in the ways we have structured our school day are partly to blame, too. As with the arts, opportunities for physical activity have been infringed upon during the school day because of the increased emphasis on academic skills and the decreased emphasis on physical education (National Association for Sport and Physical Education and the American Heart Association, 2006). ASPs can either contribute to or ameliorate the problem of the lack of MVPA.

ASPs can definitely be part of the solution to raising elementary school children's physical activity levels. If direct attention is not paid to ensuring that children are moving around, it is not clear that they will receive the amount of MVPA that they should. Many programs assume that if a lot of time for free play is allocated, elementary school children will get enough exercise. They overlook the fact that a lot of children, particularly overweight children and girls, will simply sit or stand around during free play time. Furthermore, as noted by Gullotta, Bloom, Gulotta, and Messina (2010), free play can have unintended consequences such as wrestling free-for-alls that leave children injured. It may be preferable to have a more structured program around physical activity.

As to the amount of physical activity that children typically receive in ASPs, Beets et al. (2015) measured the physical activity received in 19 ASP programs using an accelerometer that children wore during the ASP. There was great variation among programs in the amount of MVPA children received in these programs, and virtually no child in any program met the 60 minutes of MVPA recommended by national standards. On average, children spent an average of 16–18 minutes of MVPA in ASPs. Similarly, Trost, Rosenkranz, and Dzewaltowski (2008) determined that children spent an average of 20 minutes of MVPA in 7 ASPs, but an additional 41 minutes doing light physical exercise. Similarly, Schuna, Lauersdorf, Behrens, and Liebert (2013) evaluated the biweekly *Keep It Moving!* program developed with the express goal of increasing MVPA. Even in this program children spent only 22 minutes of MVPA, although they also spent 27 minutes doing light physical exercise. So, ASPs might begin to ameliorate the issue of lack of exercise, but probably not enough to fully reverse the problem.

Experimental and quasi-experimental studies have generated the firmest evidence of whether ASPs can increase children's MVPA compared to controls not attending the program. For example, Crouter and colleagues (2015) randomly assigned children either to a 10-week ASP including nutrition education and supervised physical activity or simply nutrition education alone. Children receiving the physical activity component increased their light and MVPA physical activity by around 30 minutes per day, while the children in the nutrition-only group actually declined in the amount of physical activity they participated in by 50 minutes over the course of the intervention. Unfortunately, there were no corresponding changes in health measures (blood pressure, total cholesterol, waist circumference, or body mass index) for intervention children. Similarly, an evaluation of the Coordinated Approach to Child Health (CATCH) Kids Club ASP program (*www. CATCHUSA.org*; Kelder et al., 2004), which combines nutrition education with physical activity, also found that the program nearly doubled the percentage of time children spent in MVPA in ASPs, while control children actually decreased the percentage of time spent in MVPA in ASPs. Again, the conclusion seems to be that participation in ASPs does not solve the problem of low activity level, but it can help lessen the problem of inactivity when some attention and staff training are dedicated to it.

Some ASPs have attempted to improve children's health by educating children about nutrition. For children, snacks represent 24% of their daily calorie intake, so ASPs snack choices can potentially make a meaningful difference in the prevention of obesity. Most ASPs offer snacks, although they are not always healthy ones, as required in some states, and these snacks themselves can actually contribute directly to children's weight and fitness issues. The CATCH Kids Club introduces children to tasty and healthful foods and provides hands-on snack lessons emphasizing whole grains, fruits, vegetables, and low-fat dairy items. Findings indicate that the program improved children's knowledge about nutrition, but it did little to increase the likelihood of choosing vegetables and fruits as snacks (Kelder et al., 2004). Similar effects were shown in another experimental evaluation of an after-school nutrition program designed for African American 10-year-old girls at risk for obesity (Story et al., 2003). The 12-week training dealt with nutrition facts, such as the importance of drinking water or low fat milk, eating more fruits and vegetables, watching less television, and exercising more. Compared to a self-esteem training control group, there were a few statistically significant benefits for nutritional knowledge and intentions to eat healthier, but no real changes in most variables examined. Again, the effects were mostly on nutritional knowledge and not on actual healthy behaviors. Other nutrition education programs for elementary children have had more success in producing change (Choudhry et al., 2011), but certainly the particulars of the conditions that make these programs effective or not is not well understood.

Given how difficult it is to improve children's healthy eating choices, it makes sense to ensure that ASPs do not exacerbate the obesity problem. Weight gain can occur with as little as an extra 110–165 calories per day, and the snacks offered at ASPs can easily contribute to these extra calories. Ensuring that ASPs are not part of the problem involves increasing staff awareness of the importance of providing healthy snacks. Gortmaker et al. (2012) evaluated a staff training program offered by the YMCA ASPs about providing healthy snacks (see *www.hsph.harvard.edu/ prc/proj_YMCA_guidelines_jun06.pdf*), and the staff began to offer better quality snacks, with a fewer calories, trans fats, and added sugars than those offered before the training.

In summary, research has suggested that ASPs can contribute meaningfully to the goal of increasing children's fitness and decreasing "fatness" (Yin et al., 2005). Participation in ASPs might help forestall the development of obesity as long as children participate in ASPs on a regular basis (Mahoney, Lord, & Carryl, 2005). Training staff and instituting ASP goals regarding improving children's health are part of this equation. After-school instructors can be instructed in how to ensure that children are offered only healthy, lower-calorie snacks and how to structure activities that keep children moving. Chapter 5 of this volume describes the physical activity program that is used within the PAL Program, which is structured to keep children moving without a direct emphasis on sports. In the PAL Program, we only offered healthy snacks, although our choices had to be negotiated with the school system personnel providing the snacks. It is clear that ASPs cannot (and should not be expected to) solve the problem of childhood obesity and sedentariness, but they can operate in such a way as to ameliorate some of the issues associated with these problems.

ASP Program Quality

Given the diverse types and goals of ASPs, it is difficult to make generalizations regarding what constitutes a high-quality ASP for elementary school children. Many studies have tried to determine which practices of high-quality ASPs are associated with positive child outcomes, regardless of the specifics of their aims. Often such studies look at a wide range of evaluations of programs showing effectiveness. Then researchers try to isolate the common features that are associated with good programs.

The Little, Wimer, and Weiss (2008) of the Harvard Family Research Project have made an extensive analysis of the qualities of effective programs. They have identified six features associated with effective programs. According to Little et al., effective programs

1. *Encourage high attendance.* Benefits seem to be correlated with how often children attend the program. Children with spotty attendance do not benefit nearly as much, so having program attendance goals matters. Programs need to encourage children to attend.

2. *Are structured and have intentional, goal-driven programming.* No single goal or single program is necessarily better than any others, but having a goal or several goals around which the curriculum is structured is important. Communicating those goals to schools, parents, and children is important too. Being structured and goal driven is necessary to prevent problematic behavior from developing and to enable children to get the most out of the program.

3. *Have a well-prepared staff.* That is, in well-functioning programs, the directors' salaries are higher than less well-functioning programs, and more staff have advanced education credentials. They know how to coordinate and partner with schools, families, and the community. They have experience and training in how to work with children in positive ways.

4. *Involve families when they can.* They help families work with the child's teachers. They hold open houses for the program or coordinate with the school's open houses. They help families connect to community resources where necessary.

5. *Use community resources to create a better program.* They reach out to the community for needed expertise and help. For example, in the PAL Program, we have utilized experts from the local university, for example, mathematics educators, reading experts, child behavior experts, public health experts, and kinesiologists to develop the program. We asked scientists to participate in science days to enrich the science literacy curriculum.

6. *Build strong relationships with the school principals, teachers, and staff.* They use the school as a resource to build a better program. They ask school personnel to help them recruit children who might best benefit from the program. They communicate with the child's teachers about homework, behavior, and academic skills. They are consistent in following school and district rules. They view themselves as an extension of the school, particularly when the program is held on school grounds.

Durlak, Berger, and Celio (2010) have argued that creating a logic model may be key to developing a coherent high-quality program. A *logic model* is a systematic way to represent and share the program's understanding of the relation-ships between the resources available to operate the program, the activities that are planned for the children, and the changes that the program hopes to bring about. This model can be used as a communication device between the program staff and the parents, school, and community, and the funding agencies to which the pro-gram wishes to appeal. For example, if your goal is to improve children's fluency in the reading informational text (as it was in the reading enrichment program presented in Chapter 10), what types of books and materials will you need that will best accomplish your goals, and how much money will that cost? What sorts of activities are you planning that might improve children's informational text flu-ency? How will you determine that those activities have been implemented? How will you measure this improved fluency? What is the timeline in which you wish to achieve this improved fluency? The key is to develop clarity in the link between goals and outcomes.

Others have argued that we can focus on quality by considering *regulatable program qualities*. Regulatable qualities are those features of programs that can be directly regulated and identified by outside monitors. For example, Wade (2015) focused on identifying the regulatable program qualities of ASPs that were associ-ated with higher social–emotional functioning in elementary school children.

Like Little et al. (2008), she identified staff training and experience as a key variable to supporting positive child outcomes. After-school instructors perform better when they are more knowledgeable about what they are doing and when they have skills related to the goals of the program.

Successful programs have staff that are paid well, as higher wages tend to reduce turnover. Turnover interferes with the development of strong relationships between children and adults. Why should a child become close to her ASP instruc-tor if he or she is merely going to move on to another, better-paying job when one becomes available? Why should an ASP instructor invest his emotional resources in children when he is hoping to find a better job soon? Turnover, therefore, is dila-tory to child outcomes.

Good programs have low child-to-instructor ratios. Low ratios tend to pro-mote positive interactions and relationships between the instructors and children and help to keep the after-school climate positive (Rosenthal & Vandell, 1996).

Durlack, Weissberg, and Pachan (2010) suggest that the following SAFE acro-nym can distinguish high-quality programs from low-quality programs.

1. *Sequential,* step-by-step skill building activities are provided over time; the activities are broken down into their component parts and arranged in such a way as to allow children to master a specific set of skills;
2. *Active,* hands-on forms of learning rather than lectures or discussion are emphasized; the goal here is for children to be actively engaged in the pro-gram.

3. *Focused* time, attention, and resources are dedicated to this skill building. Attendance is part of this time and attention.
4. *Explicit* learning goals are emphasized, and these learning goals are communicated to the children. The staff need to have lesson plans and training to know how to help children reach these goals.

According to Durlack, Weissberg, and Pachan (2010), if any of these features are missing from a given program, children will not experience positive benefits from it. Children attending programs they examined that had the SAFE features were found to have improved social–emotional behaviors and academic skills.

Metz, Goldsmith, and Arbreton (2008) also developed a set of guiding principles for high-quality after-school programs:

First, programs should have *clear and specific goals*. Some programs have too many goals. This approach scatters program energies, making it hard for program goals to be effectively communicated to staff, parents, and schools. It soon becomes impossible for staff to organize their activities effectively. A program that has too many goals is one that cannot pay enough attention to any one of them. Programs with clear, manageable goals are more successful.

Second, programs should have *enough intensity,* that is, children should attend on a regular basis, and the program duration should be long enough to make a difference. What dosage is needed in terms of child attendance and how long the program will need to last to make a difference will depend on program goals. Some goals simply take longer to attain than others. But the importance of attendance should be emphasized.

Third, programs should emphasize positive, *supportive adult–child relationships*. That is, teachers need to be caring and responsive rather than harsh and negative to have lasting positive effects. Caring, responsive teachers create an atmosphere of safety and support that encourages children to develop positive social skills. It makes children enjoy the program and get the most out of it. One aspect of this is staff turnover, which can be problematic and can undermine the development of supportive relationships. Another aspect is the teacher to child ratio, as noted earlier. Large ratios do not allow teachers to attend to children's particular learning and social–emotional needs.

Fourth, programs should encourage *family involvement*. This can take the form of informing parents of how well children are doing in the program. It can motivate families to volunteer in the program, and can provide a welcoming environment for family members to drop in and participate.

Fifth, programs should encourage *cultural competence*. Teachers should value and try to understand the cultural backgrounds of the children in the program. Children should be required to do this too. Programs should support the development of a positive ethnic identity among children. They should offer translation assistance for families whose dominant language is not English.

Finally, programs should *strive for improvement*, by engaging in extensive staff training in areas of weakness identified by evaluation measures and observations. They should evaluate their progress both formally and informally.

You should by now be able to identify the features that researchers associate with high-quality programs, which we have outlined in Table 2.1. Programs need to be well thought out and endure long enough to provide meaningful skill building and then strongly encourage children to attend regularly so that they receive sufficient dosage. Having a structure around and clarity about program goals is vital. Having enough knowledgeable, experienced, well-trained, and well-paid staff who can execute programming to fulfill these goals is also important. These features will help in the creation of a positive climate and the development of supportive relationships. Working to engage schools, families, and communities is also beneficial because these entities are valuable resources that can provide needed expertise.

Directions for the Future

It is clear that the benefits of ASPs are many and that participation in ASPs supports the development of children in many ways. We applaud the varied and imaginative goals that ASPs have for children's development. We are impressed by the concerted efforts of the many professionals who work diligently in this field to provide the best care for children after school. We still need more fundamental research to determine how to best structure ASPs so that they are maximally effective in supporting the academic, social, and emotional needs of the whole child. Adequate funding of ASPs, particularly for children of working class and impoverished families, remains a fundamental concern. As a society, we have not really aligned our funding priorities and our schooling needs with the reality that most families now comprise parents who must work long and hard to support their families. We need to find better ways for ASPs to partner with schools and families to provide the best care for children after school.

GLOSSARY

Homework—Academic work assigned by the school that is designed to elaborate on and extend the practice of academic skills and that is carried out during nonschool hours.

Latchkey kids—Children who care for themselves after school because their parents or caregivers have to remain at their workplace.

Light physical activity—A slow and casual level of exercise in which breathing and heart rate are not increased, but the person is still not sedentary.

Moderate physical activity—A level of exercise akin to moderate walking or biking on a

TABLE 2.1. Features That Characterize High-Quality and Effective ASPs

Feature	Little et al. (2008)	Wade et al. (2015)	Durlak & Weissberg (2007)	Metz et al. (2008)
Sufficient dosage (attendance, duration)	✓		✓	✓
Structured and sequenced	✓		✓	
Clear program goals	✓		✓	✓
Staff training and experience	✓	✓	✓	
Family–community–school involvement	✓			✓
Adequate resources to meet goals		✓	✓	
Using assessment to improve				✓
Well-paid staff		✓		
Low staff turnover		✓		✓
Low student: teacher ratio		✓		✓
Positive climate/supportive relationships		✓		✓
Active learning			✓	
Cultural competence				✓

flat terrain. The breathing and heart rate are increased somewhat, but the person is still able to carry on a conversation.

Parents' after-school stress—Stress that working parents experience related to after-school care issues such as lack of care and the consistency and quality of care. This stress is an aspect of workplace stress.

Regulatable program qualities—Features of programs that can potentially be regulated and easily identified by outside monitors.

Vigorous physical activity—Exercising at a level that requires breathing hard and fast, and at which a person's heart rate is increased significantly.

References

21st Century Community Learning Centers Act, S. 1990, 103rd Congress, 2nd Sess. (1994a).

21st Century Community Learning Centers Act, H.R. 3734, 103rd Congress, 2nd Sess. (1994b).

Afterschool Alliance. (2014). *America after 3pm: Afterschool programs in demand.* Washington, DC: Author.

Beck, E. L. (1999). Prevention and intervention programming: Lessons from an after-school program. *Urban Review, 3,* 107–124.

Beets, M. W., Shah, R., Weaver, R. G., Huberty, J., Beighle, A., & Moore, J. B. (2015). Physical activity in after-school programs: Comparison with physical activity policies. *Journal of Physical Activity and Health, 12*, 1–7.

Black, A. R., Doolittle, F., Zhu, P., Unterman, R., & Grossman, J. B. (2008). *The evaluation of enhanced academic instruction in after-school programs: Findings after the first year of implementation* (NCEE 2008-4021). Washington, DC: National Center for Education Evaluation and Regional Assistance, Institute of Education Sciences, U.S. Department of Education.

Black, A. R., Somers, M.-A., Doolittle, F., Unterman, R., & Grossman, J. B. (2009). *The evaluation of enhanced academic instruction in after-school programs: Final report* (NCEE 2009-4077). Washington, DC: National Center for Education Evaluation and Regional Assistance, Institute for Education Sciences, U.S. Department of Education.

Bureau of Labor Statistics (2016, April 22). *Employment characteristics of families—2015* (USDL-16-0795). Washington, DC: U.S. Department of Labor. Available at *www.bls.gov/news.release/pdf/famee.pdf.*

Carson, V., Ridgers, N. D., Howard, B. J., Winkler, E. A., Healy, G. N., Owen, N., . . . Salmon, J. (2013). Light-intensity physical activity and cardiometabolic biomarkers in US adolescents. *PLOS ONE, 8*(8), e71417.

Catterall, J. S. (2012). *The arts and achievement in at-risk youth: Findings from four longitudinal studies. Research Report #55*. Washington, DC: National Endowment for the Arts.

Choudhry, S., McClinton-Powell, L., Solomon, M., Davis, D., Lipton, R., Darukhanavala, A., . . . Salahuddin, R. (2011). Power-up: A collaborative after-school program to prevent obesity in African American children. *Progress in Community Health Partnerships: Research, Education, and Action, 5*(4), 363.

Cosden, M., Morrison, G., Gutierrez, L., & Brown, M. (2004). The effects of homework programs and after-school activities on school success. *Theory into Practice, 43*(3), 220–226.

Crouter, S. E., de Ferranti, S. D., Whiteley, J., Steltz, S. K., Stavroula, K. S., Feldman, H. A., Hayman, L. L. (2015). Effect on physical activity of a randomized afterschool intervention for inner city children in 3rd to 5th grade. *PLOS ONE, 10*(10), e0141584.

Dabney, K. P., Tai, R. H., Almarode, J. T., Miller-Friedmann, J. L., Sonnert, G., Sadler, P. M., & Hazari, Z. (2012). Out-of-school time science activities and their association with career interest in STEM. *International Journal of Science Education, Part B, 2*(1), 63–79.

Deke, J., Dragoset, L., Bogen, K., & Gill, B. (2012). *Impacts of Title I supplemental educational services on student achievement* (NCEE 2012-4053). Washington, DC: National Center for Education Evaluation and Regional Assistance, Institute of Education Sciences, U.S. Department of Education.

Dentro, K. N., Beals, K., Crouter, S. E., Eisenmann, J. C., McKenzie, T. L., Pate, R. R., . . . Katzmarzyk, P. T. (2014). Results from the United States' 2014 report card on physical activity for children and youth. *Journal of Physical Activity and Health, 11*(Suppl. 1), S105–S112.

DeWitt, J., Archer, L., Osborne, J., Dillon, J., Willis, B., & Wong, B. (2011). High aspirations but low progression: The science aspirations-careers paradox amongst minority ethnic students. *International Journal of Science and Mathematics Education, 9*, 243–271.

Dumont, H., Trautwein, U., Nagy, G., & Nagengast, B. (2014). Quality of parental homework involvement: Predictors and reciprocal relations with academic functioning in the reading domain. *Journal of Educational Psychology, 106*(1), 144–161.

Durlak, J., Berger, S., & Celio, C. (2010). After-school programs. In T. P. Gullotta & M. Bloom (Eds.), *A blueprint for promoting academic and social competence in after-school programs* (pp. 43–62). New York: Springer.

Durlak, J. A., & Weissberg, R. P. (2007). *The impact of after-school programs that promote personal and social skills.* Chicago: Collaborative for Academic, Social, and Emotional Learning.

Durlak, J. A., & Weissberg, R. P. (2011). Afterschool programs that follow evidence-based practices to promote social and emotional development are effective. *Big Views Forward: A Compendium on Expanded Learning* (pp. 1–6). Available at *www.expandinglearning.org.*

Durlak, J. A., Weissberg, R. P., & Pachan, M. (2010). A meta-analysis of after-school programs that seek to promote personal and social skills in children and adolescents. *American Journal of Community Psychology, 45*(3–4), 294–309.

Dynarski, M., James-Burdumy, S., Moore, M., Rosenberg, L., Deke, J., & Mansfield, W. (2004). *When schools stay open late: The national evaluation of the 21st Century Community Learning Centers Program, new findings.* Washington, DC: Mathematica Policy Research. Available at *http://EconPapers.repec.org/RePEc:mpr:mprres:c78bef58be334cd287908403c4e72cf9.*

Gareis, K., & Barnett, R. C. (2006). *After-school worries: Tough on parents, bad for business.* New York: Catalyst.

Gortmaker, S. L., Lee, R. M., Mozaffarian, R. S., Sobol, A. M., Nelson, T. F., . . . Roth, B. A. (2012). Effect of an after-school intervention on increases in children's physical activity. *Medicine and Science in Sports and Exercise, 44*(3), 450–457.

Greenberg, J. (2013). Determinants of after-school programming for school-age immigrant children. *Children and Schools, 35*(2), 101–111.

Gullotta, T. P., Bloom, M., Gullotta, C. F., & Messina, J. C. (Eds.). (2010). *A blueprint for promoting academic and social competence in after-school programs* (Vol. 10). New York: Springer.

Halpern, R. (2002). A different kind of child development institution: The history of after-school programs for low-income children. *Teachers College Record, 104*(2), 178–211.

Heinrich, C. J., Burch, P., Good, A., Acosta, R., Cheng, H., Dillender, M., . . . Stewart, M. (2014). Improving the implementation and effectiveness of out-of-school-time tutoring. *Journal of Policy Analysis and Management, 33*(2), 471–494.

Huang, D., & Dietel, R. (2011). *Making afterschool programs better* (CRESST Policy Brief). Los Angeles: University of California, Los Angeles.

Hynes, K., & Sanders, F. (2010). The changing landscape of afterschool programs. *Afterschool Matters, 12*, 17–27.

Hynes, K., & Sanders, F. (2011). Diverging experiences during out-of-school time: The race gap in exposure to after-school programs. *Journal of Negro Education, 80*(4), 464–476.

James-Burdumy, S., Dynarski, M., & Deke, J. (2007). When elementary schools stay open late: Results from the national evaluation of the 21st Century Community Learning Centers program. *Educational Evaluation and Policy Analysis, 29*(4), 296–318.

Katzir, T., & Goldberg, A., Ben Aryeh, T. J., Donnelley, K., & Wolf, M. (2013). Intensity vs. Duration: Comparing the effects of a fluency-based reading intervention program, in after-school vs. summer school settings. *Journal of Education and Training Studies, 1*(2), 61–73.

Kelder, S., Hoelscher, D. M., Barroso, C. S., Walker, J. L., Cribb, P., & Hu, S. (2004). The CATCH Kids Club: A pilot after-school study for improving elementary students' nutrition and physical activity. *Public Health Nutrition, 8*(2), 133–140.

Krishnamurthi, A., Ballard, M., & Noam, G. G. (2014). *Examining the impact of afterschool STEM programs.* Washington, DC: Afterschool Alliance.

Leos-Urbel, J. (2015). What works after school?: The relationship between after-school program quality, program attendance, and academic outcomes. *Youth and Society, 47*(5), 684–706.

Little, P., Wimer, C., & Weiss, H. B. (2008, February). After school programs in the 21st century: Their potential and what it takes to achieve it. *Issues and Opportunities in Out-of-School Time Evaluation, 10*, 1–12.

Lundh, P., House, A., Means, B., & Harris, C. J. (2013). Learning from science: Case studies of science offerings in afterschool programs. *Afterschool Matters, 18*, 33–41.

Mahoney, J. L., Lord, H., & Carryl, E. (2005). Afterschool program participation and the development of child obesity and peer acceptance. *Applied Developmental Science, 9*(4), 202–215.

Mason, M. J., & Chuang, S. (2001). Culturally-based after-school arts programming for low-income urban children: Adaptive and preventive effects. *Journal of Primary Prevention, 22*(1), 45–54.

Metz, R. A., Goldsmith, J., & Arbreton, A. J. A. (2008). *Putting it all together: Guiding principles for quality after-school programs serving preteens.* Philadelphia: Public/Private Ventures. Available at *www.ppv.org/ppv/youth/youth_publications. asp?section_id=8#pub234.*

Montgomery, D., Rogouin, P., & Persaud, N. (2013). *Something to say: Success principles for afterschool arts programs for urban youth and other experts.* New York: Wallace Foundation.

Moore, K. A., Murphey, D., Bandy, T., & Cooper, M. (2014, March). *Participation in out-of-school time activities and programs.* (Research Brief, Publication #2014-13). Bethesda, MD: Child Trends.

Moritz, C., Yampolsky, S., Papadelis, G., Thomson, J., & Wolf, M. (2013). Links between early rhythm skills, musical training, and phonological awareness. *Reading and Writing, 26*(5), 739–769.

National Association for Sport and Physical Education & American Heart Association. (2006). *Shape of the nation report: Status of physical education in the USA.* Reston, VA: Author.

National Research Council. (2009). *Learning science in informal environments: People, places, and pursuits.* Washington, DC: National Academies Press.

Newell, A. D., Zientek, L. R., Tharp, B. Z., Vogt, G. L., & Moreno, N. P. (2015).

Students' attitudes toward science as predictors of gains on student content knowledge: Benefits of an after-school program. *School Science and Mathematics, 115*(5), 216–225.

Olympia, D. E., Sheridan, S. M., & Jensen, W. (1994). Homework: A natural means of home-school collaboration. *School Psychology Quarterly, 9*(1), 60–80.

Osborne, J. F., Simon, S., & Collins, S. (2003). Attitudes towards science: A review of the literature and its implications. *International Journal of Science Education, 25*(9), 1049–1079.

Parsad, B., & Lewis, L. (2009). *After-school programs in public elementary schools: First look* (NCES 2009-043). Washington, DC: National Center for Educational Statistics, Institution of Education Sciences, U.S. Department of Education.

Patall, E. A., Cooper, H., & Robinson, J. C. (2008). Parent involvement in homework: A research synthesis. *Review of Educational Research, 78*(4), 1039–1101.

Phillips, S. F. (2010). *Honoring 15 years of the 21st Century Community Learning Centers program: A polity-centered analysis.* Washington, DC: Afterschool Alliance.

Reisner, E. R., White, R. N., Russell, C. A., & Birmingham, J. (2004). *Building quality, scale, and effectiveness in after-school programs: The TASC program approach.* Washington, DC: Policy Studies Associates.

Rosenthal, R., & Vandell, D. L. (1996). Quality of care at school-aged child-care programs: Regulatable features, observed experiences, child perspectives, and parent perspectives. *Child Development, 67*(5), 2434–2445.

Sahin, A., Ayar, M. C., & Adiguzel, T. (2014). STEM Related After-School Program Activities and Associated Outcomes on Student Learning. *Educational Sciences: Theory and Practice, 14*(1), 309–322.

Sandoval, J., & Echandia, A. (1994). Behavior assessment system for children. *Journal of School Psychology, 32,* 419–425.

Schuna, J. M., Lauersdorf, R. L., Behrens, T. K., & Liebert, M. L. (2013). An objective assessment of children's physical activity during the Keep It Moving! after-school program. *Journal of School Health, 83*(2), 105–111.

Story, M., Sherwood, N. E., Himes, J. H., Davis, M., Jacobs, D. R., Cartwright, Y., . . . Rochon, J. (2003). An after-school obesity prevention program for African-American girls: The Minnesota GEMS pilot study. *Ethnicity and Disease, 13*(1), S1–54.

Troiano, R. P., Berrigan, D., Dodd, K. W., Masse, L. C., Tilert, T., & McDowell, M. (2008). Physical activity in the United States measured by accelerometer. *Medicine and Science in Sports and Exercise, 40,* 181–188.

Trost, S. G., Rosencranz, R. R., & Dzewaltowski, D. (2008). Physical activity levels among children attending after-school programs. *Medicine and Science in Sports and Exercise, 40,* 622–629.

Wade, C. E. (2015). The longitudinal effects of after-school program experiences, quantity, and regulatable features on children's social-emotional development. *Children and Youth Services Review, 48,* 70–79.

Yin, Z., Gutin, B., Johnson, M. H., Hanes, J., Moore, J. B., Cavnar, M., . . . Barbeau, P. (2005). An environmental approach to obesity prevention in children: Medical College of Georgia FitKid Project year 1 results. *Obesity Research, 13*(12), 2153–2161.

Young, C., & Rasinski, T. (2009). Implementing Readers Theatre as an approach to classroom fluency instruction. *The Reading Teacher, 63*(1), 4–13.

Zimmer, R., Hamilton, L., & Christina, R. (2010). After-school tutoring in the context of No Child Left Behind: Effectiveness of two programs in the Pittsburgh public schools. *Economics of Education Review, 29,* 18–28.

3

The Importance of Process Evaluation for After-School Programs

Katherine Wargo
Jennifer L. Gay

The evaluation of educational and other programs usually is conducted for the outcomes of an intervention; for example, it measures whether academic achievement has increased or whether behavior management has improved. Most of the focus is placed on program outcomes because stakeholders and participants are most interested in an intervention's results. However, *process evaluation*, which is conducted to determine if the program was delivered as intended, is equally important. Process evaluation may explain why program outcomes were or were not achieved (Saunders, Evans, & Joshi, 2005). For example, information collected during process evaluation may reveal that students did not attend enough sessions to make meaningful improvements in mathematics, or that the lesson plans were not followed and so reading skills did not increase. Together, outcome and process evaluation create a summary and explanation of an intervention's results. This chapter will detail how process evaluation was conducted for the Physical Activity and Learning (PAL) Program, including our method for calculating an intervention score and how the score was used to understand results of the *outcome evaluation*.

Introduction to the PAL Program Process Evaluation

As described in Chapter 1, the PAL Program strived to deliver high-quality after-school care in accordance with the 21st CCLC program framework. In order to know whether the goals of the PAL Program were being accomplished, a process evaluation was conducted. This evaluation allowed the staff to determine the extent to which the PAL Program was being implemented as planned (Harris, 2010, p. 207). The components of recruitment, reach, response, dose delivered, dose received, and fidelity of a program are central to the process evaluation. The process evaluation occurred in parallel with program implementation. The data gathered allowed program personnel to determine the acceptance, relevance, and appropriateness of the program activities in real time to determine whether any modifications to the program might be necessary to reach its goals. Program partners and stakeholders also played a key role in contributing data. The evaluation was continuously conducted from the start of the program. Further, PAL Program personnel used process evaluation to better understand the results of the outcome evaluation.

The process-evaluation objectives for the PAL Program were

1. To what extent was the PAL Program implemented as planned or modified to be more effective?
2. What was the quality of PAL Program implementation?
3. Did implementation vary by the implementation characteristics of the site, and if so, how did this factor influence the outcome evaluation results?

Documenting Operational Procedures

In order to conduct a process evaluation, procedures for program implementation needed to be established and communicated to relevant parties. The operational procedures were much more specific than the overarching process evaluation objectives described in the grant application. For example, time stamps, program locations, and step-by-step directions were written for each activity. The Project Codirector (see the organizational chart presented in Chapter 1, Figure 1.1) documented the program's procedures in handbooks, which were created for both the program personnel and the participants and their parents. The handbooks provided a programmatic framework for evaluation. The table of contents for the staff handbook is provided in Figure 3.1.

The PAL Program staff handbook served to document the roles and responsibilities of all program personnel as well as the logistics for program implementation. During the week before the program began, PAL Program personnel attended four 2-hour training sessions, led by the Program Directors. The first 3 days of training focused on the implementation plans for each activity of the program:

homework time, physical activity games (PAGs), and academic enrichment. On the fourth day site visits to the schools were made. These trainings provided staff with the knowledge and skills needed for conducting the program. All program personnel signed an acknowledgment sheet that they had attended all training sessions. Additionally, copies of the acknowledgment sheets were kept on file as part of the implementation-monitoring requirements of the Georgia Department of Education.

Table of Contents

Rationale	3
PAL Program Sites	3
PAL Program Goals and Objectives	5
PAL Program Activities	5
Recruitment and Application Process	7
Daily Schedule	8
Program Duration	9
Program Assessment and Evaluation	10
Program Staff	11
Staff Responsibilities	15
Staff Expectations	15
Rules for Instructors	16
Staff Communication	18
Time and Effort Documentation	20
Observation and Performance Evaluation	20
Instructional Staff Absences	20
PAL Program Documentation	22
PAL Program Materials	24
Lesson Planning	25
PAL Program Students	25
Parent Engagement	31
Emergency Procedures	31
University System of Georgia Ethics Policy	37
Conflicts of Interest	38
Reporting of Suspected Child Abuse	38
Nepotism Policy	40
Reporting Fraud, Waste, and Abuse	40
Non-Discriminatory and Anti-Harassment Policy	42
Non-Discriminatory Expectations	48
Complaint Procedure	49
Staff Handbook Agreement	53

FIGURE 3.1. PAL Program handbook table of contents.

As seen in Figure 3.1, the PAL Program staff handbook began with the background of the program, explanations of the physical activity and the academic enrichment components, and the overall program goals and objectives to better understand the program's rationale. The next section outlined the process for recruiting and enrolling participants and the daily itinerary that needed to be followed each day in order to achieve the required program dose. Logistics, including the physical space, maps of the program site, medical emergency procedures, transportation arrangements, and safety and emergency procedures, were then described. Finally, legal notices, such as ethics policies, conflicts of interest, and complaint procedures were discussed. It was important for information in this legal section to be consistent with established school and district policies.

The last section of the handbook discussed the rules and expectations for the instructional staff. It provided protocols for uploading lesson plans to the staff-shared computer drive, and procedures for tracking time and effort, for scheduling absences and substitute instructors, and for communicating with program staff and school staff. All documents relevant to the program personnel working at the program sites, including a copy of the handbook, important contacts, and the behavior rules for students, were placed in a binder to be kept at each program site. The use of handbooks and training staff well are important for program implementation and therefore process evaluation.

A handbook also was developed for participating students and their parents or caregivers. Similar to the staff handbook, the student–parent handbook begins with the background of the program, explanations of the program's components, and overall program goals and objectives. The sections describing the recruitment and enrollment process, daily itinerary, logistics, and legal notices also were the same as those in the staff handbook. The section describing behavior rules and expectations is tailored to the student. Additional protocols describing ways that parents may contact the PAL Program personnel should behavioral issues with their child arise were included.

On the first day of the PAL Program intervention, key information in the handbook was reviewed with the students, focusing primarily on the itinerary, safety and emergency procedures, and behavior expectations. Parent handbooks were sent home with students for their parents to read, and the parents were asked to return a form acknowledging receipt of the handbook. Instructional staff collected the signed acknowledgment forms from students and filed them in accordance with the monitoring requirements of the Georgia Department of Education.

LESSONS LEARNED

During the first months of the PAL Program and thereafter, some sections of the handbook were revised to better align with actual program implementation procedures and expectations. This is a normal part of program development and requires annual handbook updates. Informing all personnel of handbook changes can be challenging, particularly when they work at multiple sites. When a section has been revised, it is important to notify all staff and stakeholders of the changes and to document the changes that were made. When possible, obtaining documentation that staff received the revised policy is helpful.

Data Management

Process evaluation involves a tremendous amount of data collection and record keeping. Therefore, we briefly review the data management system used by the PAL Program: the CAYEN After School software, a database system recommended by the Georgia Department of Education to manage data, information, and documentation for evaluation purposes. The CAYEN database was managed by the Project Codirector. The CAYEN software system automatically identified information required by the Georgia Department of Education, and it also provided options for internal PAL Program use. Examples of quantitative data recorded in CAYEN included the days, hours, and weeks of program operation, daily attendance, and participant demographics. Examples of qualitative data included staff information, such as certifications, trainings, professional development, surveys, and direct observations.

PAL Program data were obtained from multiple sources. Daily attendance and site debriefings were submitted by PAL Program instructional staff via an online survey link. Lesson plans were submitted weekly through an online storage account by instructional staff at all sites. Lesson plans also were placed into a permanent electronic filing system, which was accessible by all PAL Program personnel. Hard copies of paper data forms also were filed to meet the Georgia Department of Education 21st CCLC team monitoring requirements. While these methods of data management may not be necessary for all after-school programs (ASPs), it is useful to maintain detailed records either in hard copy or electronic form or both for the purposes of process evaluation. We found that both the CAYEN and hard copy database were instrumental in conducting annual monitoring. The information from the data management system was used by both PAL Program personnel and the Georgia Department of Education personnel, who used the databases during monitoring to determine whether the PAL Program objectives were "met," "not met," or "unable to be measured."

LESSONS LEARNED

It was not feasible for each member of the instructional staff to directly enter data into the CAYEN software, given the need to ensure consistency and accuracy in data management. Additionally, the instructional staff had many responsibilities beyond data collection and management. Consequently, one primary data manager was assigned to enter the registration, attendance, and debriefing report information into CAYEN (described in section "Dose Received"). Having one primary person enter all data for the PAL Program ensured that data fidelity was maintained.

Components of Process Evaluation

When planning and managing a process evaluation, it is important to consider all of the components that may affect the program's outcomes. Table 3.1 outlines the components of process evaluation for the PAL Program, the definitions of each component, and a PAL Program example of documentation. Each component is described in greater detail below.

Recruitment, Reach, and Response

The components of recruitment, reach, and response were evaluated first, as they coincided with the first steps of PAL Program implementation.

The component of recruitment refers to whether a person in the target population had an opportunity to participate in a program (Saunders et al., 2005; Steckler

TABLE 3.1. Components of Process Evaluation

Component	Definition	PAL Program example
Recruitment	Communication about the availability of the program to the target population	Information flyer sent to parents whose children were eligible for PAL
Reach	Methods to ensure the entire target population has the opportunity to participate in the program	Identification of eligible students using school records, demographic information, and group consensus
Response	Expressed interest in the program by the target population	Completion of the PAL Program registration form
Dose delivered	The number of program elements offered	3-hour program, offered 5 times per week
Dose received	The number of times a PAL student was exposed to the program	Up to 166 PAL Program days; measured by attendance
Fidelity	The degree to which the program is being implemented as planned	Direct observation of the instructional staff, lesson plans

& Linnan, 2002). The students targeted for the PAL Program were in grades 2–5, had low academic standing, and met additional "at risk" criteria, such as single-parent families, lack of parent contact, large family size, limited transportation options, or parents with limited education. For the PAL Program, stakeholders and partners were vital to successful recruitment. A meeting with PAL Program staff, school principals, faculty, guidance counselors, parents, and community business partners was held prior to the start date of the program to determine the most appropriate methods to identify and recruit students who were part of the target population. The date and time of the meeting and names of attendees were recorded in the CAYEN database.

Recruitment refers to how awareness was raised about the PAL Program and the means through which it was advertised to parents and eligible students (Saunders et al., 2005; Steckler & Linnan, 2002). During initial recruitment planning, meetings methods were identified for contacting parents of targeted students, including the use of established school student–parent information exchange and phone calls to parents from the school staff, with a follow-up text if no response was obtained. A copy of the original recruitment flyer for the PAL Program is shown in Figure 3.2.

The *reach* component describes how many people were contacted within the target population and how much information they were provided. This component facilitates recruitment by ensuring that a large number of families in the target population are informed about the program so, in turn, they have the opportunity to participate. To maximize the reach of the program, the group employed two methods for identifying students to participate in PAL.

- A review of school records, such as school attendance records, financial assistance lists, and disciplinary records
- Interviews of school staff, including teachers, nurses, counselors, social workers, and family engagement specialists

Then the school staff identified approximately 35 students (30 to enroll, and 5 alternate students in case some declined to participate). Additional students were identified and were placed on a wait list in anticipation that some students would become ineligible for the program or drop out during the year and the program would require replacements to maintain full program capacity.

To measure the *response,* or enrollment, component PAL Program personnel issued the school staff a recruitment packet, which included a one-page information sheet, in English and Spanish, about the PAL Program and a registration form to use when contacting the parents of identified students. This registration form is shown in Appendix 3.1. For consistency and ease of data entry, the registration form mirrored the required information fields in the CAYEN database. A response of verbal confirmation of enrollment was given to the school staff at the time

WELCOME TO PAL AFTER-SCHOOL PROGRAM!

The Physical Activity and Learning (PAL) program is a one-of-a-kind after-school program designed by UGA faculty that combines four parts designed to improve academic skills and health:

Physical Activity

Safe and fun games for all ages that fulfill physical activity guidelines and increase brain activity.

Math Session

Applied activities to increase math and problem-solving skills.

Reading Session

Readings fit for different grade levels used to increase reading confidence, vocabulary, and word knowledge.
Readings will be about science and general topics.

Family Events

Families and guardians are invited to attend events held during the year that will showcase the PAL program.

WHY SIGN UP?

Free after-school care

Free bus ride home

A healthy snack served

Activities and sessions lead by trained teachers from University of Georgia

Math and reading sessions go with classroom instruction

Healthy children do better in school

IMPORTANT

Be aware that there are attendance rules for this program due to terms from the GA Department of Education.

DAILY SCHEDULE

2:30 P.M.	3:30 P.M.	4:30 P.M.	5:30 P.M.
Snack and Homework	Physical Activity Games	Math and Reading Sessions	Dismissal and Transportation Home

Fill out and return the registration form to sign up!

Dr. John D. Barge, State School Superintendent
"Making Education Work for All Georgians"

FIGURE 3.2. PAL recruitment flyer.

of initial contact. The receipt of the completed registration form then confirmed a student's enrollment in the program. Instructional staff gave the forms to the Project Codirector, who then inputted the information into the CAYEN database.

The same procedure was followed if a student was moved from the wait list to the enrollment list after the intervention started. The Project Codirector changed the status of students who were no longer in the program from *active* to *inactive* in the CAYEN database before adding new enrollments. For process evaluation it is important to track the timing of enrollment. As discussed later in the section on "Dose Received," not all students were enrolled for the full 166 program days or attended 100% of the time.

LESSONS LEARNED

The Georgia Department of Education required that each site have 30 enrolled students, with each student maintaining at least 70% attendance. Students could be removed from the PAL Program if that threshold was not met. One challenge, particularly early in the program, was being able to quickly identify new students and enroll them into the program. The PAL Program relies heavily on school personnel (e.g., principals, guidance counselors, and administrative staff) to assist with identifying eligible students. This challenge highlights the importance of working closely with school staff, especially for programs run by outside organizations.

Dose

Dose is another component of process evaluation. It consists of two elements, dose delivered and dose received. Each is described below.

Dose Delivered

Dose delivered refers to the amount of program offered by an intervention. In our case, the dose delivered was measured in terms of the number of days and the number of hours the program was made available to participating students. Mirroring the school year calendar, the PAL Program had an operation goal of 166 days.

To satisfy dose-delivered requirements established by the Georgia Department of Education, the daily itinerary was set for 2 hours, 45 minutes. Thirty-five minutes were allocated for snack and homework help, then 45 minutes were spent playing physical activity games (PAGs), followed by 50 minutes spent in either math or reading enrichment. Ten-minute transition periods were allowed between homework, game, and academic sessions because these involved moving children from one location in the building to another. Students in the PAL Program received one semester of reading or math enrichment; for example, the second and third graders received reading enrichment, while the fourth and fifth graders received math enrichment. At the midpoint of the school year, the academic enrichment subjects for each group were switched to the alternate subject.

LESSONS LEARNED

One way in which process evaluation can be helpful is by illustrating ways in which the program might benefit from adaptation. In the first year of the PAL Program, 35 minutes were allocated for snack and homework help, then students participated in 45 minutes of PAGs, and the day finished with 1 hour of reading or math enrichment. However, direct observations and feedback from the instructional staff led to changes during the second year. One key change was the schedule. Instructional time in math and reading was reduced by 10 minutes. Teacher observations reflected that after a long school day many students' attention waned. In addition, transitions between sessions were increased from 5 to 10 minutes to better accommodate bathroom breaks and to reduce interruptions during the sessions. Programmatic changes such as these exemplify the need for programs to be open to feedback from program staff and to observe the levels of engagement and enthusiasm of the children.

Dose Received

Dose received refers to the amount of program received during the intervention. The PAL Program dose was measured by participant attendance, student-to-staff ratio, and participation in additional events, such as family engagement nights. Student attendance was critical for students to reap the full benefits of the intervention. Attendance in the PAL Program was registered daily by the instructional staff using an electronic survey that reflected registration data. This allowed attendance to be entered into the database in real time. An example of this daily survey is presented in Figure 3.3 below.

Students' attendance of at least 70% of the PAL Program sessions during the academic year was mandated by the Georgia Department of Education. Attendance data were provided monthly to the Program Director, and low-attendance students were flagged. The Program Director then provided written notification to the student's parent/guardian if there were concerns about meeting attendance goals. An example of the letter mailed to the student's home is presented in Figure 3.4. After notification, the student would continue to be allowed to attend the PAL Program, with the expectation that a 70% attendance rate would be met thereafter. A child who did not attend at least 70% of PAL Program sessions after this notification could be removed from the program and replaced with a child from the waiting list. Data were updated both in CAYEN and the electronic attendance survey accordingly.

Additionally, to ensure that PAL Program participants received an appropriate dose, staffing was scheduled such that an adequate student-to-staff ratio was maintained throughout the program day. In the PAL Program, a 10:1 ratio was

1. What is the date for which you are entering attendance? Please enter in MM/DD/YYYY.

2. Please select the school for which you are reporting attendance.
○ School 1
○ School 2

3. Indicate which students attended School 1 PAL for the date entered above.

	Attendance				
	Present (1)	Absent (2)	No-show (3)	Not registered (4)	Dropped (5)
Student (1)	○	○	○	○	○
Student (2)	○	○	○	○	○
Student (3)	○	○	○	○	○
Student (4)	○	○	○	○	○
Student (5)	○	○	○	○	○

4. Did any new students attend today?
○ Yes
○ No

5. Please enter the names of new students who attended today:

FIGURE 3.3. Web survey of daily PAL Program attendance.

required for snack/homework session, and the ratio ranged from 7.5:1 to 15:1 when participants were split into groups for math and reading enrichment sessions. To help adhere to ratio requirements, volunteer college students were trained to assist the program personnel. Some of these college student volunteers received field experience course credit for their volunteer hours. The Project Codirector maintained volunteer information in CAYEN and served as the point of contact for issues related to them. The student volunteers received the same background

The University of Georgia

College of Education

Department of Kinesiology

DATE

PARENT NAME
PARENT ADDRESS

Dear PARENT:

I am writing in regard to the attendance of your child, STUDENT NAME, in the *PAL Program*. In the first 12 days of this year's program, **STUDENT has eight (8) absences** in the *PAL Program*. Regular attendance at the *PAL Program* will ensure your child reaps the full benefits of the physical activity and academic enrichment provided by this program. As stated on pages 6–7 of the *PAL Program Student/ Parent Handbook,* students being served must be present for at least 70% of the sessions, which means not missing five (5) or more days per month. Currently, your child's attendance rate falls below that standard.

I am contacting you via this letter and US mail for two reasons. The first reason is to let remind you that as stated on page 7 of the *Student/Parent Handbook,* your child will still be allowed to attend the *PAL Program* but will be expected to maintain a 70% attendance rate. The second reason is to notify you that if STUDENT NAME is not able to attend at least 70% of the *PAL Program* sessions a second time he will be removed from the program so a child on the waiting list can be added.

Please note that excused absences do not count against the amount of absences for a child. To be considered an excused absence, one of the following criteria must be met: (a) documentation is provided from a doctor or other certified medical personnel indicating a child was unable to participate in the *PAL Program* or (b) the child is on a school-sponsored field trip that includes after-school hours.

Should you have any questions and/or would like to discuss this situation, please feel free to contact me via e-mail or phone at the address and number listed after my signature. It is my hope that we can work together to rectify this situation and help STUDENT NAME receive all the benefits of the *PAL Program*.

Most sincerely,

NAME
Co-Director, *PAL Program*

FIGURE 3.4. Letter to notify a parent of a child's low attendance.

checks and followed the same time and effort documentation protocols as the regular instructional staff.

Dose received was calculated for overall attendance in the PAL Program and for each component separately (i.e., snack/homework, PAGs, reading, and math). This level of detail proved necessary as some students left the PAL Program early to attend other appointments or arrived late. Tracking the attendance at each session allowed for the dose received to be considered as part of the outcome evaluation. A central assumption of academic programs is that students with higher attendance rates should have better outcomes relative to students with lower participation rates, which has been borne out by research as discussed in Chapter 2.

The PAL Program site coordinators and instructional staff were asked to complete a daily debriefing form that detailed the start and end times of each session and the number of students in attendance, which were cross-checked with the attendance rosters. The debriefing form also was used to document any deviations from the lesson plans, strategies for engaging the students, and feedback about student engagement. In addition to cross-referencing these data with other data collected through attendance and observations (shown in Figure 3.5), the debriefing form was used to determine if instructional personnel varied in their approaches during the enrichment sessions, as well as how engaged they thought the students were during instruction. Although the dose received in ASPs is generally determined by attendance, programs may consider it worthwhile to examine engagement concurrently with attendance.

Fidelity

Fidelity measures the degree of adherence to the planned protocols and activities of a program. Fidelity may be the most important component of process evaluation, as it determines if process goals and objectives are being met. The PAL Program used a variety of methods to measure the fidelity of both the program and instructional staff: site-level documentation, independent observations, and parent and student satisfaction with the PAL Program.

To ensure that data measured the fidelity to the PAL Program goals, strategies, and methods, a site binder, which contained numerous resources, was created for each program site. The site binder included checklists of tasks that were to be completed daily, weekly, and monthly by the instructional staff onsite. The Project Codirector regularly checked the lists for completion. Other resources included an itinerary for staying on schedule to ensure the proper program dose, a contact list, a calendar, and a copy of the behavior rules should disciplinary action be needed. Also, the instructional staff uploaded lesson plans at the beginning of each week to a shared computer server. The Project Codirector referenced these plans prior to monthly direct observations of the instructional staff, which ensured lesson plans were implemented. The Project Codirector also took note of adherence to the appropriate staff to student ratio, to the program itinerary, and to school rules and regulations.

In addition, independent observations were conducted on a random schedule at each school. For example, observers used the form shown in Appendix 3.2 to document whether the reading enrichment sessions were being conducted according to the weekly plan.

Name: _____

Date: _____

Session: _____

❏ Reading   ❏ Math   ❏ Physical Activity

Start time of session: _____

End time of session: _____

Provide the number of students from your session in attendance today. _____

Which parts of the lesson did you conduct? Please describe.

Did you make any changes to your lesson plan?   ❏ Yes   ❏ No
If so, please describe below.

What were some of the strategies used to implement the lesson?

❏ Small-group work/activities   ❏ Large-group discussion/activities
❏ Role playing   ❏ Other

If other is selected, please describe below.

Please list all of the materials you used today to conduct your lesson (e.g., jump ropes, gymnasium, boards).

Please provide some notes about student engagement or student feedback during the session.

FIGURE 3.5. Instructor debriefing form.

Satisfaction from Key Stakeholders: Student and Parent Satisfaction

Students and parents are key stakeholders in ASPs. A satisfaction survey was distributed to parents of PAL Program students to obtain measures of their level of satisfaction with the intervention. Student surveys were distributed during the homework and snack time. There were two versions of the student survey: one for second and third graders and one for fourth and fifth graders. The types of questions were the similar, but the response format for younger students utilized happy and sad faces rather than the traditional numeric scoring used in the older student survey. Parent surveys were sent home with students in their homework folders from school. Examples of questions from these surveys can be found in Table 3.2. All surveys were available in both English and Spanish. Data from the surveys were entered into data management system.

LESSONS LEARNED

In the first year of the PAL Program, the response rate for parent surveys was extremely low. In subsequent years, children were told that if they returned their parent's survey they would receive a prize. Prizes included a sheet of stickers, fun pencils and erasers, folders with cartoon or movie characters, and other similar items. Students were allowed to pick one prize when they returned the parent survey. The return rate for parent surveys significantly improved after small prizes were awarded to students.

Aggregate Implementation Scoring

Each item of process evaluation data can be valuable on its own. For example, we can learn that students who attended more after-school sessions did better on science tests than those who attended fewer sessions. However, it may be important to create an aggregate implementation score to be able to compare program sites or even classrooms within a program site. An *implementation score* allows us to quantifiably measure the extent to which a program has been implemented the way that it was intended. Using PAL Program data as an example, we illustrate how to develop an aggregate score. Methods in this section are derived from previously published examples of implementation scoring (Saunders, 2016; Saunders et al., 2013).

The first step in creating an implementation score is taken early in the program planning phase. Stakeholders should decide on the desired dose received and what level of fidelity will be acceptable. For the PAL Program, the desired dose was for children to attend a minimum of 70% of the provided sessions. A key decision point is how to calculate the proportion of sessions attended. The program offered

TABLE 3.2. Questions from Parent and Student Surveys

Item	Response options
Parent Survey	
1. The program is helping my child's behavior improve.	Strongly agree, somewhat agree, neither agree nor disagree, somewhat disagree, strongly disagree
2. The program is helping my child to complete and turn in his/her homework on time.	
3. The program is helping my child's math skills improve.	
4. The program is helping my child's reading skills improve.	
5. How satisfied are you with your child's 21st CCLC program?	Very satisfied, somewhat satisfied, neither satisfied nor dissatisfied, somewhat dissatisfied, very dissatisfied
6. Prior to your child participating in the 21st CCLC program, where did your child usually go after school?	My child stayed at home alone; my child stayed home with a sibling, parent, guardian, or sitter; my child went to the home of someone else (like a friend, relative, or sitter); my child went someplace for activities; other
7. How did you find out about the 21st CCLC program?	From the school or agency; from another parent; from another community organization or agency; from another student; other
Student Survey	
1. I like the 21st CCLC program.	Strongly agree, somewhat agree, neither agree nor disagree, somewhat disagree, strongly disagree
2. My overall behavior has improved because of the 21st CCLC program.	
3. The 21st CCLC program helps me complete and turn in my homework on time.	(Smiley faces instead of labels used for younger grades)
4. I'm doing better in school since I started coming to the 21st CCLC program.	
5. I feel better about myself because of the 21st CCLC program.	
6. I have made new friends because of the 21st CCLC program.	

166 program days each school year; thus, 70% of the program days would be 116 days. However, not all children enrolled in the PAL Program at the beginning of the school year. Some started but then dropped out, while other children began midterm. An alternative strategy is to calculate 70% of each term's or quarter's program days. For the PAL Program, we calculated 70% of the total days in which a child was enrolled; if a child started in the middle of the school year and had a maximum dose delivered of 80 program days, then we determined that this student met the desired dose at 56 days of attendance. Although using this calculation method means that each individual student may have a different desired dose, this approach does not penalize or discount students who enrolled midyear or dropped out early.

The desired fidelity for the PAL Program is more difficult to characterize because the some of the measures employed were more subjective than attendance scores. Each week the teachers submitted their lesson plans to the process evaluation team. Using the direct observation form such as the one shown in Appendix 3.2, we determined whether the lesson plans for the PAGs and math and reading enrichment sessions had been followed. We also wanted to know if students were engaged in the program's activities. The start and end times of each activity were documented to assess the dose delivered. For each implementation item, a rating scale was used to determine the extent to which implementation was met. Appendix 3.3 outlines the implementation scoring criteria for the PAL Program.

Using criteria such as the ones shown in Appendix 3.3, a score can be created for each site by adding the points from the Criteria column. The scores created for each implementation item, and the aggregate score, can be used to compare classrooms within a program site or across program sites to determine high- or low-implementing sites. This was important when considering the outcomes for the PAL Program and for each of our participating schools. The implementation scoring can help identify areas of improvement for future years.

Summary

Process evaluation is useful for understanding how well a program is being implemented relative to the program plan. For the PAL Program, monitoring provided useful feedback through which it has been improved. In this chapter, the components of the PAL Program process evaluation were described. It is important to note that different after-school programs should tailor the process evaluation to their needs, expectations, and resources. Some process evaluations may be more basic, such as only documenting attendance for example, whereas other programs may incorporate a more complex process-evaluation methodology. Regardless, process evaluation can be used to improve programs during implementation and serve as a basis for determining the reasons for particular results of an outcome evaluation.

GLOSSARY

Dose delivered—The amount of program components offered in which students participate.

Dose received—The amount of program components received by the participants, generally measured by participant attendance, student-to-staff ratio, and participation in additional events.

Fidelity—The degree of adherence to the planned protocols and activities of a program.

Implementation score—A score that allows us to quantitatively measure the extent to which a program has been implemented the way that it was intended.

Outcome evaluation—An evaluation of the effects of a program or intervention in the target population carried out by assessing progress toward reaching intended outcomes that the intervention is designed to achieve.

Process evaluation—A method of program assessment designed to measure how well a program was actually implemented relative to what was planned or proposed.

Reach—How many people were contacted within the target population and how much information they were provided.

Response—Decision to enroll in a program once information about the program has been received.

References

Harris, M. J. (2010). *Evaluating public and community health programs.* San Francisco: Jossey-Bass.

Saunders, R. P. (2016). *Implementation monitoring and process evaluation.* Los Angeles: SAGE.

Saunders, R. P., Evans, A. E., Kenison, K., Workman, L., Dowda, M., & Chu, Y. H. (2013). Conceptualizing, implementing, and monitoring a structural health promotion intervention in an organizational setting. *Health Promotion Practice, 14*(3), 343–353.

Saunders, R. P., Evans, M. H., & Joshi, P. (2005). Developing a process-evaluation plan for assessing health promotion program implementation: A how-to guide. *Health Promotion Practice, 6*(2), 134–147.

Steckler, A., & Linnan, L. (2002). Process evaluation for public health interventions and research: An overview. In A. Steckler & L. Linnan (Eds.), *Process evaluation for public health interventions and tesearch* (pp. 1–23). San Francisco: Jossey-Bass.

Appendix 3.1. PAL Program Registration Form

Student Information Form

Name (Last, First):

_____

_____

Grade: _____

Teacher: _____

School:

_____

_____

Birth Date (dd/mm/yyyy):

Gender:
___ Male ___ Female

Lunch Status:
□ Free/Reduced   □ Full   □ Unknown

Ethnicity:
□ American Indian/Alaskan Native   □ Asian
□ Black (not of Hispanic origin)   □ Hispanic
□ White   □ Native Hawaiian or Pacific Islander
□ Other _____

Mailing Address: _____

_____

_____

_____

Student lives with:
□ both parents   □ foster care   □ grandparents   □ guardian   □ joint custody   □ single-parent father
□ single-parent mother □ other _____

Special Needs (school needs, allergies, medications, diet, etc.):

Sibling 1: _____ **Grade:** _____ **Lives at home?** □ Yes □ No
Sibling 2: _____ **Grade:** _____ **Lives at home?** □ Yes □ No
Sibling 3: _____ **Grade:** _____ **Lives at home?** □ Yes □ No

Parent/Guardian Last Name:	**First Name:**	**Phone #:** (Cell phone)	**Relationship:**
Address:		**Other Phone #:** (Work or Home)	
Parent/Guardian Last Name:	**First Name:**	**Phone #:** (Cell phone)	**Relationship:**
Address:		**Other Phone #:** (Work or Home)	

Email Address (please provide one per household):

Parents' Preferred Method of Contact: □ Phone   □ Text   □ Email

ADDITIONAL CONTACTS:

- List additional contacts for the child(ren) and use the check boxes to indicate if these individuals are authorized to **pick up** the child(ren) and/or will serve as an **emergency contact**.
- Checking the "Lives with" box indicates that the person listed is a member of the same household.
- *If no adults are listed below, and no boxes are checked, ONLY THE PARENT(S)/GUARDIAN(S) will be able to pick up the student(s).*

Last Name	First Name	Phone	Pick Up?	Emergency	Lives with?
			□ Yes □ No	□ Yes □ No	□ Yes □ No
			□ Yes □ No	□ Yes □ No	□ Yes □ No
			□ Yes □ No	□ Yes □ No	□ Yes □ No

Check box if legal restrictions are in effect.   □ Yes □ No
List persons **not allowed** to see student at Site and/or persons **not allowed to pick up** student per legal restrictions.

(continued)

Sibling 1 information			

Name (Last, First): _____ _____

Grade: _____

Teacher: _____

School:

Birth Date (dd/mm/yyyy): _____

Gender: ___ Male ___ Female

Lunch Status: □ Free/Reduced   □ Full   □ Unknown

Ethnicity:
□ American Indian/Alaskan Native   □ Asian
□ Black (not of Hispanic origin)   □ Hispanic
□ White   □ Native Hawaiian or Pacific Islander
□ Other _____

Mailing Address: _____
_____
_____
_____
_____

Student lives with:
□ both parents □ foster care   □ grandparents □ guardian □ joint custody □ single-parent father
□ single-parent mother □ other _____

Special Needs (school needs, allergies, medications, diet, etc.):

If parent information different from page 1, please explain here: _____
_____

Check box if legal restrictions are in effect.   □ Yes □ No
If Yes, please explain and provide documentation:

List persons **not allowed** to see student at site and/or persons **not allowed to pick up** students per legal restrictions.

Sibling 2 Information			

Name: (Last, First) _____ _____

Grade: _____

Teacher: _____

School:

Birth Date (dd/mm/yyyy):

Gender: ___ Male ___ Female

Lunch Status: □ Free/Reduced   □ Full   □ Unknown

Ethnicity:
□ American Indian/Alaskan Native   □ Asian
□ Black (not of Hispanic origin)   □ Hispanic
□ White   □ Native Hawaiian or Pacific Islander
□ Other _____

Mailing Address: _____
_____
_____
_____
_____

Student lives with:
□ both parents □ foster care   □ grandparents □ guardian □ joint custody □ single-parent father
□ single-parent mother □ other _____

Special Needs: (school needs, allergies, medications, diet, etc.)

If parent information different from page 1, please explain here: _____
_____

Check box if legal restrictions are in effect   □ Yes □ No
If Yes, please explain and provide documentation:

List persons **not allowed** to see student at site and/or persons **not allowed to pick up** student per legal restrictions.

(continued)

	Parent Initials Required
	Please initial next to the 21st Century Expectations.
(Parent initials)	• I understand that the expectation for good behavior in the 21st Century After-School Program is the same as during the regular school day. • **All regular school day rules apply, including dress and behavior rules. Students who refuse to follow these procedures will not be allowed to continue in the program.** • Parents/guardians will be contacted if a child misbehaves. Chronic misbehavior may result in dismissal from the program.
(Parent initials)	• I understand that transportation from the school will be provided for my child. • **Misbehavior on the bus can result in suspension from the bus, as well as from the 21st Century program.** • **In the event that I choose to transport my child, I understand that I must pick him/her up NO LATER than 5:30 P.M. from the parent pick-up location. I understand I may be required to show an ID to confirm my identification.** • If a child is consistently not picked up on time, the child may be dismissed from the program.
(Parent initials)	• I understand due to the active nature of the PAL Program proper footwear includes closed-toed tennis, cross-training, or basketball shoes. • Sandals such as flip flops, Crocs, or gladiator sandals that have open toes or open heels may prohibit a child from running and therefore make participating much harder. • I understand that my child may wear sandals to school, but he/she should bring tennis shoes in his/her backpack if he/she plans to attend the PAL Program and participate in the activities. • If a child does not bring the proper shoes chronically, he/she may be removed from the program.
	TRANSPORTATION HOME
(Parent initials)	• If I wish to pick up my student before 5:30 P.M., I **MUST** sign him/her out at the front desk of the elementary school to ensure student safety. • After 5:30 P.M. all students will be located with PAL Program staff near the bus loop or front entrance of the building and must be signed out at that location.
	Please check all that apply below.
☐ Yes ☐ No	• My child will ride the bus in the afternoon.
☐ Yes ☐ No	• I will pick my child up at 5:30 P.M.
Parent Signature for Page 3	
I agree with all the listed procedures on this page.	
Parent signature: _____ Date: _____ / _____ / _____	

(continued)

Appendix 3.1. (page 4 of 4)

Program Policies		
Accept	**Decline**	
☐	☐	I agree to participate in the Community Learning Center (CLC) programs and activities and I hereby give permission for the participant(s) listed on the previous pages to take part in the school district's 21st Century CCLC activities, which may include off-site events (parents will be notified in advance), academic assistance, continuing education, and physical activity games.
☐	☐	If a medical emergency arises, program staff will take all steps necessary to ensure the safety of the participant and will call, if necessary, a public emergency vehicle for transport to an emergency facility. I understand that I will be responsible for any transportation charges and medical expenses incurred.
☐	☐	I agree that if a health condition exists now or in the future that would impact the participation of those listed on the front, I will notify the 21st Century CLC staff.
☐	☐	I hereby give my consent to the school district's 21st Century CLC programs to take the participant's photograph during program activities, to be used for education and public relations purposes in conjunction with the school district's 21st Century CLC programs, including creating ID badges for substitutes and volunteers of the program. I will be contacted in advance if CLC wishes to use my child's photo or video on our website and/or promotional media.
☐	☐	I hereby give permission for my child's artwork, poetry, or other work produced in conjunction with the school district's 21st Century CLC programs to be used for education, staff training, and public relations purposes.
☐	☐	I understand that the information to be posted may include information from my child's academic, guidance, permanent, or cumulative record (i.e., grades or attendance records). I also understand that the information to be posted does not include other personal identifiable information, such as my child's address, phone number, or Social Security number.
☐	☐	I understand that the school district will use participant records to evaluate individual progress and improvement, as well as to evaluate the impact of the program on student achievement and to obtain continued funding for the program.
☐	☐	I hereby certify that I have read and do understand the above information.
☐	☐	I understand that students enrolled in the program will be expected to come (Monday through Friday) each week. In the event a student cannot maintain his/her attendance at 21st Century, his/her spot will be given to a student on the waiting list after multiple consecutive days absent.
☐	☐	I understand that this program is provided free of charge to families. To ensure continuation of funding parents/guardians are asked to attend at least one family event each year (parent orientation, parent coffee, etc.).

SIGNATURES
By your signature on this document, you hereby agree and consent that your child may participate in the 21st Century CLC program. You have been informed of the policies and procedures of the program, and understand that no medical expenses will be paid in connection with any injury incurred while participating in the activities of this program.

Name of Parent/Guardian: (PRINT)

Parent/Guardian Signature:	Date:

Appendix 3.2. PAL Program Observation Fidelity Instrument for Reading

Date: _____

Start Time: _____

End Time: _____

Weekly lesson plan includes one enrichment activity related to topic.

To what extent did the instructor follow the lesson plan?
- ❏ Followed the sequence of topics and activities listed in the lesson plan.
- ❏ Changed one of the topics/activities listed in the lesson plan.
- ❏ Did not follow the sequence of topics and activities listed in the lesson plan.

Instructor's lesson plan includes one of the three related texts. *Refer to lesson plans.*
- • Please identify which book was being used: _____

To what extent did the instructor's lesson plan relate to a science topic?
- ❏ Scientific content was included throughout most of the lesson.
- ❏ Scientific content was included in less than half of the lesson.

Instructor has used at least one of the following fluency-related practices during the hour. *Please check all that apply to the lesson:*
- ❏ Teacher read-aloud
- ❏ Echo reading
- ❏ Choral reading
- ❏ Partner reading

Instructor has used at least one of the following comprehension-related practices during the hour. *Please check all that apply to the lesson:*
- ❏ Activating prior knowledge
- ❏ Emphasis on vocabulary words
- ❏ Instruction on word affixes
- ❏ Identification of informational text strategies: ID subgenres, ID key words
- ❏ Asked comprehension questions or has children ask comprehension questions

(continued)

To which extent were students able to direct the lesson?
- ❏ The instructor frequently gave room for students to raise questions and issues about reading that are relevant even if the questions are not planned in the lesson plan.
- ❏ Occasionally gave room to students to raise questions and issues about reading even if they are not planned in the curriculum.
- ❏ Followed the lesson sequence and structure.

How would you describe the participation in this group?
- ❏ Participation is balanced (everyone participates more or less equally).
- ❏ Participation is semi-balanced, but some students may dominate while others are often withdrawn.
- ❏ Participation is very much dominated by a few students.

Do you see the students learning new reading skills and strategies at this point?
- ❏ Most students demonstrate/report using new fluency or comprehension-related strategies in reading.
- ❏ A few students demonstrate/report using fluency or comprehension-related strategies in reading.
- ❏ Students don't demonstrate/report using fluency or comprehension-related strategies in reading.

	All of the time	Most of the time	Some of the time	None of the time
The teacher encourages participation.				
The students as a group are attentive.				
Students are respectful of each other.				
Students are quiet or uncomfortable during the lesson.				
Students are having fun.				

Did students express any concerns about the observer in the room?

_____

_____

_____

Did the facilitator notice any marked differences in the students because of the observer?

_____

_____

_____

Additional Notes:

Appendix 3.3. Fidelity Measures, Examples, and Implementation Scoring

Process evaluation component	PAL Program measurement tool	Example item	Rating scale	Criteria
Dose delivered	Debriefing form	Indicate the session start and end time.	Calculate the proportion of total minutes.	Calculate the proportion of total possible session time: > 90% = 1, < 90% = 0.
Dose received	Attendance records	Indicate whether each student was present for each session.	Calculate the number of students who completed 70% of program days in which they were enrolled.	70% of program days in which at least 30 students were enrolled*: ≥ 70% attendance = 1, < 70% attendance = 0.
Physical activity games	Direct observation form	To what extent did the instructor follow the lesson plan?	Score each item on the observation form as yes/no, or as a Likert scale, where higher scores are better.	Calculate the percent fidelity by dividing the observed score by the total possible points. Scores of 80% or higher represent a high level of fidelity (3 points); scores of 50%–79% represent moderate levels of fidelity (2 points); scores lower than 50% represent low fidelity (1 point).
Reading enrichment	Direct observation form	To what extent were students able to direct the lesson?		
Math enrichment	Direct observation form			
Student engagement	Direct observation form	How would you describe participation in this group?	Score the last two items on the observation form as a Likert scale, where higher scores are better.	Calculate the percent fidelity by dividing the observed score by the total possible points. Scores of 80% or higher represent a high level of student engagement (3 points); scores of 50%–79% represent moderate levels of student engagement (2 points); scores lower than 50% represent low student engagement (1 point).

Note. Based on Saunders et al. (2013).

*Dose received threshold for PAL was determined by the funder.

4

The Development of Physical Activity Games

Theory and Research Overview

Phillip D. Tomporowski
Bryan A. McCullick

Adages advocating a sound mind in a sound body (*Mens sana in corpore sano*) have been expressed since the times of the ancient Greeks and Romans. The phrase is often used in contemporary education to highlight the importance of physical activity for mental and psychological well-being. In some ways the physical activity games (PAGs) that are central to the Physical Activity and Learning (PAL) Program are nothing new. Educators have long developed many developmentally appropriate games for children. What sets the PAGs apart from most traditional games, however, is the manner in which the games are played. Considerable research over the past two decades has led scientists to elucidate how specific physical activity experiences, performed in specific ways, can favorably affect and enhance children's mental development. As described in Chapter 1, the PAGs are purposely taught before the academic enrichment interventions. The PAGs are carefully constructed so that children are not just engaging in moderate to vigorous bouts of exercise; rather, they are also put in situations that require them to inhibit movements, switch actions, and update information while they are exercising. That is, the games intentionally require the use of executive functions and strategies.

The driving force behind the PAL Program is the continually growing evidence base regarding the effects of exercise on cognition. To develop a clear understanding about the PAL Program, we feel it is necessary to have an overview of the evidence and theories that have both made contributions to and driven its design. This chapter provides summaries of several areas of research that have explored the exercise–cognition connection and the hypotheses that attempt to explain this connection. The PAGs developed for the PAL Program are the product of research that has focused on (1) specific types of physical activity interventions, (2) methods of movement instruction, (3) theories of skill acquisition, and (4) indirect psychosocial consequences of physical activity.

Types of Physical Activity Interventions

The terms *exercise* and *physical activity* are often thought of as being interchangeable. However, researchers define physical activity as any bodily movement produced by skeletal muscle contraction that requires energy expenditure, whereas exercise is a subset of physical activity and is defined by methods that are planned, structured, and purposeful in the sense that the improvement or maintenance of one or more components of physical fitness is the objective (Dishman, Heath, & Lee, 2012). Thus, exercise interventions focus specifically on cardiorespiratory function, muscular strength, muscular endurance, or flexibility. Physical activity interventions may involve the components of physical fitness, but the goals may focus on skill development, social interactions, and pleasures that are derived though movements. The distinction between exercise and physical activity is central to the PAGs designed for the PAL Program. While the games may indeed improve children's bodies in terms of physical fitness and optimal weight, they also serve as vehicles for training children's minds. The nature of the PAGs may be best explained by comparing the types of interventions that can be offered to children and adolescents.

Quantitative versus Qualitative Interventions

Historically, the role of physical education teachers has been to teach children movement skills that are necessary to engage in later sport, recreation, leisure, and everyday activities that promote physical literacy (National Association for Sport and Physical Education, 2011). *Physical literacy* is defined as the capacity to move with competence in a wide variety of physical activities benefitting the development of the whole person (Mandigo, Francis, Lodewyk, & Lopez, 2009; National Association for Sport and Physical Education & American Heart Association, 2012).

Over the past few decades, the role of physical educators has expanded beyond movement-skill instruction to include guidance in physical fitness, health, and wellness. Some may argue that this trend has been at the expense of movement-skill instruction and that physical *education* is now viewed by laypersons as physical *activity*. Research conducted in the field of pediatric exercise science has elucidated the benefits of aerobic exercise on children's physical and mental development. The global rise in the prevalence of overweight and obesity early in life and its associated impact on the individual, the family, the community, and the nation has drawn the attention of physical educators and health providers. National guidelines have emerged from many studies that demonstrate the importance of physical activity to health outcomes. The American Physical Activity Guidelines (Physical Activity Guidelines Advisory Committee, 2008) and the Exercise is Medicine (EIM) global health initiative managed by the American College of Sports Medicine (ACSM; Exercise is Medicine, 2016) have greatly influenced how contemporary physical educators, parents, and policymakers view interventions designed to improve children's lives. The EIM focuses on encouraging primary care physicians and other health care providers to include physical activity when designing treatment plans for patients and to refer their patients to EIM-credentialed exercise programs and exercise professionals. The EIM is committed to the belief that physical activity is integral to the prevention and treatment of diseases and should be regularly assessed and "treated" as part of all health care.

Proponents of the health-related models often recommend *quantitative exercise interventions,* whose purpose is to increase the components of children's physical fitness. These interventions emphasize aerobic exercises. Indeed, the 2008 American Physical Activity Guidelines recommend that children and adolescents should engage in 60 minutes or more of exercise daily, with most of the 60 minutes allocated to either moderate- or vigorous-intensity aerobic activities. As part of the 60-minutes-plus dose amount, children should include muscle-strengthening activities, such as playing on playground equipment, climbing trees, and playing tug-of-war, and bone-strengthening activities, such as basketball, tennis, and hopscotch (Physical Activity Guidelines Advisory Committee, 2008). Children's levels of involvement in these types of activities are classically defined in terms of intensity, frequency, and duration (Garber et al., 2011). Typically, the interventions are rhythmic and purposely designed to require minimal levels of movement skills.

By contrast, *qualitative exercise interventions* are characterized as those involving physical activity together with cognitive effort and/or skill learning (e.g., exergames, multilimb coordination games, or strategy/learning games), and whose intervention fidelity is based on indices of mental engagement (e.g., observational methods, self-reports). *Mental engagement* reflects thoughtfulness and exertion of attentional effort to comprehend new information and to master new skills (Tomporowski, McCullick, Pendleton, & Pesce, 2015).

Children can benefit from both quantitative and qualitative physical activity interventions. Quantitative, aerobic-based activities promote physical health and fitness and offset the detrimental effects of a sedentary lifestyle (e.g., weight gain). Qualitative, skill-based activities foster the acquisition of knowledge that underlies physical literacy. While intervention programs that blend aerobic and skills train-ing are ideal, it is important to remember that many quantitative interventions designed for adult fitness training (e.g., distance running, swimming, and cycling) are not well suited for children, whose physical activity patterns differ markedly from those of adults (Welk, Corbin, & Dale, 2000). The PAGs developed for the PAL Program intervention were based on the assumption that qualitative activities resembling play, games, and sports that are developmentally appropriate give chil-dren opportunities to master physical and cognitive skills and to learn to control thoughts and actions (Tomporowski, McCullick, & Pesce, 2015). Furthermore, these types of games appeal to children's natural inclination to want to play games, as opposed to running on a treadmill or participating in activities whose only pur-pose is to raise heart rates. At the risk of oversimplifying this notion, we ask you to think back to your childhood and ponder this scenario. If given the chance to play a game in which you would be physically active and required to think about and change your actions, or walk or jog laps around a track or on a treadmill, which would you enjoy more?

Acute versus Chronic Interventions

Acute bouts of physical activity are individual events that occur within a specific time frame. A 30-minute yoga session, for example, would constitute an acute exer-cise bout characterized by a brief warm-up period, a longer period during which specific postures and breathing techniques would be practiced, and a brief cool-down period. The yoga session would elicit multiple physiological changes in par-ticipants' skeletal, muscular, organ, endocrine, and nervous systems. Numerous studies suggest that physical activity increases general physiological and psycho-logical arousal (Brooks, Fahey, & White, 1996). Physical arousal alters an indi-vidual's levels of attention, vigilance, and emotions (Ekkekakis & Acevedo, 2006; Williamson, 2006); it also leads to the release of hormones that moderate mem-ory consolidation and learning (McGaugh, 2015). Emotional learning reflects the adaptive nature of movement-induced learning in humans. The capacity to recall emotional events and the context in which they occur has tremendous survival value for the individual as well as for the evolution of the species (Kempermann et al., 2010). Several anthropologists and neuroscientists have highlighted the impor-tance of the evolution of memory systems for the successful survival of our species (Mithen, 1996). Our ancient ancestors experienced many life-or-death experiences on a regular basis. Retaining the memories of escape from predators or remember-ing the location of water or food would provide a substantial survival benefit. The evidence amassed on the neurobiology of emotional memory consolidation support hypotheses generated in the field of evolutionary psychology. Our ancient ancestors may have had limited language or capacity to store general knowledge, but they certainly possessed memories of "fight-or-flight" situations that aided survival.

The observed memory-enhancing properties of acute bouts of physical activity have been supported by recent research results showing that both children and adults remember more academic material (e.g., word lists, prose) following a single exercise bout than they do without exercising (Etnier, Labban, Piepmeier, Davis, & Henning, 2014; Labban & Etnier, 2011). These and other observations led us to begin every after-school day with a 45-minute bout of game play to induce physical and mental arousal. Mathematics and reading interventions follow thereafter. The organization of the PAL Program in this respect differs from that seen in typical after-school programs (ASPs), which involve children first in academic enrichment programs followed by time for free play and sports.

Chronic exercise programs are defined by repeated acute bouts of physical activity, typically several times per week over periods of months (Dishman et al., 2012). Research conducted first with older-age participants (Hillman, Erickson, & Kramer, 2008) and then with children (Davis et al., 2007) revealed that chronic exercise training can lead to alterations in brain structure and function. It is well established that chronic exercise activity can affect neurological integrity. Routine exercise results in increased production of brain growth factors that are critical for maintaining the continuity of neural networks. Children who are physically fit evidence greater white-matter volume and integrity than less-fit children (Chaddock, Pontifex, Hillman, & Kramer, 2011), which is related to the brain's information-processing efficiency (Gomez-Pinilla & Hillman, 2013). Brain growth factors not only alter existing neurons but also instigate the creation of new neurons, particularly in those brain areas such as the prefrontal cortex that are involved in planning and decision making (Chaddock et al., 2010; Erickson et al., 2011). Moreover, these morphological changes are associated with mathematics and linguistic achievement scores (Chaddock-Heyman et al., 2016). Physical fitness is also associated with brain blood flow and utilization in the hippocampus, which is believed to be critical for forming new memories (Erickson et al., 2011).

The design of our PAGs guarantees that children benefit from both acute bouts of physical activity and routine chronic training. Each day, children's levels of physical arousal are altered in ways that are developmentally appropriate. Observations of children's activity levels reveal patterns that differ greatly from those of adults (Bailey et al., 1995). Children engage in multiple, rapid bursts of activity followed by periods of lower-level activities. These developmental differences help explain why games created to fit children's natural movements (brief actions followed by recovery) may be more engaging for children than aerobic training methods preferred by adults (treadmill running, cycling, distance swimming).

Laboratory versus Translational Interventions

Researchers attempt to understand relationships that exist in nature. For example, the belief that exercise improves the mind has been generally accepted for over 2 millennia; however, evidence for a causal connection between exercise and cognition was demonstrated experimentally only relatively recently. At the most basic level, an experiment requires that individuals be assigned randomly to a treatment or a nontreatment (control) group. Members of the treatment group are provided an intervention hypothesized to change a specified outcome (e.g., long-term memory); members of the control group do not receive the intervention. Support for a causal connection is provided when the outcome measures obtained from the treatment group differ significantly from those of the control group. When little information is known about the causal connection between an intervention (independent variable) and outcome variable (dependent variable), experiments are often performed under laboratory conditions. In laboratory experiments researchers have the opportunity to control the factors that might interfere with or cloud evidence of a causal connection. Much of what we know about the causal connection between exercise and children's mental functioning has taken place under this rather constrained laboratory context. Several well-designed experiments have demonstrated causality: exercise altered children's cognitive performance (Donnelly et al., 2016). These experiments provide evidence of the *efficacy* of an intervention; that is, evidence that the intervention works. Experimental research conducted on the relationship between exercise and children's cognition is also supported by evidence obtained from other research approaches, including case, cross-sectional, longitudinal, and prospective studies, for example. Taken as a whole, this body of research provides solid evidence for the benefits of both acute and chronic exercise interventions.

Translational interventions involve the uptake, implementation, and sustainability of research findings within standard care (Gaglio, Shoup, & Glasgow, 2013). Such research is concerned with the *effectiveness* of an intervention; that is, whether the intervention will reap benefits under real-world conditions. For many decades, much basic science research was predicated on the assumption that the transfer of the methods employed in research laboratories to the real world would follow a linear pathway; that is teachers, practitioners, clinicians, and policymakers would be able to understand and adapt laboratory interventions to meet their needs without difficulty. Beginning in the 1990s, researchers began to examine successful translational research programs and to promote a *relationship model*, which is based on the assumption that successful translational work depended on knowledge exchange among individuals, organizations, institutions, and social networks.

The framework of the 21st Century Community Learning Centers (CCLC) Program closely parallels the relationship model. As such, the PAL Program was designed in accordance with the RE-AIM model developed by Glasgow and colleagues (2004). The central components of the model are *Reach,* which targets individuals with specific needs; *Effectiveness,* which identifies how the intervention will affect participants' quality of life; *Adoption,* which brings school administrators and parents into decision-making processes; *Implementation,* which reflects teacher preparation and training; and *Maintenance,* which addresses the sustainability of the intervention.

Methods of Movement Instruction

Given that the goals of PAGs are to enhance children's cognitive functioning and increase their physical literacy, questions arise as to instructional methods that most efficiently achieve these goals. Many health- and skill-related training programs have been developed by highly respected sport coaches, physical educators, and concerned parents. However, there have been just as many programs designed by researchers, whose only goals were to elicit physiological changes, with little heed paid to the importance of the programs' instructional delivery. Instructional approaches are not inherently "good" or "bad" for children; they are designed with particular goals in mind. The approach used in the PAL Program places a high value on the instructional approach and depends greatly on the person working as the instructor. In this section, we want to highlight some important distinctions between types of movement instruction that are often believed to be synonymous.

Sport versus Physical Literacy

Research conducted by pediatric exercise scientists sheds light on the impact of fitness training on children's developing bodies. Some aspects of physical fitness can be enhanced through systematic exercise training programs (Malina, Bouchard, & Bar-Or, 2004). Endurance training produces improvements in the children's cardiorespiratory efficiency; however, the gains are, at best, only a third of those achieved in adults. Children's aerobic capacity is guided primarily by maturation and is influenced little by physical activity levels. Resistance training can improve children's muscular strength and endurance, but to a lesser degree than in adults. Further, improvements in children's muscular strength and endurance are explained primarily by neuromuscular integration that arises from motor skill development rather than by changes in skeletal muscle morphology. Chronic exercise training, particularly weight-bearing activity, favorably affects bone mineral content. This observation is important because bone mineral levels established early in life set the levels in adulthood.

These findings have led some teachers to develop training activities similar to those typically used by adults. Specialized sport-specific training programs from baseball to golf to swimming have become popular over the past decade. Training camps and sport schools focus on adapting children's bodies and developing skills that are required for elite levels of performance. If the goal of a training program is to improve performance at sports, then specialized training programs have merit. However, if the goal is to improve children's physical literacy and cognitive function, developmentally appropriate games may be more suitable. Of course, it is helpful to understand the course of children's development when creating and implementing effective games. Our PAGs draw upon two bodies of literature that address children's development. The first describes physical development and the emergence of fundamental motor skills, and the second describes cognitive development and the emergence of executive functions and metacognitive processes.

Physical Development

Motricity is a biological property of the nervous system that is involved in both reflective unlearned movement patterns and learned goal-directed actions (Llinas, 2001). Physical movement begins at conception and continues throughout the life span. Newborns' movements are primarily reflexive in nature and consist of those actions essential to survival (e.g., grasping, sucking, and the startle response). Locomotor reflexes are observed soon after birth, with infants displaying involuntary movement patterns that are prototypical of climbing, walking, stepping, and swimming. During early childhood (ages 3–5 years), fundamental motor skills emerge. Three broad categories of fundamental movement behaviors have been identified: locomotor, nonlocomotor, and manipulative. Locomotion involves voluntarily moving from one place to another. Children develop a wide array of movements, and use them to transport themselves forward, up, and down. Walking is observed first as a reflexive pattern in infants and, then, as a voluntary action by most children by 13 months. The skill becomes fully matured by the age of 4–5 years. Running differs from walking in that it requires the child to use leg force to propel the body into space. Most children become proficient at running by age 5. Increases in leg strength and movement control play an important role in complex movements required of sprinting, jumping, and hopping. These movement patterns are refined with experience. Nonlocomotive behaviors include balance control, which is a very complex process involving the integration of sensory inputs, such as focal and ambient vision and vestibular and proprioceptor information. Manipulative behaviors include catching, throwing, striking, and kicking. The ability to intercept objects in space, such as catching a ball, is extremely complex and reflects rudimentary psychomotor abilities. The capacity to time or pace movements is critical to manipulative skills; it is not typically observed in mature form until age 5 or 6. As a result, a young child's abilities to dribble, kick, or strike a ball are not well developed. Although children as young as 6 years may exhibit mature throwing movements, they do not become proficient until adolescence. During later childhood (6–12 years) movement skills are typically refined. Movement patterns made by young children are performed inefficiently, but become increasingly more controlled and skilled as neuromuscular control improves and skeletal muscle increases.

With practice, fundamental movement skills become habitual patterns of action that are ingrained and enduring. Without access to exercise programs that promote motor skill practice, children miss the opportunity to develop health-promoting habits. Children who fail to refine the basic skills of hopping, throwing, jumping, and kicking will tend to doubt their abilities when asked to participate in games. By middle school, children are cognizant of their skill levels; children who see themselves as lacking in these basic skills choose sedentary, solitary activities over games and sports that promote socialization and physical activity habits. Focusing on developmentally appropriate motor skill instruction promotes not only fundamental motor skills and enhances coordination, but it also encourages self-confidence (Faigenbaum, Best, MacDonald, Myer, & Stracciolini, 2014; Faigenbaum, Stracciolini, & Myer, 2011).

Cognitive Development

Systematic observations of children's behaviors have led several researchers to posit general theories of cognitive development. One of the earliest and most influential theories was developed by Jean Piaget (1896–1980), who proposed that children's mental development, like physical development, is characterized by a progression through distinct stages (Piaget, 1963). Piaget posited that children's experiences and personal interaction with their environments drive their cognitive development; he also proposed that children are forced to reorganize their thoughts or schemas when challenged by new problems.

Since Piaget's seminal early conceptualizations, considerable attention has been focused on children's cognitive development. As infants learn to control their movements, they begin to understand implicitly how actions provide the means to achieve goals (Thelen, 1996, 2004). Early forms of learning depend on sensory and motor experiences. The environment in which actions occur plays a vital role in children's mental development. An unchanging, predictable environment allows few opportunities for children to learn from their movements, but complex, changing, and unpredictable environments are assumed to broaden potential learning opportunities. These very early learning experiences have been hypothesized to benefit mental imagery (Adolph, 2008; Sommerville & Decety, 2006), reasoning and problem solving (Gallese & Metzinger, 2003; Jackson & Decety, 2004), and operations necessary for children and adults to solve mathematical and science problems (Kontra, Lyons, Fischer, & Beilock, 2015; Newcombe & Frick, 2010). Cognitive processes are deeply embedded in infants' interactions with their world (Koziol, Budding, & Chidekel, 2011; Koziol & Lutz, 2013; Wilson, 2002). Results obtained from numerous studies suggest that children's mental development is bound closely to physical activity and movement (Moreau, 2015).

Young children's mental development is linked to the emergence of executive processes, which are central to decision making, goal planning, and choice behavior (Miyake et al., 2000; Naglieri & Johnson, 2000; Posner & Dahaene, 1994). While debate concerning the structure of executive functions is ongoing, there is a general consensus among researchers that executive functioning is not a unitary process; rather, it reflects a number of more elemental, underlying processes. Purported component processes include planning, which reflects the ability to utilize strategies to attain goals; updating, which is closely linked to working memory and the need to monitor its representation; inhibition, which involves the deliberate suppression of a prepotent response; and switching, which requires individuals to disengage the processing operations of an irrelevant task and to engage the operations involved in a relevant task. Psychoneurological research suggests that the prefrontal cortex, which has been associated with basic information processing and intellectual functioning, develops in a nonlinear fashion from infancy through young adulthood (Bunge & Wright, 2007; Casey, Giedd, & Thomas, 2000; Diamond, 2000, 2002; Diamond & Goldman-Rakic, 1989; Luciana, 2003). In general, executive functions develop rapidly through the elementary school years and then at a slower pace during adolescence (Brocki & Bohlin, 2004; Huizinga, Dolan, & van der Molen, 2006). During later childhood, children and adolescents evidence metacognition, which refers to the higher-order thinking that controls thought processes required for complex, long-term problem solving (Borkowski, Carr, & Pressely, 1987; Flavell, 1979). Metacognition differs from executive functioning in terms of the depth of monitoring involved. Unlike executive functions, which are important for making decisions in the "here and now," metacognition involves continuous bottom-up and top-down feedback loops that are critical when considering future actions to be taken. "Mulling over" the solution to a problem allows time to consider the costs and benefits of actions and brings into play such factors as emotional states, social demands, and personality factors, which may have minimal influence on rapid decision making that is characteristic of most methods of assessing executive functions (Roebers, 2017; Tomporowski, McCullick, Pendleton, & Pesce, 2015).

The research data from these two fields of investigation provide the academic rationale for our PAGs and the manner in which they are taught to children. Similar to other researchers (Diamond, 2013, 2015), we view executive processes and metacognition as skills that can be refined with training and practice.

Discovery Instruction versus Direct Instruction

Environmental enrichment research suggests that the benefits of physical activity interventions depend not only on the timing of interventions but also on how they are administered (Curlik & Shors, 2012; Hertzog, Kramer, Wilson, & Lindenberger, 2008). Clearly, the instructional methods developed for preschool, young, and older children would be expected to differ. Our PAGs reflect a combination of two approaches to teaching: discovery instruction and direct instruction.

Discovery-instruction methods of teaching emphasize environments that allow children the opportunity to choose the actions that best allow them to achieve a goal. Discovery games promote exploration, which encourages multiple solutions to a problem. They allow players to consider the broad range of actions that are possible, rather than being constrained to only one correct solution (Corbetta & Vereijken, 1999). Sometimes called divergent discovery, these games are typically open ended, which means that the starting point, the rules, and the goals are explained, but how to perform the games is not (Mosston & Ashworth, 2008). Open-ended games are particularly useful with young children, who typically engage in fantasy (Memmert, 2011; Memmert, Baker, & Bertsch, 2010). Discovery games are thought to promote children's mental dexterity, which is the ability to find a solution for a problem using available physical and mental resources (Scibinetti, Tocci, & Pesce, 2011). High levels of mental effort are generated during open-ended movement games; this supports creativity. In our games, children go over or under obstacles and find as many solutions as possible. In order for children to generate novel ideas, they think about, plan, execute, and observe the consequences of their movements, which may foster creativity.

Direct-instruction methods of teaching emphasize environments in which the teacher prescribes how students will accomplish a specific goal and then requires the students to do what he or she instructed. The direct instruction model (DIM) is characterized by six key elements: (1) a review of previously learned material, (2) a presentation of content and skills, (3) initial student practice, (4) the provision of feedback and correctives, (5) independent student practice, and (6) periodic reviews during class time (Metzler, 2011). The DIM addresses two issues central to effective teaching: management and engagement. To learn from their actions, children must be mentally engaged and in the control of their movements; it is not enough simply to be physically active.

Intentional and focused observation of the children's performance is key to inducing child engagement; this is where the teacher's expertise is vital. A teacher needs to recognize when children are bored or frustrated because the game is too easy or too difficult. When children are bored or experience frustration, the likelihood of continued engagement drops drastically. At best, disengagement leads them to stop altogether. At worst, it leads to managerial issues that disrupt the environment for everyone.

As a teaching model, DIM is the best way to engage a learner in an activity, which is important for any exercise or physical activity program (i.e., the PAL Program). The fundamental assumption is that "learning occurs when students make incremental progress on small tasks that lead to the acquisition of larger and more complex, skills/knowledge" (Metzler, 2011, p. 179). This approach requires a teacher who is able to not only recognize students' performance and make judgments about it, but also who knows when and how to provide appropriate and valid feedback, and when and how to modify games so that they neither get stale nor are too challenging and cause learner disengagement. Perhaps the teacher's most important skill is the ability to modify conditions to promote learning—an act termed "extending the task" (Rink, 2010, p. 145). Examples of this instructional skill are changing the variables of the activity, such as the distance to the target, the time allotted for completion, boundaries, and equipment used. While the term "extend" might connote making something more difficult, it refers only to changing the activity so that it is most appropriate for the learner.

Discovery-instruction and direct-instruction approaches differ in their use of teacher feedback and questioning. Feedback that describes the quality of the child's movements is critical to comprehending how specific skills are used to play a game. Teachers provide extrinsic feedback that children can use to improve their understanding of game challenges and how those challenges can be overcome. While general feedback, such as saying "good job" in response to a child's specific action, is something anyone can give, this type of statement does not promote learning as much as specific feedback, both positive and corrective. Especially when working with children, providing positive statements about what a child is doing correctly not only helps the child to learn, but also motivates him or her to stay engaged. An example of a positive-specific feedback statement is "I like how you kept your elbow high on that throw, Adaline." Corrective feedback is sometimes misinterpreted as negative feedback; inexperienced instructors are often hesitant to use it because they may feel it would be demotivating. However, an informed and skilled instructor knows that it is prescriptive in nature and essential to correcting performance, which is crucial for learning. An example of a corrective feedback statement would be "Adaline, you need to keep your elbow higher on your throw." Purposive questioning from the teacher requires children to think about the question, contrast it with their current knowledge or performance, and then use the answer to inform themselves. The decision to use either direct feedback or questioning to inform children about performance is dependent on the context and on the teacher, emphasizing again the importance of the teacher in our exercise intervention.

Our PAGs are predicated on the belief that effective teaching is part science and part art. When a teacher is prescriptive and directive and guides a child to meet specific instructional goals, he or she is reflecting the "science" of teaching. When a teacher relies on intuition and reflection and lets children freely explore and discover on their own, he or she is exhibiting the "art" of teaching (Hellison & Templin, 1991). Thus, DIM and discovery-instruction methods are two sides of the same coin—both are valid ways of teaching children. We recommend that teachers use both methods and avoid a "one-size-fits-all" approach to instruction. The processes of physical and mental development are complex; as such, they require teachers to adapt learning approaches that best fit the child at a specific time.

Repetitive Practice versus Variable Practice

Practice is necessary to increase skilled performance. However, the manner in which skills are practiced can have a profound effect on what is actually learned by children and adults. A critical assumption of our PAGs is that the mental processes children employ when playing games will transfer from the context of playing games to the academic classroom, home, and community. *Transfer* is the degree to which knowledge transfers from one condition to another. Over the past decade, several studies conducted with children demonstrate that cognitive skill training conducted in specific ways does generalize across conditions (Diamond & Lee, 2011). These findings are consistent with our view that the mental processes children use and the strategies they acquire during physical games will transfer to other, nongame conditions.

The basis for successful knowledge transfer appears to lie in the type of practice employed during training. Motor skill teachers often used *repetitive training* methods in which novice learners repeat the same movement patterns over and over. For example, a baseball pitcher may be taught to throw a ball from the mound to a catcher. The repetition and sequencing of movements typically result in changes in neuromuscular integration and improved performance (Chin, 2010). With extended practice, the novice learns a very specific motor program that controls a specific type of throwing movement. Specificity of training prepares the player to perform a very specific task. Repetition is desirable for many psychomotor performance skills that involve doing one thing well. However, research shows that transfer of training using repetition practice is minimal. *Variable training* involves practice in which learners do not repeat the same movement pattern, but rather, alter their movements from trial to trial, for example, mixing throws to the catcher with throws to other players. Variable training introduces *contextual interference,* which is a practice schedule that results in less efficient performance but produces better long-term memory and improves transfer (Tomporowski, McCullick, & Horvat, 2010). Under varied practice conditions, every change in successive practice trials requires the individual to inhibit previously used movement action plans and to call into action a different movement plan. Successfully shifting movement action plans from one task to another involves multiple mental operations. The child must recognize the environmental conditions that define the task, retrieve a movement program from long-term procedural memory, and apply movement parameters to actions that are planned to perform the task.

The improved learning that is due to the contextual interference effect has been explained in terms of *mental engagement,* which is reflected in persistence, concentration, and the allocation of attentional resources and mental effort (Christenson, Reschly, & Wylie, 2012). Children's mental engagement increases when they are involved in novel activities or when activities challenge their skill levels. Researchers have proposed that mental engagement is greatest at an *optimal challenge point,* which is an unstable point of balance between the degree of task complexity and the learner's skill level (Guadagnoli & Lee, 2004; Pendleton, Sakalik, Moore, & Tomporowski, 2016). The results obtained from several recent studies conducted with children (Best, 2013; Lakes et al., 2013; Lakes & Hoyt, 2004) provide evidence for the optimal challenge point/complexity hypotheses (See reviews by Best, 2010; Diamond, 2012, 2015; Diamond & Lee, 2011; van der Fels et al., 2015.) Of particular interest are studies conducted by Curlik and his colleagues (Curlik & Shors, 2012; Shors, Anderson, Curlik, & Nokia, 2012), which explicitly hypothesize that mentally challenging physical activities generate greater learning through their influence on brain plasticity.

Teachers who use our PAGs should determine the optimal challenge point for each child, as it is crucial for the developing of executive functions. Researchers have found that executive functions must be continually stimulated to instigate improvements in performance. Children who perform the same activities, but do not experience cognitive challenge, evidence no gain in executive functioning (Cairney, Bedard, Dudley, & Kriellaars, 2016; Diamond & Lee, 2011). Movement games should be neither too simple nor too difficult for children in order to maximize cognitive challenge. While children are primed to learn, optimal learning requires specific instructional conditions. The practice context sets the stage for learning. A game without a movement problem that attracts and channels children's attention will not encourage learning. The greatest challenge that teachers face is to understand how to create the optimal context for each child and to keep that child on the learning curve. Effective teachers learn how to change instructional and game demands in order to maintain an optimal challenge point.

Theories of Skill Acquisition during Childhood

Our PAGs have been influenced by two theories of motor-skill learning: schema theory and dynamic systems models. While the two theories make very different assumptions concerning how movements are controlled and learned, both provide useful points of view and, together, support our assumptions concerning the design and implementation of our PAGs.

Schema Theory

The emergence of cognitive psychology in the late 1960s spurred interest in the role of mental processes that guide coordinated movements. Several proposed theories explained motor control and motor learning in terms of information-processing components, such as short-term sensory buffers, stimulus identification, response selection, and response preparation, much like the components of a modern computer. Mental components and processes, because they operate internally, are considered latent variables; that is, their existence is linked to observable behavior. The schema theory had a significant impact on researchers in the field (Schmidt, 1975, 1988). At the core of the theory is the generalized motor program, which is an abstract representation of a movement plan. The execution of a specific motor program is believed to be directed by a general rule, or *schema*, which specifies the selection, sequencing, and timing of muscles.

Strategy development and utilization play a key role in our PAGs. As games are introduced to younger children, specific strategies may not be explicitly described by the teacher. Children are placed in decision-making conditions in which there are several alternative ways to play a game. For older children, teachers may suggest possible strategies and allow them the opportunity to test and evaluate the consequences of their decisions. In both conditions, children either independently or in concert with others go through the four processing steps hypothesized to initiate or reinforce schema development (Schmidt & Wrisberg, 2008): (1) initial game conditions, which involves the environment conditions that a child can observe; (2) movement specification, which involves the selection of a motor movement program judged best to execute movements needed to play the game; (3) feedback, which is derived from internal and external sensory input and knowledge of results or knowledge of performance provided by the teacher; and (4) evaluation and correction, which reflects the correspondence between what the child expected to occur and what actually occurred and if corrective actions are required. Over repeated actions, children's strategic knowledge of how to play a specific game is increased.

Dynamical Systems Models

Behavioral psychologists during the first half of the 20th century developed research approaches that focused on the relationship between stimuli and responses. Researchers such as B. F. Skinner (1904–1990) hypothesized that both simple reflexive behaviors and complex behaviors were explained in terms of associations between environmental conditions and the consequences of actions on the environment (Skinner, 1938). Paralleling Skinner's work was that of Nikolai Bernstein (1896–1966), a Russian scientist who focused on the analysis of movements of factory workers (e.g., using a hammer to hit nails) (Gurfinkel & Cordo, 1998). He observed how variability in workers' movements decreased with practice, and he focused on environmental conditions that influenced how actions were performed across multiple training trials, such as hammering nails with a hammer.

Bernstein's research and others (Gibson, 1969) influenced a number of contemporary motor behavior scientists who, like Skinner and Bernstein, deemphasized the role of internal cognitive mechanisms, such as schemas, and emphasized the role of the environment on motor actions (Newell, 1991). The dynamic systems approach highlights three types of constraints that together govern physical action: (1) environmental constraints, such as gravity, temperature, and wind, which affect movements; (2) organismic constraints, such as body shape, weight, and height, which play a role in movements; and (3) task constraints, which are imposed by the skill to be learned and how movements related to that skill need to be made. A similar approach to movement production and skill development has been proposed by proponents of embodied cognition, which emphasizes the bonds between perception and actions and deemphasizes the roles of internal cognitive mechanisms, such as the schema (Moreau & Conway, 2014; Pick, 2004).

The central tenets of the dynamical systems approach are incorporated in our PAGs. There is clear evidence that many motor actions are learned implicitly; that is, without direct attention or mental engagement. The games are taught in ways that require children to make rapid decisions in actions that, with practice, come to be performed more and more automatically. Our work and the development of our PAGs were influenced by theories of skill development that stress the interaction between top-down (schema) and bottom-up (embodied learning) processing (Ackerman, 1987; Fitts & Posner, 1967; Proctor, Reeve, & Weeks, 1990).

Indirect Psychosocial Consequences of Physical Activity

Physical activity may influence children's mental function in a variety of ways. As described in Figure 4.1, data supports a direct causal relation between exercise and cognition (Donnelly et al., 2016; Hillman, 2014). However, there is good reason to expect that indirect relations exist as well. The case has been made that enhancement of children's cognition is mediated by changes in other factors. Four potential mediators are described in the figure: (1) physical fitness factors, (2) health factors, (3) psychosocial factors, and (4) skill-development factors. Researchers have examined chronic exercise studies to determine whether improvements in cardiorespiratory fitness are related to changes in adults' cognitive functions. The evidence failed to support the hypothesis that changes in aerobic fitness lead to changes in adults' cognition (Etnier, Nowell, Landers, & Sibley, 2006); however, the strength of the relation may differ for children (Chaddock-Heyman, Hillman, Cohen, & Kramer, 2014). Physical activity has been associated with improved health status via the regulation of weight gain (Gutin, 2008, 2011a, 2011b), sleep duration (Youngstedt, O'Connor, & Dishman, 1997), and fatigue (Puetz, O'Connor, & Dishman, 2006) and associations with these changes

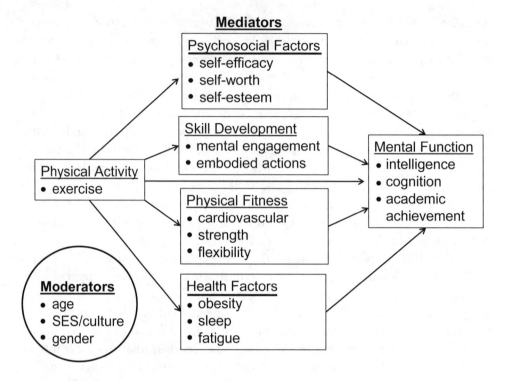

FIGURE 4.1. Working model of mediators and moderators that may play a role in physical activity effects on children's mental function; SES, socioeconomic status.

have been associated with cognitive function. A large literature has addressed the effects of acute bouts of exercise and chronic exercise training on psychosocial outcomes, such as self-efficacy (Bandura, 1997) and self-esteem (Strong, Malina, & Blimkie, 2005). The main premise of our PAGs is that the children acquire skills that lead to changes in mental functioning, as measured in terms of academic achievement and cognitive performance.

Besides factors that potentially moderate the association between physical activity and mental functioning, the impact of physical activity interventions, such as the PAGs, on children's mental functioning are influenced by a number of moderators. These include the developmental stage of the children, their socioeconomic level, and their gender.

Clearly, enhancing children's physical and mental development is a complex endeavor that requires a multidisciplinary approach. Hence, the PAL Program has been designed to integrate the expertise of specialists in physical education and mathematics and reading instruction and the involvement of family members. Each of the components of the PAL Program contributes to its overall impact.

Conclusion

As one of the three components of the PAL Program, the PAGs have unique features that separate them from other ASPs. Their design reflects contemporary theories of physical and mental development and instructional practices as applied to authentic after-school settings and to children who have multiple academic and social needs. As you would expect, the laboratory is not the real world, and if we are to benefit from what is learned in the laboratory, its findings must be rigorously tested in conditions that represent the messy nature of the world outside it.

Educators know there are no quick fixes for maximizing every child's potential to learn. The impact of PAGs on children may not always be immediately apparent, as children accumulate knowledge over many years of interacting with others. Teachers are uniquely positioned to create environments that foster children's development, and PAGs may provide one of many vehicles that can improve children's lives.

GLOSSARY

Chronic exercise programs—Exercise regimens characterized by repeated acute bouts of physical activity, typically occurring several times per week over periods of months.

Direct instruction—Methods of teaching in which the instructor prescribes how students will accomplish a specific goal, and the students are required to do as the teacher instructs.

Exercise—A subset of physical activity defined by planned, structured, and purposeful methods whose objective is to improve or maintain one or more components of physical fitness.

Optimal challenge point—An unstable point of balance between the degree of task complexity and the learner's skill level, so that the skill is neither too difficult to be mastered nor too simple to be interesting.

Physical activity—Any bodily movement produced by skeletal muscle contraction that requires energy expenditure.

Physical literacy—The capacity to move with competence in a wide variety of physical activities benefitting the development of the whole person.

Qualitative exercise interventions—Interventions involving physical activities together with cognitive effort and/or skill learning.

Quantitative exercise interventions—Interventions that involve physical activities that require minimal mental engagement or allocation of attention.

Transfer—Degree to which knowledge can be used from one condition to another.

Variable training—Practice in which learners do not repeat the same movement pattern, but alter movements from trial to trial to produce better long-term memory and transfer of skill.

References

Ackerman, P. L. (1987). Individual differences in skill learning: An integration of psychometric and information processing perspectives. *Psychological Bulletin, 102*, 3–27.

Adolph, K. E. (2008). Learning to move. *Current Directions in Psychological Science, 17*(3), 213–218.

Bailey, R. C., Olson, S. L., Pepper, S. L., Porszasz, J., Barstow, T. J., & Cooper, D. M. (1995). The level and tempo of children's physical activities: An observational study. *Medicine and Science in Sports and Exercise, 27*, 1033–1041.

Bandura, A. (1997). *Self-efficacy: The exercise of control.* New York: Freeman.

Best, J. R. (2010). Effects of physical activity on children's executive function: Contributions of experimental research on aerobic exercise. *Developmental Review, 30*(4), 331–351.

Best, J. R. (2013). Exergaming in youth. *Zeitschrift für Psychologie, 221*(2), 72–78.

Borkowski, J. H., Carr, M., & Pressely, M. (1987). "Spontaneous" strategy use: Perspectives from metacognitive theory. *Intelligence, 11*, 61–75.

Brocki, K. C., & Bohlin, G. (2004). Executive functions in children aged 6 to 13: A dimensional and developmental study. *Developmental Neuropsychology, 26*(2), 571–593.

Brooks, G. A., Fahey, T. D., & White, T. P. (1996). *Exercise physiology* (2nd ed.). Mountain View, CA: Mayfield.

Bunge, S. A., & Wright, S. B. (2007). Neurodevelopmental changes in working memory and cognitive control. *Current Opinion in Neurobiology, 17*, 243–250.

Cairney, J., Bedard, C., Dudley, D., & Kriellaars, D. (2016). Toward a physical literacy framework to guide the design, implementation and evaluation of early childhood movement-based interventions targeting cognitive development. *Annals of Sports Medicine and Research, 3*(4), 1073.

Casey, B. J., Giedd, J. N., & Thomas, K. M. (2000). Structural and functional brain development and its relation to cognitive development. *Biological Psychology, 54*, 241–257.

Chaddock, L., Erickson, K. I., Prakash, R. S., Kim, J. S., Voss, M. W., VanPatter, M., & Pontifex, M. B. (2010). A neuroimaging investigation of the association between aerobic fitness, hippocampal volume, and memory performance in preadolsecent children. *Brain Research, 1358*, 172–183.

Chaddock, L., Pontifex, M. B., Hillman, C. H., & Kramer, A. F. (2011). A review of the relation of aerobic fitness and physical activity to brain structure and function in children. *Journal of the International Neuropsychological Society, 17*, 1–11.

Chaddock-Heyman, L., Erickson, K. I., Chappell, M. A., Johnson, C. L., Kienzler, C., Knecht, A. M., . . . Kramer, A. F. (2016). Aerobic fitness is associated with greater hippocampal cerebral blood flow in children. *Developmental Cognitive Neuroscience, 20*, 52–58.

Chaddock-Heyman, L., Hillman, C. H., Cohen, N. J., & Kramer, A. F. (2014). III. The importance of physical activity and aerobic fitness for cognitive control and memory in children. *Monographs of the Society for Research in Child Development, 79*(4), 25–50.

Chin, E. R. (2010). Intracellular Ca2+ signaling in skeletal muscle: Decoding a complex message. *Exercise and Sport Science Reviews, 38*(2), 76–85.

Christenson, S. L., Reschly, A. L., & Wylie, C. (Eds.). (2012). *Handbook of research on student engagement*. New York: Springer.

Corbetta, D., & Vereijken, B. (1999). Understanding development and learning of motor coordination in sport: The contribution of dynamic systems theory. *International Journal of Sport Psychology, 30*, 507–530.

Curlik, D. M., & Shors, T. J. (2012). Training your brain: Do mental and physical (MAP) training enhance cognition through the process of neurogenesis in the hippocampus? *Neuropharmacology, 64*, 506–514.

Davis, C. L., Tomporowski, P. D., Boyle, C. A., Waller, J. L., Miller, P. H., Naglieri, J. A., & Gregoski, M. (2007). Effects of aerobic exercise on overweight children's cognitive functioning: A randomized controlled trial. *Research Quarterly for Exercise and Sport, 78*(5), 510–519.

Davis, C. L., Tomporowski, P. D., McDowell, J. E., Austin, B. P., Yanasak, N. E., Allison, J. D., . . . Miller, P. H. (2011). Exercise improves executive function and achievement and alters brain activation in overweight children: A randomized, controlled trial. *Health Psychology, 30*(1), 91–98.

Diamond, A. (2000). Close interrelation of motor development and cognitive development and of the cerebellum and prefrontal cortex. *Child Development, 71*(1), 44–56.

Diamond, A. (2002). Normal development of prefrontal cortex from birth to young adulthood: Cognitive functions, anatomy, and biochemistry. In D. T. Stuss & R. T. Knight (Eds.), *Principles of frontal lobe function* (pp. 466–503). New York: Oxford University Press.

Diamond, A. (2012). Activities and programs that improve children's executive functions. *Current Directions in Psychological Sciences, 21*(5), 335–341.

Diamond, A. (2013). Executive functions. *Annual Review of Psychology, 64*(1), 135–168.

Diamond, A. (2015). Effects of physical exercise on executive functions: Going beyond simply moving to moving with thought. *Annals of Sports Medicine and Research, 2*(1), 1011.

Diamond, A., & Goldman-Rakic, P. S. (1989). Comparison of human infants and rhesus monkeys on Piaget's A-not-B task: Evidence for dependence on dorsolateral prefrontal cortex. *Experimental Brain Research, 74*, 24–40.

Diamond, A., & Lee, K. (2011). Interventions shown to aid executive function development in children 4 to 12 years old. *Science, 333*(6045), 959–964.

Dishman, R. K., Heath, G. W., & Lee, I.-M. (2012). *Physical activity epidemiology* (2nd ed.). Champaign, IL: Human Kinetics.

Donnelly, J. E., Hillman, C. H., Castelli, D., Etnier, J. L., Lee, S., Tomporowski., P. D., . . . Szabo-Reed, N. (2016). Physical activity, cognitive function and academic achievement in children: American College of Sports Medicine Position stand. *Medicine and Science in Sports and Exercise, 48*(6), 1197–1222.

Ekkekakis, P., & Acevedo, E. O. (2006). Affective responses to acute exercise: Toward a psychobiological dose-response model. In E. O. Acevedo & P. Ekkekakis (Eds.), *Psychobiology of physical activity* (pp. 91–110). Champaign, IL: Human Kinetics.

Erickson, K. I., Voss, M. W., Prakash, R. S., Basak, C., Szabo, A., Chaddock, L., . . . Kramer, A. F. (2011). Exercise training increases size of hippocampus and improves memory. *Proceedings of the National Academy of Sciences, 108*(7), 3017–3022.

Etnier, J. L., Labban, J. D., Piepmeier, A. T., Davis, M. E., & Henning, D. A. (2014). Effects of an acute bout of exercise on memory in 6th grade children. *Pediatric Exercise Science, 26,* 250–258.

Etnier, J. L., Nowell, P. M., Landers, D. M., & Sibley, B. A. (2006). A meta-regression to examine the relationship between aerobic fitness and cognitive performance. *Brain Research Reviews, 52,* 119–130.

Exercise is Medicine. (2016). Available from *http://exerciseismedicine.org.*

Faigenbaum, A. D., Best, T. M., MacDonald, J., Myer, G. D., & Stracciolini, A. (2014). Top 10 research questions related to exercise deficit disorder (EDD) in youth. *Research Quarterly for Exercise and Sport, 85*(3), 297–307.

Faigenbaum, A. D., Stracciolini, A., & Myer, G. D. (2011). Exercise deficit disorder in youth: A hidden truth. *Acta Paediatrica, 100*(11), 1423–1425.

Fitts, P., & Posner, M. I. (1967). *Human performance.* Belmont, CA: Brooks/Cole.

Flavell, J. H. (1979). Metacognition and cognitive monitoring: A new area of cognitive-developmental inquiry. *American Psychologist, 34,* 906–911.

Gaglio, B., Shoup, J. A., & Glasgow, R. E. (2013). The RE-AIM framework: A systematic review of use over time. *American Journal of Public Health, 103*(6), e38–e46.

Gallese, V., & Metzinger, T. (2003). Motor ontology: The representational reality of goals, action and selves. *Philosophical Psychology, 16*(3), 365–388.

Garber, C. E., Blissmer, B., Deschenes, M. R., Franklin, B. A., Lamonte, M. J., & Lee, I.-M. (2011). Quantity and quality of exercise for developing and maintaining cardiorespiratory, musculoskeletal, and neuromotor fitness in apparently healthy adults: Guidance for prescribing exercise. Position stand. *Medicine and Science in Sports and Exercise, 43,* 1334–1359.

Gibson, E. J. (1969). *Principles of perceptual learning and development.* New York: Academic Press.

Glasgow, R. E., Klesges, L. M., Dzewaltowski, D. A., Bull, S. S., & Eastbrooks, P. (2004). The future of health behavior change research: What is needed to improve translation of research into health practice? *Annals of Behavioral Medicine, 27*(1), 3–12.

Gomez-Pinilla, F., & Hillman, C. H. (2013). The influence of exercise on cognitive abilities. *Comprehensive Physiology, 3,* 403–428.

Guadagnoli, M. A., & Lee, T. D. (2004). Challenge point: A framework for conceptualizing the effects of various practice conditions in motor learning. *Journal of Motor Behavior, 36*(2), 212–224.

Gurfinkel, V. S., & Cordo, P. J. (1998). The scientific legacy of Nikolai Bernstein. In M. L. Latash (Ed.), *Progress in motor control: Berstein's traditions in movement studies* (Vol. 1, pp. 1–19). Champaign, Il: Human Kinetics.

Gutin, B. (2008). Child obesity can be reduced with vigorous activity rather than restriction of energy intake. *Obesity, 16*(10), 2193–2196.

Gutin, B. (2011a). Diet vs. exercise for the prevention of pediatric obesity: The role of exercise. *International Journal of Obesity and Related Metabolic Disorders, 35,* 29–32.

Gutin, B. (2011b). The role of nutrient partitioning and stem cell differentiation in pediatric obesity: A new theory. *International Journal of Pediatric Obesity, 6,* 7–12.

Hellison, D. R., & Templin, T. J. (1991). *A reflective approach to teaching physical education.* Champaign. Il: Human Kinetics.

Hertzog, C., Kramer, A. F., Wilson, R. S., & Lindenberger, U. (2008). Enrichment effects on adult cognitive development. *Psychological Science in the Public Interest, 9*(1), 1–65.

Hillman, C. H. (2014). I. An introduction to the relation of physical activity to cognitive and brain health, and scholatic achievement. *Monographs of the Society for Research in Child Development, 79*(4), 1–6.

Hillman, C. H., Erickson, K. I., & Kramer, A. F. (2008). Be smart, exercise your heart: Exercise effects on brain and cognition. *Nature Reviews Neuroscience, 9*(1), 58–65.

Huizinga, M. M., Dolan, C. V., & van der Molen, M. W. (2006). Age-related change in executive function: Developmental trends and a latent variable analysis. *Neuropsychologia, 44,* 2017–2036.

Jackson, P. L., & Decety, J. (2004). Motor cognition: A new paradigm to study self-other interactions. *Current Opinion in Neurobiology, 14,* 259–263.

Kempermann, G., Fabel, K., Ehninger, D., Babu, H., Leal-Galicia, P., Garthe, A., & Wolf, S. A. (2010). Why and how physical activity promotes experience-induced brain plasticity. *Frontiers in Neuroscience, 4,* 189.

Kontra, C., Lyons, D. J., Fischer, S. M., & Beilock, S. L. (2015). Physical experience enhances science learning. *Psychological Science, 26*(6), 737–749.

Koziol, L. F., Budding, D. E., & Chidekel, D. (2011). From movement to thought: Executive function, embodied cognition, and the cerebellum. *Cerebellum, 11*(2), 505–525.

Koziol, L. F., & Lutz, J. T. (2013). From movement to thought: The development of executive function. *Applied Neuropsychology: Child, 2*(2), 104–115.

Labban, J. D., & Etnier, J. L. (2011). Effects of acute exercise on long-term memory. *Research Quarterly for Exercise and Sport, 82*(4), 712–721.

Lakes, K. D., Bryars, T., Sirisinahal, S., Salim, N., Arastoo, S., Emmerson, N., . . . Kang, C. J. (2013). The Healthy for Life Taekwondo pilot study: A preliminary evaluation of effects on executive function and BMI, feasibility, and acceptability *Mental Health and Physical Activity, 6,* 181–188.

Lakes, K. D., & Hoyt, W. T. (2004). Promoting self-regulation through school-based martial arts training. *Applied Developmental Psychology, 25,* 283–302.

Llinas, R. (2001). *I of the vortex: From neurons to self.* Cambridge, MA: MIT Press.

Luciana, M. (2003). The neural and functional development of human prefrontal cortex. In M. de Haan & M. H. Johnson (Eds.), *The cognitive neuroscience of development* (pp. 157–179). New York: Psychology Press.

Malina, R. M., Bouchard, C., & Bar-Or, O. (2004). *Growth, maturation, and physical activity* (2nd ed.). Champaign, IL: Human Kinetics.

Mandigo, J., Francis, N., Lodewyk, K. R., & Lopez, R. (2009). *Position paper: Physical literacy for educators.* Ottawa, Ontario: Physical and Health Education Canada.

McGaugh, J. L. (2015). Consolidating memories. *Annual Review of Psychology, 66,* 1–24.

Memmert, D. (2011). Sports and creativity. In M. A. Runco & S. R. Pritzker (Eds.),

Encyclopedia of creativity (2nd ed., Vol. 2, pp. 373–378). San Diego, CA: Academic Press.

Memmert, D., Baker, J., & Bertsch, C. (2010). Play and practice in the development of sport-specific creativity in team ball sports. *High Ability Studies, 21,* 3–18.

Metzler, M. W. (2011). *Instruction models for physical education* (3rd ed.). Scottsdale, AZ: Holcomb Hathaway.

Mithen, S. (1996). *The prehistory of the mind.* London: Thames and Hudson Ltd.

Miyake, A., Friedman, N. P., Emerson, M. J., Witzki, A. H., Howerter, A., & Wager, T. D. (2000). The unity and diversity of executive functions and their contributions to complex "frontal lobe" tasks: A latent variable analysis. *Cognitive Psychology, 41,* 49–100.

Moreau, D. (2015). Brains and brawn: Complex motor activities to maximize cognitive enhancement. *Educational Psychology Review, 27,* 475–482.

Moreau, D., & Conway, A. R. A. (2014). The case for an ecological approach to cognitive training. *Trends in Cognitive Training, 18*(7), 334–336.

Mosston, M., & Ashworth, S. (2008). *Teaching physical education* (5th ed.). Upper Saddle River, NJ: Pearson Education.

Naglieri, J. A., & Johnson, D. (2000). Effectiveness of a cognitive strategy intervention to improve math calculation based on the PASS theory. *Journal of Learning Disabilities, 33,* 591–597.

National Association for Sport and Physical Education. (2011). Physical education position statements. Available at *www.aahperd.org/naspe/standards/upload/Physical Education-Is-Critical-to-Educating-the-Whole-Child-Final-5-19-2011.pdf.*

National Association for Sport and Physical Education & American Heart Association. (2012). *2012 shape of the nation report: Status of physical education in the USA.* Reston, VA: American Alliance for Health, Physical Education, Recreation and Dance.

Newcombe, N. S., & Frick, A. (2010). Early education for spatial intelligence: Why, what, and how. *Mind, Brain and Education, 4*(3), 102–111.

Newell, K. M. (1991). Motor skill acquisition. *Annual Review of Psychology, 42,* 213–337.

Pendleton, D. M., Sakalik, M. L., Moore, M. L., & Tomporowski, P. D. (2016). Mental engagement during cognitive and psychomotor tests: Effects of task type, processing demands, and practice. *International Journal of Psychophysiology, 109,* 124–131.

Physical Activity Guidelines Advisory Committee. (2008). *Physical activity guidelines advisory committee report.* Washington, DC: U.S. Department of Health and Human Services.

Piaget, J. (1963). *The origins of intelligence in children* (M. Cook, Trans.). New York: Norton.

Pick, H. L. J. (2004). Interrelation of action, perception, and cognition in development: An historical perspective. In I. J. Stockman (Ed.), *Movement and action in learning and development: Clinical implications for pervasive developmental disorders* (pp. 33–48). New York: Elsevier.

Posner, M. I., & Dahaene, S. (1994). Attentional networks. *Trends in Neurosciences, 17,* 75–79.

Proctor, R. W., Reeve, E. G., & Weeks, D. J. (1990). A triphasic approach to the acquisition of response-selection skill. In G. H. Bower (Ed.), *The psychology of learning: Advances in research and theory* (pp. 207–240). New York: Academic Press.

Puetz, T. W., O'Connor, P. J., & Dishman, R. K. (2006). Effects of chronic exercise on feelings of energy and fatigue: A quantitative sysnthesis. *Psychological Bulletin, 132*(6), 866–876.

Rink, J. E. (2010). *Teaching physical education for learning* (6th ed.). Boston: McGraw-Hill.

Roebers, C. M. (2017). Executive function and metacognition: Towards a unifying framework of cognitive self-regulation. *Developmental Review.*

Schmidt, R. A. (1975). A schema theory of discrete motor skill learning theory. *Psychological Review, 82*, 225–260.

Schmidt, R. A. (1988). Motor and action perspectives on motor behaviour. In O. G. Meijer & K. Roth (Eds.), *Complex movement behaviour: The motor-action controversy* (pp. 3–44). Amsterdam: Elsevier.

Schmidt, R. A., & Wrisberg, C. A. (2008). *Motor learning and performance.* Champaign, IL: Human Kinetics.

Scibinetti, P., Tocci, N., & Pesce, C. (2011). Motor creativity and creative thinking in children: The divergent role of inhibition. *Creativity Research Journal, 23*(3), 262–272.

Shors, T. J., Anderson, M. L., Curlik, D. M., & Nokia, M. S. (2012). Use it or lose it: How neurogenesis keeps the brain fit for learning. *Behavioural Brain Research, 227*, 450–458.

Skinner, B. F. (1938). *The behavior of organisms: An experimental analysis.* New York: Appleton-Century.

Sommerville, J. A., & Decety, J. (2006). Weaving the fabric of social interaction: Articulating developmental psychology and cognitive neuroscience in the domain of motor cognition. *Psychonomic Bulletin and Review, 13*(2), 179–200.

Strong, W. B., Malina, R. M., & Blimkie, C. J. (2005). Evidence based physical activity for school-age youth. *Journal of Pediatrics, 146*, 732–737.

Thelen, E. (1996). Motor development. *American Psychologist, 50*(2), 79–95.

Thelen, E. (2004). The central role of action in typical and atypical development: A dynamical systems perspective. In I. J. Stockman (Ed.), *Movement and action in learning and development: Clinical implications for pervasive developmental disorders* (pp. 49–74). New York: Elsevier.

Tomporowski, P. D., McCullick, B. A., & Horvat, M. (2010). *Role of contextual interference and mental engagement on learning.* New York: Nova Science.

Tomporowski, P. D., McCullick, B., Pendleton, D. M., & Pesce, C. (2015). Exercise and children's cognition: The role of task factors and a place for metacognition. *Journal of Sport and Health Science, 4*, 47–55.

van der Fels, I. M. J., te Wierike, S. C. M., Hartman, E., Elferink-Gemser, M. T., Smith, J., & Visscher, C. (2015). The relationship between motor skills and cognitive skills in 4–16 year old typically developing children: A systematic review. *Journal of Science and Medicine in Sport, 18*, 697–703.

Welk, G. J., Corbin, C. B., & Dale, D. (2000). Measurement issues in the assessment of physical activity in children. *Research Quarterly for Exercise and Sport, 71*(2), 59–73.

Williamson, W. A. (2006). Brain activation during physical activity. In E. O. Acevedo & P. Ekkekakis (Eds.), *Psychobiology or physical activity* (pp. 30–42). Champaign, IL: Human Kinetics.

Wilson, M. (2002). Six views of embodied cognition. *Psychonomic Bulletin and Review, 9*(4), 625–636.

Youngstedt, S. D., O'Connor, P. J., & Dishman, R. K. (1997). The effects of acute exercise on sleep: A quantitative synthesis. *Sleep, 20*(3), 203–214.

5

The PAL Physical Activity Games Program in an Experimental After-School Setting

E. Nicole McCluney

As you have learned in Chapter 4, one characteristic of the Physical Activity and Learning (PAL) Program that distinguished it from the typical after-school program (ASP) was the type and delivery of the *physical activity* (PA) provided. Chapter 4 discussed why we used these kinds of activities and delivered them in the way we did. As one of the physical activity games (PAGs) instructors, my goal is to give you a sense of the kinds of activities that were carried out as part of the PAL Program. More specifically, this chapter describes the types of activities used, important areas for implementation, the evidence obtained regarding changes in children's general fitness levels, and a discussion about the challenges in teaching PAGs in an ASP like ours.

PAGs as a Vehicle to Enhance Body and Mind

While *physical education* (PE) tends to be a marginalized subject in schools (Lux & McCullick, 2011), research has shown that there are significant benefits to students being physically active. Not only are physically active students healthier, but they demonstrate better academic performances than those who lead sedentary lifestyles (Abadie & Brown, 2010). Neuroscientists have recognized and acknowledged that students' learning processes can be significantly enhanced through regular participation in PA (Jensen, 2000). Tremarche, Robinson, and

Graham (2007) suggest that student engagement in a wide variety of developmentally appropriate experiences within a PE program can produce profoundly beneficial academic achievement results. Since students rarely receive sufficient amounts of physical activity during a typical school day, despite PE inclusive curriculums, ASPs are an excellent place to enhance children's physical and mental skills. Beyond the health benefits directly attributable to improved fitness, the evidence presented in Chapter 4 suggests that moderate-to-vigorous PA is important for educational achievement.

Both psychological and physiological factors contribute to the relationship between PA and academic performance (Abadie & Brown, 2010). For example, the type of activity, whether aerobic or anaerobic, and the length of time a student is engaged in any given activity are factors that consistently arise in the discussion of PA or exercise in relation to student learning. Aerobic exercise is intense enough to increase heart rate and breathing in a way that can be sustained for an entire exercise session. Anaerobic exercise, by contrast, is short-duration, high-intensity exercise that causes one to become quickly out of breath. Consequently, the intensity of an activity is an important factor. Tomporowski (2003) found that, under particular circumstances, acute bouts of exercise can enhance response speed and accuracy, which is believed to underlie goal-directed actions and problem-solving skills. Seldom addressed by researchers, however, are individual differences in abilities that moderate the effects of exercise on physical and mental development. For example, attentional capacity is central to the ability to select and respond to relevant information while blocking out irrelevant material. The ability to read and decide which components are significant as opposed to trivial or supplemental is a critical element in reading comprehension, which ultimately affects learning in most academic areas. If a student is presented with a mathematical word problem that contains more information than necessary to solve it, the student must be able to accurately identify which pieces of information are essential to correctly solve the posed problem. Similarly, engagement in a science experiment will demand attention to detail and the most pertinent information for conducting such experiments.

Diamond (2014) suggests that students perform better on academic outcome measures when they are given the opportunity to engage in more playtime rather than spend all their time in direct academic instruction. This recommendation has led some educators to integrate PA into the classroom itself. In summary, children's PA habits have significant implications for their educational advancement (Tomporowski, Davis, Miller, & Naglieri, 2008). Considerable evidence presented in this book points to PA as a practical strategy for influencing cognitive processes that underlie reading comprehension and mathematics fluency, which in turn, directly affect other academic subject areas.

Effectively designed and implemented ASPs can assist students not only by helping them meet national PA guideline recommendations, but also by improving their academic achievement. The next section describes the structure and implementation of the PAGs in the PAL Program and the rationale for the organizational structure of the games.

Design and Delivery of PAGs

There are many commonalities among ASP PA interventions. In a typical ASP, homework and academic enrichment are completed before any PA is allowed. PA is usually provided toward the end of the ASP's daily schedule. This PA is predominantly free play that is only occasionally or marginally organized by an adult. Typically, the role of ASP staff is merely to monitor this PA for safety. There is minimal, if any, instructional component or leadership—merely supervision from the ASP staff.

PAGs Design

There are two considerations related to PAGs design: when PAGs should be scheduled and what they should accomplish. So, let us address the question of "when" first. The daily PAL Program schedule began with a 35-minute snack and homework assistance period. The children were engaged in movement soon after. Children need to move, especially considering they have been mostly sitting at desks for approximately 7 hours up to this point. Accordingly, it can be difficult to motivate children if the after-school setting mimics much of the same structure as the school day.

Offering PA earlier rather than later in the ASP schedule also leads to improved cognition during the following academic enrichment activities. It allows students to release some built-up energy from the monotony of sitting and reduces the chance that behavioral and attentional issues will occur during the academic enrichment. That is, the transition from playful, physical activities to classroom settings, in fact benefits instruction and learning in core academic content subjects.

If you were to walk in off the street and visit the PAL Program you would see children engaged in PAGs and, at first glance, likely would not have seen much that would surprise you. However, under closer examination you might have noticed three things: (1) the children were engaged in moderate-to-vigorous levels of activity, (2) the PAGs required mental engagement, and (3) they were having fun.

Other features of our PAGs are intentionally incorporated into the program. Because we served 30 children in grades 2–5 at each site, the games had to be as inclusive as possible—this is no small task when you consider the variety of skill abilities, experiences, and physical sizes that exist among these age groups. Generally speaking, the PAGs of the PAL Program did not include playing specifically for the enhancement of sport skills. While many of our games had a sports theme or were related to a sport, they were deliberately modified versions that used equipment, space, and rules that were developmentally appropriate for children of these diverse ages.

The PAGs design supported executive functioning as intended; that is, the games required mental engagement. By doing so, the games fostered problem-solving and decision-making skills, as well as creativity. Moreover, the games increased heart rate while the children were cognitively engaged. When students become physiologically aroused, blood flow increases which, in turn, increases the flow of oxygen to the brain (Gabbard, 2012). As discussed in Chapter 3, PA is thought to prime the brain to learn. The basic outline of our 45-minute PAG lesson is presented in the next sections.

Instant Activity

Upon arriving at the gymnasium, our students engaged in an *instant activity*, which is a short, fun warm-up session. As implied by the name, this is an activity that happens almost instantly after students arrive to PAGs. It is essential because the sooner students begin moving, the better. Designating time for students to release their energy at the beginning of the class benefits both the students and the instructor because it is likely students will pay closer attention if they have had a break from sitting and listening. Sometimes, we provided instructions to children as they transitioned into the PAGs area, so they did not even sit down, but began the activity immediately.

Examples of instant activities used in the PAL Program included stretching, tag games, dance sessions, or activities directly related to the game for the day. Two tag games "Fish, Ship, Shore" and "Alligator, Alligator" were instant activities most preferred by our students (see Appendices 5.1 and 5.2). Dance sessions, referred to as dance parties by students, were usually offered as reward for good behavior. On dance days, we played popular songs (edited for children) with choreographed dance moves. Most of the children already knew the dances and even made frequent requests for dance time. Songs used for dancing included, but were not limited to, "Hit the Quan," "Whip and Nae Nae," "The Wobble," and "The Cupid Shuffle." Other instant activities were linked to the PAGs scheduled for the day; for example, an instant activity for a soccer-based lesson may consist of activities like passing and dribbling with soccer balls. Instant activities were performed approximately 5–10 minutes prior to the main PAG.

PAL Lesson

Following the instant activity, the PAG lesson for the day was introduced. Here, students were given clear, concise instructions to prevent confusion and reduce time spent sitting or idly standing. Because lessons were designed to encourage problem solving, decision making, and creativity, students often began an activity and then the instructor added new rules, reversed rules, or switched to a completely different game. Frequent rule changes forced students to remain cognitively engaged and also reduced the likelihood of students becoming bored with activities, which kept them from becoming disengaged and off-task.

Transitions between rule or game changes also provided times for rest periods. The National Association for Sport and Physical Education (NASPE) (2004b) recommends that children play in approximately 15-minute bouts, separated by brief breaks. Many of the activities utilized in PAGs are aerobically challenging, and children can quickly tire. Planned rest breaks give children the chance to receive further instructions and/or be asked questions to check for their understanding of a strategy, skills, or concepts. We also found it helpful to ask children to share their strategies for successful games during this time, so that other students can pick up new strategies. So, these rest breaks should not be viewed as wasted time and should be used to maintain students' mental and social engagement.

Once students have adequately demonstrated the ability to effectively implement strategies that promote success in an activity, the instructor can offer children a brand-new game or a new set of rules that differs from what they have just been doing. Switches such as these keep the games challenging and the students mentally engaged and, as a result, our students tended to quickly learn successive games. Rule changes require students to continually seek different strategies to comply with the newly implemented rules and engage cognitively within the games.

Students in the PAL Program usually experienced two or three changes in game rules within a designated 45-minute PAGs period. For example, children might begin the lesson playing Hoopla (see Appendix 5.1). The objective of this game is for students to work in teams to obtain several objects of the same type to return to their home hula hoop. Because multiple teams might attempt to retrieve the same objects, students have to work together to develop a strategy to obtain and maintain possession of at least four matching objects. For instance, there might be four frisbees, four bean bags, four tennis balls, and four poly spots disbursed throughout the hula hoops positioned in each corner of the gym. If the blue team attempts to secure the frisbees but the red team also has its sights on the frisbees, it becomes a matter of which team has the best strategy to gain possession of all four frisbees the fastest. One team may decide to change their object of interest to the tennis balls, say, if they are unsuccessful in collecting the frisbees before the other team.

Once students have played Hoopla in this fashion for several rounds, the instructor may introduce a small rule change. The objective of the game will remain the same, but a defender may be added for each team, for example. So, children's strategies for obtaining objects will need to be adjusted accordingly. The defender's job is to protect their hula hoop containing objects they have retrieved that the other teams may try to obtain for their own hula hoops. If tagged by a defender, the player must return to home base and attempt to pursue the objects again. If a player is in possession of an object from a defender's hoop when tagged, he or she must return the object as well. Because the defender adds a slightly more complex element to the game, students are now forced to work more as a team to obtain objects as opposed to being able to work individually within a team as they did in the first iteration of the game without a defender. Once the children demonstrate success and can identify and explain why the strategies were successful, the instructor may change the rules or objective of the game yet again.

In this case, we frequently advanced the game from Hoopla to Guardian Hoopla. While the goal of the first version was to collect all objects of the same type, Guardian Hoopla's objective is to collect all like-colored objects. Simply stated, Hoopla required students to gain possession of either all four tennis balls, frisbees, poly spots, or bean bags, regardless of whether they were of different colors. In Guardian Hoopla, the objective is to retrieve all like-colored objects, meaning students may collect a frisbee, a poly spot, a bean bag, and a tennis ball, providing all objects are the same color. To begin this version of the game, each team may be assigned to retrieve objects that match the color of their team. For example, the blue team would be wearing blue jerseys and their home-base hula hoop would also be blue. Therefore, the blue team would be assigned to collect all blue objects before the other teams can collect their objects. These rules might change, once again, allowing teams to select whichever color objects they would like to retrieve. Students are afforded the opportunity to engage in several rounds of each game.

Finally, the 45-minute lesson ends with a brief closure that checks for student understanding of the rules and concepts of the games. Children should also be able to discuss various strategies, which target the cognitive domain. The closure may include small-group or team discussions, questions from the instructor, demonstrations from students, or students verbally identifying what the instructor is doing correctly or incorrectly in executing a specific skill or strategy. In the PAL Program, children then transitioned to reading or math enrichment activities.

Lesson Plan Organization

Effective planning is an essential element of successfully implementing any form of instruction to promote student learning. Planning occurs on multiple levels and includes yearly plans, unit plans, and lesson plans. Each planning level becomes narrower and more specific in descending order. A lesson plan will focus on objectives for a single lesson, which should aim to meet unit objectives. The unit goals should be based on the yearly goals, which are ultimately the overarching program goals. Here, we focus on the organization of lesson plans used in the PAL Program for PAGs sessions (see Appendices 5.1 and 5.2 for examples).

According to Gallahue and Cleland-Donnelly (2007), a lesson plan serves the purpose of assisting teachers with thinking about the most efficient method to guide students toward meeting a given objective. The lesson plan is a guide that allows instructors to maximize student learning time. The PAGs lesson plan comprises the following components: (1) heading, (2) instant activity, (3) instructor essentials and explanation points, (4) challenges posed by the instructor and confronted by the children, (5) modifications and moving on, and (6) strategy maps. Using an example of a PAG, the next subsections focus on teacher essentials and explanation points and the challenges posed by the instructor for the children. Further, small modifications are noted throughout these subsections (see Tomporowski, McCullick, Pendleton, & Pesce, 2015).

Teacher Essentials and Explanation Points

The instructor should clearly establish and explain the rules of the PAGs and emphasize adherence to those rules. Compliance is important because, otherwise, promotion of improved cognitive processing may not occur as intended. If students fail to follow instructions and abide by rules in the beginning, then later rule or game changes may be significantly less effective in terms of promoting mental engagement. Take Hoopla and Guardian Hoopla, for example. In Hoopla, the instructor must emphasize that the objective is to be the first team to retrieve all four of the same objects and place them in their hula hoop. Likewise, the instructor should stress the importance of being aware of what items the other teams are selecting, only bringing one item at a time, and, if a defender is involved, the expectations for what happens when and if they are tagged. We have found it helpful, and a best practice, to briefly demonstrate the game before it begins. The instructor should then check for student understanding of the game rules and expectations after the demonstration. For example, the instructor may ask, "How many objects should be in your hoop when you are finished?' or "What happens if you are tagged by a defender?" When students can correctly respond to questions concerning the rules and safety, then the game begins.

Once there is a modification such as a rule or game change, for example, to Guardian Hoopla, the instructor provides essential explanation points again. In this case, the emphasis should be on the switch to the new objective of the game. In the Hoopla version, the children were attempting to obtain objects of the same type. However, in the second version, the new goal became collecting objects of the same color. In both versions of the game, instructors should frequently check that students are grasping the concept of the game and thinking of new and creative ways to win the game and navigate through changes, such as adding or removing a defender.

Challenges Posed by the Teacher and Confronted by the Children

Continuing with the Hoopla and Guardian Hoopla examples, the instructor can pose a multitude of challenges to keep students mentally engaged by using small modifications. One such challenge, noted earlier, is the addition of a defender. Once a defender is introduced to the game and children can no longer freely approach a hula hoop containing the desired objects, they must figure out how to get around this obstacle. During the process of making a decision, the students can engage in deeper levels of cognitive processing by asking questions such as "What is the advantage of having or not having a defender?" or "How did your team work together to get past the defender?"

Besides posing questions, the instructor may challenge students by adding more objects to collect. Rather than having students collect one set of four identical items in Hoopla, have them obtain two sets of four identical items to win the game. Similarly, in Guardian Hoopla, additional colors may be added to make the game more challenging. The instructor can have students gather one object of each color or two sets of four objects of the same color. In the first case, students would need, for example, one blue, red, yellow, and green object to win the game. In the second case, students would need, for instance, four blue objects and four red objects (or whatever combination of colors they choose) to win. The challenges section of the lesson plan offers students ideas on how to experiment in the game they are playing.

This portion of the lesson plan also prompts instructors to anticipate difficulties the children might encounter throughout the activity and to offer potential solutions should those problems arise. This procedure is sometimes known as a refinement task. For example, when teaching dribbling in basketball, it can be anticipated that novice students will slap the ball. Because we are aware of this common mistake, we can offer suggestions in the lesson plan to address the issue. The challenge may be the instructor saying something like, "I noticed many of you are slapping the ball with the palm of your hand. It would be beneficial to use only your finger pads to push the ball to the floor. Let's see if we can be a little quieter with our dribbling by using only the finger pads this time." In that statement, the instructor has identified the problem, stated and demonstrated the correct way to execute the skill, and challenged the students to follow suit. If we anticipate that some students are likely to have difficulties with an activity, the instructor can also plan the feedback statements that he or she might give them during the challenges that have been posed.

Small Modifications and Moving On

Modifications can be physical or cognitive and can be adjusted according to the developmental needs of the children. In the Hoopla and Guardian Hoopla examples, modifications included changing the rules, switching the game, or posing additional challenges, such as defenders and an increased number of objects to retrieve. However, sometimes other kinds of modifications are necessary. For example, if the instructor notices during Hoopla or Guardian Hoopla, that one team is dominating the game, switching members of the teams may be necessary to help all students succeed. A change in team members would also serve to initiate a more challenging environment for the dominating team, as they will now have to work with new team members and against their former teammates who know their strategies.

Team selection is another consideration in a program designed like PAL. Team selection can occur before or after the introduction to the game, and is left to guidance of the instructor who understands the social dynamics of the students. We used a variety of methods to create teams given the wide age and ability range of students in the PAL Program. On some days, teams were selected using the Team Shake app (Rhine-o Enterprises, 2014), which allows students to be organized by age, ability, gender, or grade level and then randomly chooses team members according to specified settings. At other times, teams were selected by having students choose a partner. Because students are clever and catch on to instructor habits quickly, sometimes their partner would be their teammate and sometimes a partner would be their opponent. Regardless of the selection process, teams always had, to the extent possible, an even distribution of various ages and ability.

Promoting Fitness in PAGs

Globally, many countries report declines in children's health and levels of *physical fitness*, which is "the ability to carry out daily tasks with vigor and alertness, without undue fatigue, and with ample energy to enjoy leisure-time pursuits and respond to emergencies" (U.S. Department of Health and Human Services, Office of Disease Prevention and Health Promotion, 2008, p. 53). In the United States, PE and PA have received renewed attention by policymakers, especially concerning children who are overweight or obese. The consensus is that PA provides many health benefits, which include preventing obesity (Shephard, 2009) and hypokinetic diseases (Corbin & Cardinal, 2008). Because so many students today lead sedentary lifestyles, many school administrators, parents, and communities have begun searching for practical solutions for reducing childhood obesity. In 2008, nearly 20% of American children between the ages of 6 and 11 were considered overweight (Daniels, Jacobson, McCrindle, Eckel, & Sanner, 2009). More recently, it was reported that 32% of children and adolescents between the ages of 2 and 19 are overweight or obese, but more specifically, 17.7% of elementary school children between ages 6 and 11 were considered obese (SHAPE America, 2015).

While improving children's physical fitness levels is a worthy goal, the sole intent of our PAGs is not to increase fitness levels, nor are they solely designed to be a fitness program. Nevertheless, it is important to discuss what we have learned about students' physical fitness as a result of participation in PAGs.

As a result of inadequate levels of participation in PA, reduced or nonexistent mandates for PE in schools, and the continuous rise in obesity among children, it is safe to suggest that ASPs are the next best place to provide students with extra opportunities for adequate exercise. As we discussed, PA in the PAL Program offered daily, structured games that emphasized aerobic capacity, cognitive functioning, and socialization of students. To determine whether the intervention was effective in promoting physical fitness, students' fitness was assessed using the FITNESSGRAM Assessment, which is described in the following subsections.

How Fitness Data Were Collected in the PAL Program

The PAL Program utilized some of the fitness measures provided by the *FITNESS-GRAM*. The FITNESSGRAM is a criterion-referenced assessment that measures health-related fitness (HRF) components (Plowman et al., 2006). This assessment battery is the most consistently used fitness test in PE classes across the country and is mandated in many states.

The HRF components consist of aerobic capacity/cardiovascular endurance, muscular strength, muscular endurance, flexibility, and body composition (FIT-NESSGRAM, 2012). *Cardiovascular endurance* is the ability of the heart and lungs to efficiently deliver oxygen to the working muscles over a sustained period of time. *Muscular strength* is the ability to exert the maximum amount of force by a muscle or a muscle group for a single repetition. *Muscular endurance,* on the other hand, is the ability of a muscle or muscle group to produce repeated contractions without tiring too quickly. *Flexibility* is defined as the range of motion about a joint without suffering an injury. Finally, *body composition* is the relative amount of lean muscle tissue versus body fat.

Administration of the FITNESSGRAM

The fitness levels of PAL Program students were measured twice a year using FIT-NESSGRAM. The first measurements occurred during the beginning of the fall semester, and the second approximately seven months later near the end of the spring semester. Prior to the initial FITNESSGRAM assessment, students were taught the proper protocol for each test and given a practice FITNESSGRAM assessment. All PAL Program staff were trained to accurately identify errors and record students' scores. Each student's demographic information was recorded on a FITNESSGRAM score sheet, which was included as part of the assessment's toolkit. Student scores and score sheets were managed by the PA instructor so as to minimize the risk of lost data. Testing took place over the course of 5 days and focused on one HRF component each day. The same procedure was followed for the posttest. The FITNESSGRAM assessments were not administered in any particular order.

In accordance with the Georgia Department of Education recommendations, the following FITNESSGRAM test batteries were used to assess students in the PAL Program: the PACER Test, the Curl-Up Test, the Push-Up Test, the Back-Saver Sit and Reach Test, and BMI calculations. Below, we describe each of the FITNESSGRAM batteries used to assess PAL students.

The PACER Test

The *PACER Test* measures cardiovascular endurance (*FITNESSGRAM*, 2012). It is a 20-meter shuttle-run test in which students paced themselves according to the beeping, pacing signal as they ran back and forth in designated running lanes marked by color-coordinated cones. The cones served to help students run in a straight line while remaining in their lane, and made it easier for students to identify which running lane belonged to them. As the test continued, the pace progressively grew faster. Students were allowed only two errors before the tester ended the test. Errors included mistakes such as not crossing the designated goal line in the allotted time given to reach the 20-meter distance and beginning to run before the start signal was given.

The Curl-Up Test

The *Curl-Up Test* was used to assess abdominal muscular strength and endurance. For this test, participants were asked to lie on their backs on a mat with their fingertips about 4 inches from the end of the mat and then curl up to a sitting position. This test also allowed up to two errors for each participant (FITNESSGRAM, 2012) before the test was terminated. Curl-ups were performed to a cadence provided on the FITNESSGRAM CD. Errors included falling out of synchrony with this cadence and taking breaks in between curl-ups. Also, each student was instructed to ensure that his or her head touched the mat in between each curl-up, fingers slid to the end of the mat each time, and feet remained in contact with the ground at all times.

The Push-Up Test

The push-up portion measured upper body muscular strength and endurance (FITNESSGRAM, 2012). This test allowed two errors for each participant as well. Students were placed on a gymnastics mat, or they could opt to use the floor. The starting push-up position required students to assume a prone position while supporting their body weight on their hands and toes. Students were instructed that arms should be fully extended with their hands shoulder width apart, their bodies should form a straight line with their faces focused on the floor, and only their hands and feet contacting the surface. When the cadence signaled for a push-up, the students were to lower their bodies until the elbows were flexed to a 90-degree angle. They were expected to follow a cadence that signaled exactly when to bend and extend the arms. The speed of the cadence allowed for one push-up every 3 seconds. Errors for the push-up test included falling out of synchrony with the cadence, failing to reach a 90-degree angle at the elbows on the downward phase, failure to maintain a straight body (i.e., no bottoms lifted to the sky like a McDonald's arch or sagging the hips to the ground like an upward dog yoga pose), allowing the body (except for hands and feet) to touch the floor, or taking breaks in between push-ups.

The Back-Saver Sit and Reach Test

The *Back-Saver Sit and Reach Test* was used to separately assess the flexibility of the right and left hamstrings, as well as the lower back. The test required students to remove their shoes and sit on the floor in an upright position facing the sit and reach apparatus. After the sit and reach box was secured against the wall for stability, students were asked to place one foot flat against the sit and reach box keeping that leg fully extended (FITNESSGRAM, 2012). The nonextended leg was to be placed in a bent position so that the foot was flat on the floor and the instep of the foot was aligned with the knee of the extended leg. Further, the foot of the bent leg was to be placed approximately 2–3 inches from the extended leg. Then students placed one hand on top of the other by aligning their middle fingers with the palms facing down. They were asked to reach forward as far as they could while keeping the knee of the extended leg straight and against the ground and the foot of the bent leg flat on the ground. As the participants leaned forward, the outstretched fingers slid a metal marker on the top of the sit and reach box, which measured the distance they reached in inches. Then, the process was repeated using the other leg.

Body Composition, Utilizing Body Mass Index

For *body mass index (BMI)* calculations, participants' height and weight were measured. The weight in pounds was divided by height in inches squared, then multiplied by 703, which resulted in the BMI number (FITNESSGRAM, 2012). This number attempted to justify the appropriateness of a person's height relative to his or her weight.

Initial FITNESSGRAM Results

As primary measures of fitness, we were interested in evaluating for possible changes for two FITNESSGRAM assessments: the PACER and push-up tests.

As measures of cardiovascular endurance and muscular strength and endurance, these were the skills that our PAGs primarily focused on. Secondarily, we also calculated the children's BMI, which was also a FITNESSGRAM measure, albeit a problematic one to be used for evaluating fitness in growing children. The means and standard deviations for the three FITNESSGRAM measures described here are presented in Table 5.1.

The PACER and push-up scores were evaluated by statistical analyses to determine whether children's physical fitness had improved. Analyses of variance tests revealed that posttest scores for both primary measures of fitness were significantly higher than pretest scores ($p < .05$), indicating improved fitness. Thus, as hoped, children's cardiovascular and strength/endurance fitness had improved as a result of their participation in PAGs.

BMI scores were also statistically analyzed. Typically, among adults, decreases in BMI scores are indicative of fitness improvement. However, in our case, BMI scores increased slightly, but there were no statistically significant differences from pretest to posttest. It should be noted that BMI does not account for body fat percentages nor muscle mass gains, but rather offers a suggested weight relative to an individual's height. The raw data showed that most of the students grew taller and, consequently, gained weight from pretest to postassessment. Children of this age are constantly growing, as expected, so the increase in mean scores for BMI should not be surprising. BMI is probably better for merely evaluating fitness at a single point in time in growing children.

To summarize, we conclude that the PAGs intervention proved effective in increasing student fitness levels on aerobic capacity and muscular strength/endurance over the school year. Children improved on the number of laps they were able to complete in the PACER test, and they also increased the number of push-ups they were able to do. Research suggests that when no PA is provided by ASPs, children's fitness can be expected to decline rather than improve throughout the school year, as noted in Chapter 2. Thus, PAGs are one way that ASPs can improve children's fitness in a mixed-age and gender setting like ours.

TABLE 5.1. FITNESSGRAM Score Changes from Pretest to Posttest

Subtest	Fall pretest		Spring posttest	
	M	SD	M	SD
BMI (pounds/inches)	19.93	3.69	20.98	4.84
PACER (number of laps)	18.51	8.27	24.77	12.07
Push-up (number of repetitions)	3.90	2.00	5.20	4.87

Note. N = 60.

Challenges in Teaching PAGs in ASPs

We encountered a few challenges in successfully incorporating the PAGs in the PAL Program. These included (1) large class size, (2) planning developmentally appropriate lessons, (3) gymnasium management, and (4) administration of the FITNESSGRAM assessment.

Large Class Sizes

The challenge of managing a large group of students was overcome by soliciting the assistance of reading and math enrichment instructors and volunteers. During homework and academic enrichment activities, the program design ensured that the second- and third-grade students were segregated from the fourth- and fifth-grade students. However, during PAGs, children were taught as a single mixed group. The use of additional staff was vital in making our PAGs successful, as they assisted in monitoring student behavior and attended to any accidents that occurred. They also participated in PAG activities and helped by repeating rules and instructions children might have missed or misunderstood. They addressed logistical and practical issues, such as guiding early-dismissed children to the office and obtaining items from another part of the school building. Further, these instructors assisted in scoring during the FITNESSGRAM testing.

Planning Developmentally Appropriate Lessons

Another challenge was the need to plan lessons that were developmentally appropriate. Students ranged in age from 7 to 12, and were of various heights and weights. Imagine the problems that might ensue when a 12-year-old, fifth-grade boy who is playing basketball and football, standing at 5 feet, 9 inches, and weighing 110 pounds is playing in the same PAG as a second-grade girl standing at 3 feet, 11 inches, and weighing approximately 50 pounds. Differences in the size and stature of the children required rigorous attention to ensuring the safety of all students playing and being physically active together. One method used to ensure inclusiveness was appropriately assigning teams. For instance, in Hoopla, there are four teams. Each team should consist of different age groups, genders, and skill levels. No one team should contain all higher-skilled students, while the other contains those who are less skilled. Similarly, a single team should not have all second graders playing against all fourth graders. For the PAL Program, composing teams with these concerns in mind meant that the groups were well-mixed. As previously mentioned in the discussion on team selection, diversity offers challenging experiences that provide each person an opportunity to work both with and against others of similar ability and age.

Gymnasium Management

We stress the importance of gymnasium management for several reasons. First, although the PAL Program was conducted after school, it still took place within the school building. Beyond the fact that children needed to use the gym equipment and space with care, the instructors were not the school's teachers. Consequently, failure to establish and maintain gymnasium management might lead to lack of engagement time in PA. Careful attention to establishing rules and protocols is necessary to promote safety. In the PAL PAGs, for example, there were several rules and protocols that students were taught and had an opportunity to practice. One protocol surrounded the use of the whistle. Students were taught that when they heard the instructor's whistle, they had to stop whatever they were doing, put down any and all equipment, and sit "criss-cross applesauce." If the instructor said, "Freeze, please," students knew that it would be a brief interruption in activity (< 30 seconds), so they would stop what they were doing, put down equipment, and look at the instructor.

Moreover, there were specific rules addressing physical boundaries during all the games for safety purposes and consequences for breaking any of the rules. In our case, the boundary lines of the basketball court served as boundaries for PAGs as well. Students were to remain inside the basketball court unless instructed otherwise. Failure to adhere to these safety regulations resulted in consequences. The first consequence was usually a warning, followed by 2 minutes on the bench. When the behavior was a major disruption, such as fighting or behavior that endangered other students, the child was removed from the class, parents were contacted, and the child was potentially suspended from the program.

Free play days were earned as positive incentives for good behavior. Friday was the day of choice for free play because most students were not assigned homework over the weekend which meant homework time was much shorter than normal. For free play, we would offer children four or five different activity options, disperse equipment, and allow them to engage in the activity of their choice for a short time before PAGs instruction started. Gymnasium management was essential during unstructured free play because several activities took place at once within a confined space. For the well-being and safety of all children in the gym, rules and procedures were reiterated, and sometimes practiced, prior to participating in free play.

Challenges of Fitness Testing

Another set of challenges related to issues that occurred during the FITNESS-GRAM assessment. Students were sometimes absent, so we provided assessment make-up days, which ameliorated the missing data problem to some extent. Sometimes children were inappropriately dressed, for example, wearing sandals or skirts. To minimize the clothing issue, we provided extra tennis shoes and shorts that children could wear for testing.

A second challenge was ensuring that all instructors were trained to administer and score the FITNESSGRAM assessment so that children could be tested within a small window of time. Finding the time and resources to ensure that all assistants are properly trained can be difficult.

Further, the FITNESGRAM assessment does not tell us how much PA children participate in outside of PAL or what their nutritional habits are. It may be that these outside activities and habits also had an effect on improving fitness. Nor does the assessment measure the game-specific, skill-related fitness that may be improved as a result of the skills used in some of the PAGs the children play.

Summary

This chapter has provided an overview of the PAGs portion of the PAL Program. You have been introduced to the types of PAs children participated in during the PAL Program. A description of game activities, particularly Hoopla and Guardian Hoopla, has been provided to show the types of games that were played in the PA portion of PAL. The design and delivery, as well as a rationale for implementation, of activities were discussed. Additionally, this chapter provided a brief synopsis of the importance of lesson planning and an example of explanation points using the Hoopla example. Further, the assessment of student fitness levels, the data collection methods of physical fitness, and the results of the FITNESSGRAM assessment from the PAL Program were discussed. Finally, the chapter expressed some of the challenges of implementing such a program design and solutions for meeting these challenges.

GLOSSARY

Back-saver sit and reach test—A FITNESSGRAM test measuring flexibility of the lower back and both left and right hamstrings.

Body mass index (BMI)—A measure of fitness determined by the appropriateness of a person's height relative to his or her weight.

Curl-up test—A FITNESSGRAM test of abdominal muscular endurance requiring children to curl up from lying down into a sitting position.

FITNESSGRAM—A criterion-related standardized assessment of fitness targeting aerobic capacity/cardiovascular endurance, muscular strength, muscular endurance, flexibility, and body composition.

Instant activity—An instant activity is one that begins within the first 1 to 2 minutes of student arrival and aims to immediately engage students in fun, dynamic PA as soon as possible.

PACER test—A test of cardiovascular endurance requiring children to run while keeping up with an ever-increasing cadence.

Physical activity—Any bodily movement produced by the contraction of skeletal muscle that enhances health.

Physical education—A planned, sequential K–12 standards-based program with written curricular and appropriate instruction designed to develop the motor skills, knowledge, and behaviors of active living, physical fitness, sportsmanship, self-efficacy, and emotional intelligence; it should be taught by a certified/licensed physical educator.

Physical fitness—The ability to carry out daily tasks with vigor and alertness, without undue fatigue, and with ample energy to enjoy leisure-time pursuits and respond to emergencies.

Push-up test—A test of muscular strength requiring the student to lower the body until the elbows are flexed to a 90-degree angle and then raise the body until arms are extended while keeping the body in a straight line.

References

Abadie, B. R., & Brown, S. P. (2010). Physical activity promotes academic achievement and a healthy lifestyle when incorporated into early childhood education. *Forum on Public Policy Online, 2010*(5).

America, S. H. A. P. E., Couturier, L., Chepko, S., & Holt, S. A. (2014). *National standards and grade-level outcomes for K–12 physical education*. Champaign, IL: Human Kinetics.

Body Mass Index. (2004–2016). Retrieved September 28, 2016, from *www.diet.com/g/body-mass-index*.

Corbin, C. B., & Cardinal, B. J. (2008). Conceptual physical education: The anatomy of an innovation. *Quest (00336297), 60*(4), 467–487.

Daniels, S. R., Jacobson, M. S., McCrindle, B. W., Eckel, R. H., & Sanner, B. M. (2009). American heart association childhood obesity research summit report. *Journal of the American Heart Association, 119*, 489–517.

Diamond, A. (2014). Want to optimize executive functions and academic outcomes?: Simple, just nourish the human spirit. In *Minnesota Symposia on Child Psychology* (Vol. 37, p. 205). Washington, DC: NIH Public Access.

FITNESSGRAM. (2012). Retrieved September 28, 2016, from *www.FITNESSGRAM.net*.

Gabbard, C. P. (2012). *Lifelong motor development*. Upper Saddle River, NJ: Pearson Higher Education.

Gallahue, D. L., & Cleland-Donnelly, F. (2007). *Developmental physical education for all children*. Champaign, IL: Human Kinetics.

Jensen, E. (2000). Moving with the brain in mind. *Educational Leadership, 58*(3), 34–37. Retrieved from *www.districtadministration.com/article/report-bodymotion-gets-better-grades*.

Lux, K., & McCullick, B. A. (2011). How one exceptional teacher navigated her working environment as the teacher of a marginal subject. *Journal of Teaching in Physical Education, 30*(4), 358–374.

National Association for Sport and Physical Education. (2004). *PA for children: A statement of guidelines for children ages 5–12* (2nd ed.). Reston, VA: NASPE Publications.

Plowman, S. A., Sterling, C. L., Corbin, C. B., Meredith, M. B., Welk, G. J., & Morrow, J. R., Jr. (2006). History of FITNESSGRAM. *Journal of Physical Activity and Health, 3*(Suppl. 2), S5–S20.

Rhine-o Enterprises (2014). Team shake—A random name and team selection app. Retrieved December 19, 2016, from *http://ipadapps4school.com/2014/04/16/team-shake-a-random-name-and-team-selection-app.*

SHAPE America. (2015). *The essential components of physical education.* Reston, VA: Author.

Shepherd, A. (2009). Obesity: Prevalence, causes and clinical consequences. *Nursing Standard, 23*(52), 51.

Tomporowski, P. D. (2003). Effects of acute bouts of exercise on cognition. *Acta Psychologica, 112,* 297–324.

Tomporowski, P. D., Davis, C. L., Miller, P. H., & Naglieri, J. A. (2008). Exercise and children's intelligence, cognition, and academic achievement. *Educational Psychology Review, 20*(2), 111–131.

Tomporowski, P. D., McCullick, B., Pendleton, D. M., & Pesce, C. (2015). Exercise and children's cognition: The role of task factors and a place for metacognition. *Journal of Sport and Health Science, 4,* 47–55.

Tremarche, P. V., Robinson, E. M., & Graham, L. B. (2007). Physical education and its effect on elementary testing results. *Physical Educator, 64*(2), 58–64.

U.S. Department of Health and Human Services, Office of Disease Prevention and Health Promotion. (2008). *Physical activity guidelines for Americans.* Washington, DC: U.S. Department of Health and Human Services.

Appendix 5.1. Sample Lesson Plan 1

Game for the Day: Hoopla
Equipment Needed: Hula hoops, balls/beanbags, frisbees, poly spot/items (at least four each) of four different colors
Space Requirements: Gym

Instant Activity: Fish, Ship, Shore

- The object of this game for the instant activity is to keep the children moving and to avoid being the last person to follow the captain's orders.

- The instructor is the captain. The sailors (children and students) line up along the wall and wait for the captain to say a command. The sailors will move according to the captain's commands. The basic commands the captain will issue are the following:
  - "FISH!"—The children have to run to the line that has been designated "fish."
  - "SHIP!"—The children run to the line that has been designated "ship."
  - "SHORE!"—The children run to the line that has been designated "shore."
  - "CAPTAIN ON DECK!"—The children need to stand straight up, legs together, feet turned out at the heel to form a *v,* and with their right hands saluting next to their right eye and their left hands behind their backs.
  - "AT EASE."—The children need to stand with feet apart and both hands their behind backs.
  - "(#) IN A BOAT!"—The captain will say a number, for example, 3, and then count down from 5, and the children will have 5 seconds to form a group of three and sit one behind the other, criss-cross applesauce, and rowing with their arms.
  - "OCTOPUS!"—The captain will count down from 5, and then the children need to find a group of four, link arms, and form a circle with their feet facing out of the circle and wiggle their legs like an octopus.
  - "HIT THE DECK!"—The children need to drop to the floor in a push-up position as quickly as possible, but also as safely as possible.
  - "THE STORM IS COMING!"—The captain will count down from 5, and the children need to find a partner. One partner gets on the floor on their hands and knees and the other puts one foot lightly on their backs and holds their hands up to their eyes as if they are looking for the storm off in the distance.

- The whole point of this game is to not be the last few children to arrive at any spot the captain calls out or the last to get into whatever position the captain calls out. This makes sure the children are paying attention and following directions. If a child is one of the last ones, that child will need to jump up in the air with his/her legs and feet sprawled out and yell "BIG STAR!" then get back in line.

(continued)

Teacher Essentials and Explanation Points

Divide students into four teams with no more than four students per team. Starting with the same four objects (e.g., a ball, beanbag, frisbee, poly spot [or some flat item used as a space marker]) inside each team's hula hoop. The goal of the game is for each team to get all four of the same object in its own hoop. The instructor should place each team's hoop a few feet from each corner of the play area to allow for a balance of offense and defense at each hoop.

Rules

1. Teams decide on a target object before each round begins. *Note:* Teams may end up choosing the same target item; this is OK, as it adds to the challenge of the game.
2. An attacker may only steal one item at a time.
3. For the first few rounds, there is no defender to allow students to become familiar with the game. After two or three rounds, each team must have a defender at its home hoop (though the defender must stay outside of the coned area, if the instructor decides to use them).
4. If the defender—and only the defender—tags an opponent, the opponent must go back to his/her home hoop (and, if holding an item, return it to the defender).

Challenges Posed by the Teacher and Confronted by the Children

- "What is the advantage of having/not having a defender?"
- "How can you get your target object if another team is trying to get the same object?"

After two to three playing rounds:
- Stop the game and check for understanding of rules, concepts, strategies, and tactics.
- Switch up teams if necessary by assigning a subset of children to new teams.

Notes: Some students may try to pass stolen items back to their home hoop by tossing them to their defender. Allow this strategy initially, exploring during a pause for questions why it may or may not be a good strategy.

Feedback suggestions: Pay attention to what items the other teams have decided to go after.

Small Modifications and Moving On

Make the defender optional. Ask students the first question above after a round or two, giving teams the opportunity to explore the game with or without a dedicated defender.

(continued)

Appendix 5.1. (page 3 of 4)

Switch to a New Game: Guardian Hoopla (Version 2)
Equipment Needed: Hula hoops, balls/beanbags, frisbees, poly spot/items (at least four of each) of four different colors
Space Requirements: Gym

The instructor assigns each team a particular color and divides the play area into four distinct quadrants (one for each color). Explain that the object of the game is for each team to retrieve all items of the same color from the other teams' hoops. Depending on class size, the instructor should make sure that each quadrant's hoop contains three to five items per color, except for that quadrant's/team's color. Before beginning, show the students an example of what a particular team's hoop should look like—students will help "reset" items in the hoops after each round and should be familiar with what items belong in their hoops to start the game.

Rules

1. A student is safe from taggers only in his/her home quadrant.
2. If tagged in another color's quadrant, a student must return to his/her home quadrant.
3. If tagged while holding a stolen item, a student must return it to the hoop from which he/she stole it.
4. Students only retrieve one item at a time of the color assigned to them.
5. Defenders must stay one arm's length from the hoop they are defending.

Challenges Posed by the Teacher and Confronted by the Children

- "Should attackers spread out or try to attack one zone at a time?"
- "Should a team have more attackers or more defenders? Why?"
- Name three things that make a team successful in this game.

After two to three times:
- Stop the game and check for understanding.
- Switch up teams if necessary.

Notes: With a play area smaller than a typical basketball court, the instructor may decide not to divide the area into quadrants. In this case, have the children play the game in a manner similar to the first game, with the only difference being that teams should try to get items of their team's color.

Feedback suggestions: It may be a good idea to tag others even if they are not stealing one of your items just so they won't finish before you.

(continued)

Small Modifications and Moving On

If possible, combine play areas (e.g., two halves of a gym or two separate areas if outside) to form four larger quadrants with more students per team. Defensive and offensive strategies may change with larger quadrants and more teammates. Increase the number of items per color in each hoop accordingly.

Appendix 5.2. Sample Lesson Plan 2

Game for the Day: Pillow Polo—Trash Can (Version 1)
Equipment Needed: pinnies, pillow polo sticks, gopher balls, cones (or soccer goals or trash cans)
Space Requirements: Gym

Instant Activity: Alligator, Alligator

- The object of this game is to keep children moving and make it from one side of the "pond" to the other without being caught by an alligator.
- There will be two children in the middle circle (alligators) while the rest of the children line up on one side of the gym.
- The students will ask permission to cross the bridge, and the alligators will alternate turns calling out some characteristic or identifier to indicate when the others should attempt to cross the pond. For example,
  - Students will call out, "Alligator, alligator, may we cross your bridge?"
  - One alligator will respond with "If you have a brother."
  - Then, students who do, in fact, have a brother will attempt to run from one side of the gym to the other without being tagged. If tagged, they must kneel to the ground, until the game restarts or the instructor calls for jail break. Jail break restarts the game immediately, and everyone is back in the game.
  - After all students who had a brother were either tagged or safely to the other side, the students ask permission again: "Alligator, alligator, may we cross your bridge?"
  - The other alligator will now respond with something like "If you are wearing yellow."
  - The process repeats itself until all students are tagged, or you want to switch the alligators.

Teacher Essentials and Explanation Points

Divide the students into groups of five to six people per group. Set up cones, soccer nets, or trash cans (a goal for students to aim for) at either end of the gym. There will be no goalies in this game. The aim of the game is score on the other teams' goal while keeping the opposing team from doing the same in your own goal. The students are supposed to pass the ball using the pillow polo sticks. Students may adopt different methods with which to strike and hit the ball. Allow them to explore these, but if the method becomes dangerous to the other children, stop that method immediately. Also, make sure when a ball goes out of bounds, the defenders give the opponent hitting the ball back in enough space to do so.

Rules

1. Players may only move the ball on the ground using the pillow polo sticks.

(continued)

2. Neither team will have a goalie.
3. If the ball goes out of bounds on one team, the opposing team will now gain possession of the ball.
4. Fouls (hitting, pushing, and shoving) result in a free hit from the foul spot.
5. Players shall not raise their sticks higher than knee height.

Challenges Posed by the Teacher and Confronted by the Children

- "What is the best way to move the ball down the court?"
- "How do I get open to receive a pass?"
- "Do you have to be on the lookout for teammates? Why?"
- "Do you want more offense or defense on your team? Why?"
- "What makes receiving the ball difficult and how can you overcome this?"

After two to three times:
- Stop the game and check for understanding of rules, concepts, strategies, and tactics.
- Switch up teams if necessary by assigning a subset of children to new teams.

Notes: Make sure the children keep the polo sticks below their knees; raising it above their knee will result in a foul on the team and can be very dangerous. Some teams may focus more on offense and neglect the defensive end of the game, allowing the other team to continuously score.

Feedback suggestions: Once the game starts, it is very likely that the children will clump together and follow the ball instead of spreading out. If this happens, stop the game and suggest that it may be easier and less work if the team spreads out and passes the ball.

Small Modifications and Moving On

Divide the students into smaller teams or create bigger teams. Either way, strategies tend to change. Make the goals smaller, making it more difficult to score and forcing children to control the ball more. If it is too difficult, you can make the goals wider. Ask the questions about playing more offense or defense and why it is important. You may also allow students to experiment with a goalie for a round or two.

> *Switch to a New Game:* Four Team Pillow Polo (Version 2)
> *Equipment Needed:* four colors of pinnies, gopher balls, cones, pillow polo sticks, four trash cans, number signs
> *Space Requirements:* Gym

There will be four teams of up to five students per team playing all at once. Each team will defend one of the four goals (garbage cans) in one of the four corners. The goals

(continued)

will be labeled with numbers 1–4, and the children will need to defend their number goal while also trying to score on the other numbers. For example, if a child is labeled (2), then his/her main goal is 2, and the goal is to try to score on goals 1, 3, and 4. This can also be organized by color (if the team is wearing blue, then its goal is the blue goal) There will be three balls in play at once. The children will try to get as many points by scoring on the other goals while also defending their own goal.

Rules

1. A team may have possession of more than one ball at the same time. (although one player may not have possession of more than one ball at the same time).
2. If a team hits a ball out of bounds, the nearest player of another team will in-bound the ball.
3. The ruling for fouls remains the same as in the first game.
4. No team may have a dedicated goalie.

Challenges Posed by the Teacher and Confronted by the Children

- "How can we balance offense and defense?"
- "Is it more important to score on other goals or defend your own? Why?"
- "How can we draw our opponents away from defending our goal?"

After two to three times:
- Stop the game and check for understanding.
- Switch up teams if necessary.

Notes: Look for the children who are not getting enough play time. If this is the case, stop the game and have that student start with possession of the ball. The idea is to get everyone involved in the game.

Feedback suggestions: Encourage students to pay attention to all players in all areas rather than only the goal they are trying to score on or attempting to defend.

Small Modifications and Moving On

Increase the number of balls with different assigned point values. Offer the option of a goalie: "If your team has a goalie, do you need defenders?"

6

The Challenges Struggling Learners Face in Mathematics

Martha M. Carr

While students are in elementary school, they must construct an understanding of numbers that allows them to compute answers to increasingly complex problems, including multidigit arithmetic problems, problems that involve fractions, and multiplication and division problems. This understanding goes beyond that needed for whole numbers to include negative numbers and rational numbers. This is not an easy task. While whole numbers (i.e., numbers without fractions) are relatively easy to comprehend, students have difficulty conceptualizing negative numbers and fractions. More important, students have trouble solving problems that include these numbers.

In this chapter we discuss several factors that promote the development of a good understanding of number and skilled mathematical problem solving. Students who are more likely to do well in mathematics are fluent in basic math and multiplication facts, have a well-developed understanding of how numbers relate to each other on the number line, and transition smoothly to mental computation. Because they reflect a rich understanding of number, these skills undergird later developing mathematics skills and knowledge. This chapter also describes several major challenges students face in developing a good understanding of number and in acquiring problem-solving skills; specifically, students are challenged to understand place value, equivalence, and fractions. Finally, this chapter discusses how general cognitive skills and knowledge affect development of these skills in the mathematical realm. Chapter 7 (Yi-Jung Lee, this volume) complements this chapter in that it presents research-based practices for improving these skills and knowledge.

Critical Mathematical Knowledge and Skills

Fluency for Basic Math Facts

For a number of years, the focus of mathematics education was on the construction of conceptual knowledge about mathematics, and there was little interest in teaching children to improve mathematics *fluency*, which is defined as the ability to quickly and accurately compute or retrieve answers, during mathematics problem solving. While the focus on conceptual knowledge remains strong, it has become clear that fluency is an important component of achievement in mathematics, for both students' current performance and for learning advanced skills (e.g., Biddlecomb & Carr, 2011).

Teaching for fluency should consist of not only "drill-and-kill" practice. It has long been known that the drill-and-kill practice does little to improve fluency (Brownell & Chazal, 1935). Activities such as having children complete timed tests, fill out basic math fact worksheets, and drill memorization of basic math facts have not been effective in producing better fluency, in comparison with activities that emphasize the relationships among numbers (Henry & Brown, 2008). Specifically, games and activities that require students to think about how numbers are connected or how to decompose and reconstruct numbers appear to support emerging fluency.

A number of gamelike activities have been developed to improve computational fluency through the activation of conceptual knowledge. For example, Baroody and his colleagues (Baroody, Eiland, Purpura, & Reid, 2012; Baroody, Purpura, Eiland, Reid, & Paliwal, 2016) created a computer game for kindergarten students that highlighted conceptual connections. The game focuses on linking subtraction and addition, so that in giving students two problems, such as 7 + 1 and 8 − 7, back-to-back, the goal is for students to understand the link between them. The game also encourages students to use 10's as benchmarks so that 19 + 7 is solved by first solving 20 + 7, and then subtracting 1 from the result. The idea behind the use of benchmarks is that children typically learn doubles and 10's first, and can use this knowledge to solve other problems. As with many fluency programs, this program includes substantial practice, and it is done in a way that fosters links among families of numbers.

Activities that focus on speed can be combined with activities that focus on conceptual understanding, and this practice has been found to be more effective than non-speeded practice. Fuchs and her colleagues (2013) had first graders first participate in an activity designed to teach students about number families, for example, by having the students find all the different combinations of numbers that can add to five. The students were then split into groups that either carried out speeded practice in which students computed answers to problems as quickly as possible or non-speeded practice that involved practicing the problems as a part of a board game. They found that students who were given speeded practice performed better on arithmetic and two-digit calculations, but the advantage did not extend to word problem solving. Speeded practice was especially helpful for the at-risk students in the class.

Given what we know from this and other research, games and other afterschool activities selected to improve fluency ought to include components that support both students' understanding of the relationships among numbers and that focus on speed. The mathematics enrichment program as presented in Chapter 7 includes team competitive games that involve groups of students competing to complete families of number problem sets, for example. Fluency can be improved as students transition to mental math and learn place value by including speeded practice or competition in those activities.

Transition to Mental Math

Students typically learn to count by counting objects and then shifting over to mental calculation as they acquire a mental representation of number. *Mental math* refers to calculations people can do in their minds without using pencil and paper, calculators, or objects to count on. For addition and subtraction, the transition from a reliance on concrete objects to mental representations of number occurs during the early elementary school years, but some students fall behind, with implications for their later achievement (Biddlecomb & Carr, 2011). Failure to transition to mental computation is an indicator that the student does not have a well-developed understanding of number. Students may not fluently map their concept of a number onto the number of objects the number represents, they may be slow in their counting, or they may not recognize relationships among numbers on the mental number line. All of these problems make it difficult to move to mental computation.

Mentally representing number is more than having the number in memory. To really understand number and to accurately and quickly compute answers to problems, the student must understand how the different numbers are linked along the number line and how numbers are embedded within other numbers (Steffe, Cobb, & von Glaserfeld, 1988). For instance, a student with limited understanding of number will likely count out all numbers for the addition problem 6 + 4; that is, the student will count out 6, then count out 4, and then count all 10 items in sequence to get the answer. Students eventually understand a number as an abstract concept so that the number 4 means 4 of anything. Numbers are not tied to the objects that are counted. Through practice students realize that they can start counting at the largest number, a strategy called *counting on*. Once students begin to counton they may count-on a 4 with their fingers, which should eventually transition to counting on mentally. As students acquire a more complex, networked understanding of number, even more advanced strategies become available. They can use

10's as benchmarks for computation. For example, 29 + 4 will be transformed into 30 + 3 for easier computation. As such, the ability to mentally compute answers to problems requires a rich, complex understanding of number.

Mental computation is intertwined with developing fluency. Whereas fluent retrieval of basic math facts makes mental computation easier, the repeated efforts to mentally calculate or retrieve answers, in turn, reinforces basic math facts in memory. This is why the need for fluency with basic math facts increases as students progress into the second grade, when the complexity of problems increases. Likewise, once students begin to solve division problems, the ability to quickly and efficiently retrieve multiples, such as $5 \times 7 = 35$, allows students to efficiently solve division problems. The continued reliance on manipulatives slows computation, increases opportunities for mistakes as students count increasingly larger numbers, and makes it difficult for students to construct complex solutions.

One technique for transitioning students away from relying on concrete numbers is to cover objects and ask them to compute an answer while only imagining the items. This technique can be incorporated into after-school games and activities. Card games, in particular, provide opportunities for students to retrieve from memory the next or prior number when the game involves stacking cards in order (e.g., Skip-Bo). Card games can be modified to be more complex. Teachers can have students play addition, subtraction, or multiplication "war" with one or both numbers turned upside down after viewing. The PAL Program mathematics component has students play "hands-on-the-table," in which students solve homework problems while their hands are placed firmly on the table. Teams of students can also play "hands-on-the-table," with each team winning a point when a team member can accurately solve a math problem without counting on his/her fingers. This game can be modified so that students can score more points for faster, correct responses.

Mental Number Line

As students construct abstract representations of number, they generate a mental number line that reflects the relationship among numbers. A *mental number line* is a mental representation of the order and magnitude of numbers, with a focus on the equidistant placement of numbers on the line. A student who has a well-defined concept of a mental number line will know that 25 is halfway between 0 and 50, for instance. This representation opens up possibilities for better problem solving. First, it allows students to estimate possible responses. A student with a well-developed mental number line will know that 88 + 44 = 1212 is not a possible response and that a mistake has been made. It also supports emerging fraction knowledge, as students begin to use benchmarks to mark fractions on the number line. For instance, 50 is halfway between 0 and 100.

When young students first begin to estimate where a number belongs on a number line, their estimates tend to be significantly way off. They tend to think that the smaller numbers are much further along the number line than where they actually should be. Younger students often solve these mental number line tasks by counting from the beginning of the line and are often unaware of how far off their count is from the target. A good example of this problem is given in Figure 6.1, which shows the work of a first grader who had attempted find where 64 is located on a 0 to 100 number line. As you can see, the student had much bigger spaces between the hash marks for the smaller numbers, but then began to squeeze in hash marks as he completely overshot 64. While the counting strategy is fine for smaller numbers, it is not effective for larger numbers. It is not until the second grade that most students are able to accurately judge where a number is on the 0 to 100 number line and not until the fourth grade that students can accurately judge where a number is on the 0 to 1,000 number line (Luwel, Verschaffel, Onghena, & De Corte, 2001). Older students use benchmarks to estimate the location of a number, making it easier for them to zero in on the correct location. Students with well-defined mental number lines are higher achievers in mathematics (Booth & Siegler, 2008), and this skill supports fraction learning: Students who are good at placing whole numbers on the number line are also more likely to correctly place fractions (Fazio, Bailey, Thompson, & Siegler, 2014).

Interestingly, some research shows that simply pointing out that 50 is the midpoint of a 0 to 100 number line results in improved estimation. Many students may merely be unaware of the utility of using benchmarks. If teachers decide to teach students how to use benchmarks, they should make sure that the students correctly mark the halfway point. It is not unusual for students to mark the halfway point a significant distance from where it should be. Fischer, Moeller, Bientzle, Cress, and Nuerk (2011) performed a study based on the concept of *embodied cognition,* which is the idea that we store perceptual representations in memory (e.g., movement and sight). They had 5- and 6-year-old students stand in the middle of a 0 to 10 number line and step up toward the 10 or down toward 0

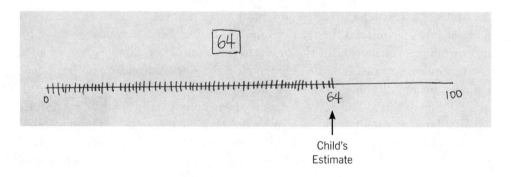

FIGURE 6.1. How a first grader or low-performing second grader might estimate the position of the number 64 on a 0 to 100 number line.

from the 5 to show whether a number was bigger or smaller than 5. They found that students who stood at the center of a line and stepped right or left to show bigger or smaller when comparing two numbers (e.g., 5 in comparison to 8) were better at paper and pencil number line estimation tests than children who did not. Embodied cognition theory assumes that we represent the mental number line in memory spatially. The use of physical movement takes advantage of that spatial representation and helps to reinforce that spatial representation in memory. Clapping to a regular beat while counting, for example, is an activity that enhances the idea of regular intervals among numbers. Certainly, these types of activities can be incorporated in any after-school program (ASP) directed at struggling mathematicians.

Understanding of Place Value Knowledge

Once students begin to work with numbers higher than 10, the issue of place value knowledge comes into play. *Place value* refers to the value that a digit has based on the location of the digit in a number. When students first work with multidigit addition and subtraction problems, they frequently treat the digits in the 10's column as 1's, ignoring the relationship between 1's and 10's. As a result, they will compute answers incorrectly: 35 + 78 = 1013. Students with both mathematics and reading disabilities have problems understanding and working with place value (Jordan, Hanich, & Kaplan, 2003), suggesting multiple or more general deficits.

While some argue that the failure to understand place value may be due to the complexity of the concept of place value (Chandler & Kamii, 2009), newer research indicates that kindergarteners can understand basic place value concepts. Specifically, kindergarteners are able to correctly select which of two multidigit numbers is the larger significantly above chance, suggesting that they have a basic understanding of place value. Mix, Prather, Smith, and Stockton (2014) believed that this competency emerged from repeated incidental learning experiences with number. As such, many children may simply not have had experiences with constructing basic place value concepts before entering school. They may need to catch up with their peers with activities that provide extra attention to these concepts in ASPs.

Problems with place value emerge as students begin to work with multidigit computation problems. Traditionally, students were taught to use the standard algorithm, which involved computing the answer in the ones column, carrying or borrowing as necessary, and computing the answer to the 10's column and so on. While many students were able to grasp the concept of place value within this context, other students struggled. These students viewed digits in the tens and hundreds columns as ones. For these students, 21 represented a 2 and a 1 as opposed to a 20 and a 1. An alternative approach is to focus on the 100's,

10's, and 1's separately. For the problem 35 + 78, students might be asked to add the 10's to equal 100, add the ones to equal 13, and then to add 100 + 13 to equal 113. Variations of this approach that required students to break down both numbers, particularly involving subtraction with regrouping, have been found to result in confusion and less than optimal learning (Beishuizen, 1993), so care must be taken to avoid cognitive overload. Another instructional strategy involved the use of an empty number line on which students wrote the first number and then jumped up the number line starting with the largest units and then jumping up in smaller units. For example, Figure 6.2, which shows the problem of adding 24 + 25, involves the student starting at 24, jumping two 10's up the number line and then five 1's (Klein, Beishuizen, & Treffers, 1998). Given that this system utilizes the mental number line, activities that improve the mental number line should also improve place value knowledge.

These programs are effective because they embed computation within contexts that provide students with different representations of 10's, 1's, and 100's, and these experiences allow students to abstract the necessary place value knowledge (Boulton-Lewis, 1998). ASPs can offer additional practice through activities that involve movement up and down a number line as students compute answers to multidigit problems. The involvement of a number line supports students' understanding of magnitude, for example, that 50 is five 10's away from 0. Other games or activities that focus on creating 10's or 100's by breaking down and recombining numbers will reinforce place value. For younger students, games like Make-a-Ten Bingo (see Yi-Jung Lee, Chapter 7, this volume) can be used to teach how numbers can be combined to create 10's. The game can be modified for older students, so that the goal can be to make 20s, 30s, or 100s.

Understanding of Fractions

Even young children have a basic understanding of fractions, such as one-half, as a result of experiencing them in everyday activities. Yet, elementary students typically struggle with fractions when they are introduced in school. One reason

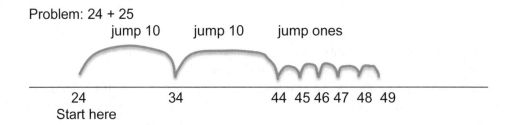

FIGURE 6.2. Empty number line method for teaching multidigit computation.

is that students fail to grasp important fraction concepts. They do not realize that all parts of the whole must be equal and often assume that parts can be different sizes. They also do not understand that all "wholes" are equal, and this misconception makes it difficult to add or subtract fractions. These misconceptions develop because teachers frequently introduce fractions through the use of a drawing showing a whole divided into portions, but often fail to tell students that the portions must be equal to be fractions and that all wholes must be equal to each other. These basic concepts are often not explicitly taught in the curriculum, but when they are taught explicitly, they produce better transfer of fraction knowledge (Yoshida & Sawano, 2002).

Understanding fractions is also problematic because it involves the integration of two conceptualizations of number. While fractions represent a relationship between two numbers, for example, ½ indicates one part of two, a fraction is a single or rational number in itself. As such, ½ can be found on a number line between 0 and 1, and it can be transposed into a decimal. Students often have trouble placing a fraction on a number line because a fraction does not conform to their understanding of a number (Behr & Bright, 1984). This becomes more problematic when problem solving requires that they understand a fraction as a whole in itself, particularly when multiplying or dividing fractions.

To complicate matters further, other factors affect the learning of fractions. Number line estimation, computation skills, and the ability to quickly and accurately count objects are predictive of later success in learning fractions (Vukovic et al., 2014). This means that difficulties with fractions may go beyond simply not understanding fraction concepts, but may indicate deficits in underlying skills in these areas.

Given that fractions can be represented in multiple ways and that focusing on only one way to teach fractions is unlikely to be effective, multiple approaches to teaching fractions are recommended. They can include the commonly used part–whole approach in which a teacher divides a whole, depicting numbers on a number line, as occurs when measuring. They can include symbolic representation in which students manipulate numbers, for example, dividing 2 with a 3 for ⅔. Regardless of the approach, the teacher needs to be aware of potential misconceptions and teach explicitly to avoid them.

ASPs can support the learning of fractions through the use of teaching activities that involve fractions and focus on potential misconceptions. Research indicates that the use of concrete manipulatives is an extremely helpful component of intervention studies aimed at improving fraction knowledge (Shin & Bryant, 2015). A number of commercially available manipulatives teach fraction concepts and can be included in after-school games and activities. Simple card games can be constructed to improve fluency and conceptual understanding. For example, Gabriel et al. (2012) had fourth- and fifth-grade students play a card game in which they matched pairs of numbers that represent the same quantity (e.g., ½ and ¾), a game of "war" in which students compared fractions to determine which was the larger. They also played a fraction version of Old Maid, in which students collect pairs of fractions with the same magnitude, Treasure Hunt, in which they figure out which pair of fractions represented the highest magnitude, and Blackjack, in which students collect fractions until they were close to two.

Equivalence

Although the equal sign seems self-explanatory, students from kindergarten to college often have trouble understanding its meaning. Instead, they incorrectly interpret the equal sign to mean "do something" instead of interpreting the sign to mean that the two sides of the equation must be balanced (Kieran, 1981). This misconception is likely the result of the tendency of teachers to introduce and teach the equal sign using the format of $3 + 4 =$ __, which reinforces the "do something" interpretation. The misconception is so well entrenched in elementary school that even including this format among nontraditional formats, such as $a = c + b$, causes students to have problems solving the nontraditional problems, such as $3 + 4 + 5 = 6 +$ __. Essentially, the "do something" interpretation trumps the "balance" interpretation given any opportunity.

The strength of the "do something" interpretation was made evident in research showing that students' ability to deal with nontraditional formats *decreases* as they progress from the second to third grade (McNeil, 2007). McNeil believes that the third-grade slump occurs when students who have become very familiar with the traditional "do something" format resist nontraditional formats, viewing them as incorrect or impossible equations. The problem with equivalence emerges again when students study algebra. When students begin to work with variables, they usually fall back to the "do something" interpretation of the equal sign, which is very problematic when dealing with variables. It is important for students to be introduced to the correct interpretation of the equal sign as early as possible and for that interpretation to be maintained through elementary school.

McNeil suggests several techniques that can be used to avoid the development of this misconception. Teachers can introduce and use nontraditional formats, such as __ $= 4 + 3$ to reinforce the "is equal to" idea (McNeil, Fyfe, & Dunwiddie, 2015). Teachers need to talk about balancing equations, as opposed to coming up with an answer. One approach is to use an array of nontraditional formats for the same problem: __ $+ 6 = 13$, $7 +$ __ $= 13$, $7 + 6 =$ __. Relatedly, teachers can have multiple numbers on both sides of the equation: $7 + 6 = 4 +$ __, which teaches students that one side of the equation does not need to be a single answer. In the PAL Program, we use a number of games that highlight the balance aspect of equivalence including a fulcrum and balance beam. Students or teams can score points when they come up with equations that balance or when they are able to correct unbalanced equations.

General Cognitive Abilities That Affect Learning Math

Students' ability to learn is affected by a number of general cognitive processes that grow and mature over time and with experience. Working memory is one such process. *Working memory* is the cognitive system that we use to temporarily store and manage all the information we need to complete difficult mental tasks, such as mathematics. Cognitive psychologists have focused primarily on two forms of working memory: verbal working memory and spatial working memory. Whereas the working memories are assumed to be responsible for our cognitive processing, long-term memory is the system that we use to store knowledge and skills that have been processed in working memory. Working memories are important because they are what we use to mentally manipulate information, including information that we are attempting to learn and use in problem solving and planning. We also hold information in working memory temporarily for later use. For example, when solving a two-part problem, the solution to one part will be held in working memory, while solving the second part of the problem. Given the role of working memory in problem solving and comprehension, it is obvious why it is important for mathematics. *Attention* is another important general cognitive skill that affects students' ability to learn mathematics. Our attention processes allow us to inhibit irrelevant or distracting information, to shift from one topic to the next, and to update information by discarding old, outdated information for new information within working memory.

We know that students who have better functioning working memories and attention in preschool are more likely to have better mathematics skills in the second grade (Bull, Espy, & Wiebe, 2008). Limited growth in attention, verbal, and spatial working memories in early elementary school also predicts problems in mathematics in children at risk for later learning problems (Swanson, 2008). As students work on more complex mathematics, these general cognitive skills become increasingly important. For example, both working memories and attention are important for word problem solving, which is more demanding than simple computation (Fuchs et al., 2010).

A number of studies have examined how verbal working memory affects different mathematics skills. Verbal working memory has been linked to performance on word-problem and whole-number calculation (Peng, Namkung, Barnes, & Sun, 2016). It is important for mental computation (Adams & Hitch, 1998) and predicts number line estimation for at-risk students (Fuchs et al., 2016). It also affects students' ability to learn how fractions are related to each other on the number line. Interestingly, having students explain how they solved fraction number line problems supports learning in students with poor working memory (Fuchs, Geary, Fuchs, Compton, & Hamlett, 2016). Having students talk or write about what they are doing in problem solving likely improves performance by focusing attention on what is being learned.

There is considerable evidence that spatial skills and spatial working memory are important for mathematics as well. *Spatial working memory* processes information in a visual or spatial form within the larger working memory system. It is particularly useful when considering children's ability to mentally manipulate numbers along a number line. Spatial working memory measured in the first grade predicts fifth graders' ability to estimate where a number falls on the number line (Cho, Ryali, Geary, & Menon, 2011). It is linked to place value knowledge and mental computation skills (Varelas & Becker, 1997). We can improve spatial skills through instruction (Cheng & Mix, 2014). Spatially based mathematics instruction, such as the use of an abacus, is less effective for students with poorer spatial skills (Barner et al., 2016).

Attention, which is an aspect of executive functioning, also influences students' ability to learn. For example, students' ability to pay attention predicts their ability to learn fraction concepts and fraction procedures (Ayalon & Livneh, 2013). All three forms of attention, including shifting, inhibition, and updating, predict mathematics achievement, but it appears that updating is the most predictive of math achievement (Bull & Lee, 2014). The importance of updating for mathematics achievement may be the result of the need to simultaneously hold and replace information in working memory as students solve math problems. Games and activities that ask students to hold information in memory, while replacing old information with new information, involves and supports updating skills. For example, a memory game may involve giving students 10 random numbers and asking the students to hold the 3 highest numbers in memory.

Students with mathematics disabilities often have problems in multiple areas, typically with spatial processing (Andersson, 2010). Many studies also reveal that they have problems in quickly retrieving number words from their mental dictionary (Bull & Johnston, 1997; D'Amico & Guarnera, 2005), which has the effect of slowing or preventing the development of fluent computation. In fact, this is sometimes so problematic that students are not able to solve multidigit computation problems by recalling basic math facts (Balfanz & Byrnes, 2006). These students often continue to rely on concrete manipulatives long after their peers have transitioned to mental math.

Teachers need to remember that students who are struggling in mathematics may have deficits in one or more general cognitive processes as well as with specific math problems. Research on ways to improve verbal and spatial working memory and attention is as yet limited. In fact, existing research is fairly pessimistic about the impact of working memory training programs on improving functioning in a way that is noticeable on real world tasks, such as mathematics (Melby-Lervåg,

Redick, & Hulme, 2016). It suggests that young students with these deficiencies will need continuous intervention designed to maintain improvements in working memory and attention. Moreover, students will need to be taught metacognitive strategies for dealing with poor working memory, such as breaking problems down into their component parts, verbally repeating or writing down key concepts they need to keep in mind, and, as we have emphasized here, practicing key concepts to automatize their retrieval (Alloway, 2006).

Environmental Factors: Challenges Due to Poverty

Home environments can have a big impact on the development of mathematical skills and knowledge, both directly through the instruction of number and indirectly through the development of the working memories and attention. Parents can play a major role in developing their children's mathematics skills and knowledge when their conversations with their children include what researchers call "number talk" (Levine, Suriyakham, Rowe, Huttenlocher, & Gunderson, 2010). Counting and simple addition and subtraction activities with everyday objects can give students an advantage. The use of board games that have children rolling dice and counting steps is another good way to improve basic math skills in young children, while having fun, particularly when the counting is along a straight line (Siegler & Ramani, 2009).

The use of puzzles and materials, such as building blocks, is linked to the development of better spatial skills and spatial working memory in children. In one study, parents were asked to work with their young children to build an array of shapes of increasing complexity using building blocks. The children whose parents used more spatial words, such as *between* or *above,* when working with the building blocks did better on a mathematics test (Verdine et al., 2014). This research shows that everyday play activities and objects can be used to improve students' mathematics achievement.

After-school staff can use these kinds of practices, too, to help students strengthen their understanding of numbers. These types of additional practices are even more important for children who might not otherwise obtain them at home.

Unfortunately, there is considerable evidence that students from low-income homes are sometimes not given the same home experiences as middle-income students. Students from such homes tend to do poorly in mathematics once they enter school. In addition, their general cognitive skills differ from middle-income students. They tend to be less able to pay attention, particularly in their ability to update information in working memory (Lee & Bull, 2016). Students from low-income homes generally have poorer spatial skills (Carr et al., 2017; Casey, Dearing, Vasilyeva, Ganley, & Tine, 2011). These differences likely occur as a result of the parents' tendency to use fewer spatial words and to have fewer spatial activities on hand, such as puzzles and building blocks, to support the development of spatial skills. It helps if instructors who teach in after-school settings are aware of the possible experience differential of their students.

General Recommendations

Attempting to teach students in ASPs can be difficult because they have been in school for at least 6 hours and are often quite tired. Even the most self-controlled student would have trouble focusing attention on yet more mathematics after a full school day. It is important, therefore, that activities in ASPs be fun and stimulating. Students from low-income homes who often do not have access to basic board games or materials that instigate mathematics achievement would particularly benefit, as we have noted above. These considerations aside, there are some general recommendations for what teachers should aim for in these activities.

There is growing evidence for the usefulness of movement in the development of spatial skills as a means of improving mathematics achievement. Movement can involve counting using a marker on a board game, but it can also involve counting steps or moving up and down on a number line. Having students clap to a count is another activity that involves movement and number. There are numerous available games that involve counting on a straight line; teachers can also develop or modify existing games to include both movement and counting.

Particularly for younger students, having adults include number talk whenever possible can be helpful. For example, simply asking a student to bring over the *two chairs* instead of *the chairs,* predicts growth in their mathematics skills (Klibanoff, Levine, Huttenlocher, Vasilyeva, & Hedges, 2006). In ASPs, teachers should create activities in which both adults and students increase their use of number words as a part of an activity. In games that involve number objects, such as dice, cards, and dominoes, a student can call out the number as opposed to just reading it. Having students verbalize counting while playing board games is also another way that number talk can be incorporated in games. Older students can be asked to verbally compute answers to multiplication or division problems as a part of a game or activity.

One point that has become clear from the research on both the concept of equivalence and on memory is that changing things up is a good thing (Chen, 1999). Using examples that are very similar may result in faster learning, but the students' understanding of the concept will be limited by the range of examples. In the case of equivalence, limiting the range of examples usually results in misconceptions. With regard to fractions, the use of whole–part models, such as pie charts, and the failure to teach other approaches, such as fraction number lines, results in a diminished understanding of fractions that leads to misconceptions. Although utilizing a range of examples slows initial learning, it is better to use multiple approaches that together communicate the concept that needs to be learned.

An ASP should also focus on supporting what is being taught in the classroom as opposed to introducing new concepts and skills. In the second grade, mental computation, place value knowledge, and multidigit computation are major areas of study, so it is important for instructors to select activities that support the learning of these skills. Games are great ways to improve fluency in basic math facts in the early years and, in later years, in multiplication. Games enhance students understanding of number line, starting with small ranges for young first-grade children and expanding to increasingly larger ranges for fourth-grade students. For older students, decimals and fractions can be placed on the number line. In sum, the focus should be on enjoyable activities that encourage children to practice the basic skills and concepts being taught in class. Keeping a supply of counting games, puzzles, and building blocks comes in handy for filling the various gaps in activities that occur, such as when children have completed their homework or when they are waiting to be picked up by parents. Likewise, these kinds of practices will help children understand that mathematics is everywhere, not just during the specific block of instructional time allocated to it in the school day.

GLOSSARY

Attention—The cognitive system that allows us to actively process specific information within working memory by ignoring irrelevant or distracting information, shifting topics, discarding old information, and replacing it with new information.

Fluency—In the context of mathematics, the speed with which students accurately compute or retrieve math facts from memory.

Mental math—Calculations people make mentally without using pencil and paper, calculators, or objects to count with.

Mental number line—A mental representation of the order and magnitude of numbers, with a focus on the equidistant placement of numbers on the line.

Place value—The value a digit has based on the location of the digit in a number.

Spatial working memory—The aspect of working memory that processes information in a visual or spatial form within the larger working memory system.

Working memory—Cognitive system used to temporarily store and manage the various types of information needed to complete difficult and complex cognitive tasks.

References

Adams, J. W., & Hitch, G. J. (1998). Children's mental arithmetic and working memory. In C. Donlan (Ed.), *The development of mathematical skills* (pp. 153–173). Hove, UK: Psychology Press/Taylor & Francis.

Alloway, T. P. (2006). How does working memory work in the classroom. *Educational Research and Reviews, 1*(4), 134–139.

Andersson, U. (2010). Skill development in different components of arithmetic and basic cognitive functions: Findings from a 3-year longitudinal study of children with different types of learning difficulties. *Journal of Educational Psychology, 102*(1), 115–134.

Ayalon, H., & Livneh, I. (2013). Educational standardization and gender differences in mathematics achievement: A comparative study. *Social Science Research, 42*(2), 432–445.

Balfanz, R., & Byrnes, V. (2006). Closing the mathematics achievement gap in high-poverty middle schools: Enablers and constraints. *Journal of Education for Students Placed at Risk, 11*(2), 143–159.

Barner, D., Alvarez, G., Sullivan, J., Brooks, N., Srinivasan, M., & Frank, M. C. (2016). Learning mathematics in a visuospatial format: A randomized, controlled trial of mental abacus instruction. *Child Development, 87*(4), 1146–1158.

Baroody, A. J., Eiland, M. D., Purpura, D. J., & Reid, E. E. (2012). Fostering at-risk kindergarten children's number sense. *Cognition and Instruction, 30*(4), 435–470.

Baroody, A. J., Purpura, D. J., Eiland, M. D., Reid, E. E., & Paliwal, V. (2016). Does fostering reasoning strategies for relatively difficult basic combinations promote transfer by K–3 students? *Journal of Educational Psychology, 108*(4), 576–591.

Behr, M. J., & Bright, G. W. (1984). Identifying fractions on number lines. Retrieved from *http://search.ebscohost.com/login.aspx?direct=true&db=eric&AN=ED24 8148&site=ehost-live.*

Beishuizen, M. (1993). Mental strategies and materials or models for addition and subtraction up to 100 in Dutch second grades. *Journal for Research in Mathematics Education, 24*(4), 294–323.

Biddlecomb, B., & Carr, M. (2011). A longitudinal study of the development of mathematics strategies and underlying counting schemes. *International Journal of Science and Mathematics Education, 9*(1), 1–24.

Booth, J. L., & Siegler, R. S. (2008). Numerical magnitude representations influence arithmetic learning. *Child Development, 79*(4), 1016–1031.

Boulton-Lewis, G. M. (1998). Children's strategy use and interpretations of mathematical representations. *Journal of Mathematical Behavior, 17*, 219–237.

Brownell, W. A., & Chazal, C. B. (1935). The effects of premature drill in third-grade arithmetic. *Journal of Educational Research, 29*, 17–28.

Bull, R., Espy, K. A., & Wiebe, S. A. (2008). Short-term memory, working memory, and executive functioning in preschoolers: Longitudinal predictors of mathematical achievement at age 7 years. *Developmental Neuropsychology, 33*(3), 205–228.

Bull, R., & Johnston, R. S. (1997). Children's arithmetical difficulties: Contributions from processing speed, item identification, and short-term memory. *Journal of Experimental Child Psychology, 65*, 1–24.

Bull, R., & Lee, K. (2014). Executive functioning and mathematics achievement. *Child Development Perspectives, 8*(1), 36–41.

Carr, M., Alexeev, N., Wang, L., Barned, N., Horan, E., & Reed, A. (2017). The development of spatial skills in elementary school students. *Child Development.*

Casey, B. M., Dearing, E., Vasilyeva, M., Ganley, C. M., & Tine, M. (2011). Spatial and numerical predictors of measurement performance: The moderating effects of community income and gender. *Journal of Educational Psychology, 103*(2), 296–311.

Chandler, C. C., & Kamii, C. (2009). Giving change when payment is made with a dime: The difficulty of tens and ones. *Journal for Research in Mathematics Education, 40*(2), 97–118.

Chen, Z. (1999). Schema induction in children's analogical problem solving. *Journal of Educational Psychology, 91*(4), 703–715.

Cheng, Y.-L., & Mix, K. S. (2014). Spatial training in children's mathematics ability. *Journal of Cognition and Development, 15*(1), 2–11.

Cho, S., Ryali, S., Geary, D. C., & Menon, V. (2011). How does a child solve 7+8? Decoding brain activity patterns associated with counting and retrieval strategies. *Developmental Science, 14*(5), 989–1001.

D'Amico, A., & Guarnera, M. (2005). Exploring working memory in children with low arithmetical achievement. *Learning and Individual Differences, 15*(3), 189–202.

Fazio, L. K., Bailey, D. H., Thompson, C. A., & Siegler, R. S. (2014). Relations of different types of numerical magnitude representations to each other and to mathematics achievement. *Journal for Experimental Child Psychology, 123,* 53–72.

Fischer, U., Moeller, K., Bientzle, M., Cress, U., & Nuerk, H.-C. (2011). Sensorimotor spatial training of number magnitude representation. *Psychonomic Bulletin and Review, 18*(1), 177–183.

Fuchs, L. S., Geary, D. C., Compton, D. L., Fuchs, D., Hamlett, C. L., Seethaler, P. M., . . . Schatschneider, C. (2010). Do different types of school mathematics development depend on different constellations of numerical versus general cognitive abilities? *Developmental Psychology, 46*(6), 1731–1746.

Fuchs, L. S., Geary, D. C., Compton, D. L., Fuchs, D., Schatschneider, C., Hamlett, C. L., . . . Changas, P. (2013). Effects of first-grade number knowledge tutoring with contrasting forms of practice. *Journal of Educational Psychology, 105*(1), 58–77.

Fuchs, L. S., Geary, D. C., Fuchs, D., Compton, D. L., & Hamlett, C. L. (2016). Pathways to third-grade calculation versus word-reading competence: Are they more alike or different? *Child Development, 87*(2), 558–567.

Fuchs, L. S., Schumacher, R. F., Long, J., Namkung, J., Malone, A. S., Wang, A., . . . Changas, P. (2016). Effects of intervention to improve at-risk fourth graders' understanding, calculations, and word problems with fractions. *Elementary School Journal, 116*(4), 625–651.

Gabriel, F., Coché, F., Szucs, D., Carette, V., Rey, B., & Content, A. (2012). Developing children's understanding of fractions: An intervention study. *Mind, Brain, and Education, 6*(3), 137–146.

Henry, V. J., & Brown, R. S. (2008). First-grade basic facts: An investigation into teaching and learning of an accelerated, high-demand memorization standard. *Journal for Research in Mathematics Education, 39*(2), 153–183.

Jordan, N. C., Hanich, L. B., & Kaplan, D. (2003). A longitudinal study of mathematical competencies in children with specific mathematics difficulties versus children with comorbid mathematics and reading difficulties. *Child Development, 74,* 834–850.

Kieran, C. (1981). Concepts associated with the equality symbol. *Educational Studies in Mathematics, 12*(3), 317–326.

Klein, A. S., Beishuizen, M., & Treffers, A. (1998). The empty number line in Dutch second grades: Realistic versus gradual program design. *Journal for Research in Mathematics Education, 29*(4), 443–464.

Klibanoff, R. S., Levine, S. C., Huttenlocher, J., Vasilyeva, M., & Hedges, L. V. (2006). Preschool children's mathematical knowledge: The effect of teacher "math talk." *Developmental Psychology, 42*(1), 59–69.

Lee, K., & Bull, R. (2016). Developmental changes in working memory, updating, and math achievement. *Journal of Educational Psychology, 108*(6), 869–882.

Levine, S. C., Suriyakham, L. W., Rowe, M. L., Huttenlocher, J., & Gunderson, E. A. (2010). What counts in the development of young children's number knowledge? *Developmental Psychology, 46*(5), 1309–1319.

Luwel, K., Verschaffel, L., Onghena, P., & De Corte, E. (2001). Strategic aspects of children's numerosity judgement. *European Journal of Psychology of Education, 16*(2), 233–255.

McNeil, N. M. (2007). U-shaped development in math: 7-year-olds outperform 9-year-olds on equivalence problems. *Developmental Psychology, 43*(3), 687–695.

McNeil, N. M., Fyfe, E. R., & Dunwiddie, A. E. (2015). Arithmetic practice can be modified to promote understanding of mathematical equivalence. *Journal of Educational Psychology, 107*(2), 423–436.

Melby-Lervåg, M., Redick, T. S., & Hulme, C. (2016). Working memory training does not improve performance on measures of intelligence or other measures of "far transfer" evidence from a meta-analytic review. *Perspectives on Psychological Science, 11*(4), 512–534.

Mix, K. S., Prather, R. W., Smith, L. B., & Stockton, J. D. (2014). Young children's interpretation of multidigit number names: From emerging competence to mastery. *Child Development, 85*(3), 1306–1319.

Peng, P., Namkung, J., Barnes, M., & Sun, C. (2016). A meta-analysis of mathematics and working memory: Moderating effects of working memory domain, type of mathematics skill, and sample characteristics. *Journal of Educational Psychology, 108*(4), 455–473.

Shin, M., & Bryant, D. P. (2015). Fraction interventions for students struggling to learn mathematics: A research synthesis. *Remedial and Special Education, 36*(6), 374–387.

Siegler, R. S., & Ramani, G. B. (2009). Playing linear number board games—but not circular ones—improves low-income preschoolers' numerical understanding. *Journal of Educational Psychology, 101*(3), 545–560.

Steffe, L. P., Cobb, P., & von Glaserfeld, E. (1988). *Construction of arithmetical meanings and strategies.* New York: Springer-Verlag.

Swanson, H. L. (2008). Working memory and intelligence in children: What develops? *Journal of Educational Psychology, 100*(3), 581–602.

Varelas, M., & Becker, J. (1997). Children's developing understanding of place value: Semiotic aspects. *Cognition and Instruction, 15*(2), 265–286.

Verdine, B. N., Golinkoff, R. M., Hirsh-Pasek, K., Newcombe, N. S., Filipowicz, A. T., & Chang, A. (2014). Deconstructing building blocks: Preschoolers' spatial assembly performance relates to early mathematical skills. *Child Development, 85*(3), 1062–1076.

Vukovic, R. K., Fuchs, L. S., Geary, D. C., Jordan, N. C., Gersten, R., & Siegler, R. S. (2014). Sources of individual differences in children's understanding of fractions. *Child Development, 85*(4), 1461–1476.

Yoshida, H., & Sawano, K. (2002). Overcoming cognitive obstacles in learning fractions: Equal-partitioning and equal-whole. *Japanese Psychological Research, 44*(4), 183–195.

7

The PAL Mathematics Enrichment Program and Challenges in the After-School Setting

Yi–Jung Lee

After-school programs (ASPs) afford a unique opportunity to extend and enrich the learning of mathematics for elementary school children. The Physical Activity and Learning (PAL) Program was specially designed to engage elementary school children from low-income or high-risk families who might not otherwise have had access to mathematics supports to achieve greater mathematics learning. In the PAL schools, end-of-year mathematics test scores had shown that approximately 20% of third to fifth graders were not meeting the standard. Students who are economically disadvantaged—many from ethnic minority groups (such as Hispanic or African American children)—are significantly more likely not to meet the standard, an issue that undermines their academic success. Although the PAL Program was geared primarily for students not meeting state academic standards, students with other kinds of risks also were included. In the mathematics enrichment program, students participated in activities that targeted improvement of conceptual knowledge related to mathematics as well as fluency in computation and problem-solving skills. A unique aspect of math enrichment in the PAL Program was the integration of mathematics, reading, and physical activity games (PAGs). By doing so, the PAL math enrichment program not only supported classroom instruction, but also offered a rich environment for improving the academic and physical skills of participating students.

The main goal of the PAL math enrichment program was to achieve the objective of having at least 70% of regularly participating students demonstrate mathematical proficiency accordant with the Georgia Standards for Excellence in Mathematics (*www.georgiastandards.org/Georgia-Standards/Pages/Math.aspx*). The purpose of this chapter is to discuss the activities that were used in the PAL Program to achieve these goals. These activities are derived from the research described in Chapter 6, which discussed problems that academically struggling children tend to have with learning mathematics, as well as potential solutions.

Preparation for the Mathematics Enrichment Intervention

In the daily schedule of the PAL Program, students first completed 1hour of homework with assistance from the PAL staff, followed by 1 hour of PAGs. One hour of academic enrichment, in either math or reading, followed the PAGs.

In the homework session, site staff and volunteers circulated around the cafeteria assisting students in the completion of their homework. During this time, the mathematics enrichment instructors in the ASP paid special attention to the content and design of the mathematics homework. Doing so informed them about which concepts needed to be focused on in the mathematics enrichment lesson. Through assisting and observing students in the homework session and in the PAGs, the math instructors also had the opportunity to become familiar with each student's character, disposition, and behaviors, particularly around the subject of mathematics. The time spent with students gave the instructors some insights into the modifications that needed to be made in the math enrichment class to improve the support given to each student. Thus, careful observations during the homework period for the instructors formed an important part of teaching preparation.

The bulk of this chapter is devoted to describing the activities in the PAL mathematics enrichment program. We explain the rationale for each activity and its implementation, including the challenges and potential solutions to the problems encountered. We also analyze the program's effectiveness. The chapter concludes by addressing the alignment of the mathematics enrichment activities in the after-school setting with the Common Core State Standards for Mathematics (CCSSM) and the eight CCSSM Standards for Mathematical Practice (SMP) (Common Core State Standards Initiative, 2010a, 2010b).

Activities Designed for Critical Mathematical Knowledge and Skills

The activities in the next sections are presented in accordance with the general order of mathematical concepts and skills discussed in Chapter 6.

Fluency in Basic Math Facts

The evolution of children's solution strategies for different problem types takes time and practice. Research shows that when children are first learning to add, they start with direct modeling strategies by using objects or fingers to represent each of the addends and then counting the union or the sum of two numbers. For example, to solve the problem 3 + 4 = __ children hold up three fingers on one hand and four fingers on another, and then count the fingers sequentially ("1, 2, 3, 4, 5, 6, 7") to find the answer (Carpenter, Fennema, Franke, & Empson, 1999). After developing fluency with the counting-words sequence (i.e., 1, 2, 3, 4, . . .) and familiarity with the relations between numbers (e.g., 4 is 1 more than 3), children are able to memorize certain number facts (e.g., the doubles, 3 plus 3 is 6). At this stage, children are ready to learn to use the memorized facts to derive new facts (Cross, Woods, & Schweingruber, 2009).

In the PAL program, students in grades 2 and 3 tended to use counting strategies to compute their answers. Based on our observations of students' computation processes on the math pretest and the strategies used as they completed their homework, more than half of our students computed the answer by counting on their fingers. Therefore, the goal of the PAL math specialists became that of improving computational fluency by scaffolding the transition from the use of counting strategies to the use of derived fact strategies. *Derived fact strategies* are strategies in which a student uses a small set of known number facts (e.g., 2 + 3 = 5, 5 + 5 = 10) to figure out the solution to unknown number facts (e.g., 12 + 13). For example, children solve the problem 2 + 4 = __ by viewing it as 2 + 3 + 1 due to the known fact that 2 + 3 = 5. In view of the crucial role of the number "10" in the development of the base-ten system, the math specialists decided to expose students to activities related to the number "10" with two Make-A-Ten activities, followed by two Math Facts board game activities. These Make-A-Ten activities aim to increase students' abilities to use derived fact strategies.

Make-A-Ten Activities

Make-A-Ten activities were designed to increase students' use of the Make-A-Ten method, which is one popular instructional method for carrying out derived facts strategies. The Make-A-Ten method requires "recomposing the given numbers into a new, easier problem (e.g., 9 + 4 becomes 10 + 3)" (Cross et al., 2009, p. 154), and it is handy when students are computing the sum of a series of single-digit numbers (e.g., 3 + 9 + 7 + 2 + 1 + 8 + 5). The props that are used for the activity include a special pair of gloves. Due to the flexibility of the copper frames beneath the soft textile gloves, the fingers on these hand models may be folded, enabling students to manipulate each finger individually (into an up or down position). Another useful prop is a Bingo set, which includes sheets with playing cards, as shown in Figure 7.1.

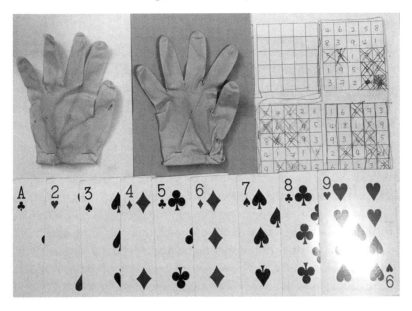

FIGURE 7.1. Materials for the Make-A-Ten activities.

Students are initially asked to find out the fact family of 10 (one form is __ + __ = 10) by using the hand model. For example, they may hold up one finger on the pair of model hands and see the nine fingers in the down position, so the sum of 1 and 9 equals 10. Manipulating these hand models strengthens students' impression of using their own hands as they learn the Make-A-Ten method. It is also effectual for students' memorization of the facts of 10 (e.g., 1 and 9, 2 and 8, and so on) when they practice the fact family by manipulating fingers on the models.

After spending sufficient time reinforcing students' mental image of the facts of 10 through working with the models, three follow-up games were introduced in class—the Make-A-Ten Bingo game, the tri-FACTa™ board game (*www.learning resources.com/product/tri-facta—8482-++addition+-+subtraction+game.do*), and the Football Multiplication board game (*www.teachercreated.com/products/football-multiplication-game-7807*). The Make-A-Ten Bingo game is an activity in which the instructor randomly draws a number from a deck of jumbo playing cards numbered 1–9, and students are asked to cross out the complementary number that will make a 10 with the drawn number (on a Bingo sheet like that shown in Figure 7.1). In this BINGO game, if any student had trouble crossing out the correct number on the worksheet, he or she was reminded by other students who said, "Check it with your fingers!" After demonstrating their fluency on the number facts of 10 in the Make-A-Ten activities, children were then exposed to two board games designed to enhance students' proficiency with additional math facts: tri-FACTa™ and Multiplication Football.

Math Facts Board Games

The tri-FACTa™ board game emphasizes the use of addition and subtraction skills to build math facts. In this game, three to four students were grouped as a team, and each player held a tray with 6 number cards (the deck has 100 cards in total, and each card has a number ranging from 0 to 20; any unused cards are kept face down in the deck). A triangular game board was placed within reach of all players in the team. The players took turns trying to make a true fact triangle with number cards and were allowed to choose cards from a deck only when there were no feasible number cards on their trays for completing the triangle. The fourth and fifth graders played this board game as described in the game guide, but students in grades 2 and 3 played a variation of the game. In this version, children were required to write down the facts (see Figure 7.2) on recording sheets because of their deficient understanding of number facts. The advantage of this variation was that students on the same team were able to reexamine and correct their team members' equations, as well as their own, on the recording sheets.

In the Multiplication Football game, multiplication facts up to 12 can be practiced on a football mat. When playing this game, each player chose a football mat with multiplication products on it and took turns picking a disc with an expression card in the form of A × B. If the expression matched one of the products on the

14 = 9 + 5	5 = 3 + 2	7 = 6 + 1	15 = 13 + 2	5 = 7 − 2	11 = 6 + 5
16 = 14 + 2	9 = 6 + 3	15 = 16 − 1	9 = 7 + 2	1 = 15 − 14	14 = 7 + 7
1 = 16 − 15	13 = 15 − 2	20 = 19 + 1	19 = 14 + 5	3 = 2 + 1	16 = 14 + 2
2 = 6 − 4	5 = 11 − 6	7 = 14 − 7	16 = 7 + 9	3 = 6 − 3	19 = 20 − 1

FIGURE 7.2. Students in grades 2 and 3 were required to write down the facts as they came up in the tri-FACTa™ board game, and other students in the group checked them for accuracy.

mat, the player covered the product with the disc. As with the tri-FACTa™ game, we used this board game as described in the game manual in the sessions for grades 4 and 5 class but created a variation for second and third graders. These students were asked to draw groups of objects, an array, or an area of a rectangle on the recording sheets (see Figure 7.3) because they had just started learning this definition of multiplication: *A groups of B objects in each group* (Common Core State Standards Initiative, 2010a). By drawing these arrays, students were able to review the definition of multiplication addressed in their school math and visualize the multiplication facts in drawings.

In the process of playing both board games, students experienced the commutative properties of addition and multiplication when they repeatedly saw that the switching of two addends or summands in addition and two factors in multiplication resulted in the same answers (such as "7 + 5 is equal to 5 + 7" and "4 × 6 is equal to 6 × 4"). Students improved their conceptual understanding of number facts in addition, subtraction, and multiplication while playing these games, and when they recognized that numbers could be recomposed in several ways, their understanding of the commutative and associative properties of addition and multiplication was reinforced.

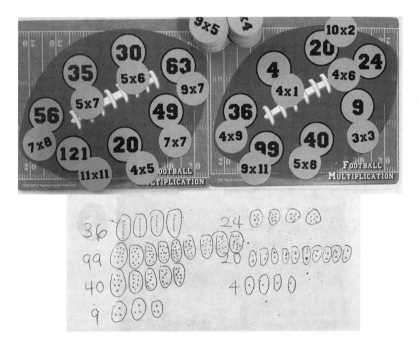

FIGURE 7.3. Students in grades 2 and 3 drew groups of objects on the recording sheets to represent multiplication expressions.

Transition to Mental Math

Mental math refers to doing math in one's mind without the aid of any calculating or recording devices (Reys, 1985; Sowder, 1990). We focused on this transition because it is linked to better number sense, as evidenced by the increased flexibility in dealing with numbers and operations shown once children are able to carry out mental math. However, we did not want mental math to be limited to simple memorization of number facts because students need to be flexible in their computation performance. That is, the most important attribute of mental math is the comprehension of arithmetic properties and the characteristics of numbers in operations.

The robust environment of the PAL math enrichment program helped students develop and practice their mental math, and the activities were constructed to avoid simple memorization of basic math facts. Burns (2007) suggested a method called "hands-on-the-table," in which students have to clear away everything and place their hands on the table when they are doing mental math. This practice prevents children from simply counting on their fingers under the table. Recall that the PAL Program groups second and third graders separately from fourth and fifth graders for reading and math enrichment activities. To make the mental math activity more appealing students in different grades, we conducted different mental math games in each class.

PAL Mathopoly Board Game.

We designed a new version of the Mathopoly® board game (*www.mathopoly.ca/mathopoly-.html*) for second and third graders in the PAL Program. PAL Mathopoly is a board game in which students have to solve diverse mental math problems, including such topics as number line, base-ten, number facts, operations, fractions, data, time, and geometry; students play this game through trading by using four types of coins (penny, nickel, dime, and quarter) and bills ($1, $2, $5, and $10). The basic idea of PAL Mathopoly is similar to the Monopoly board game (*www.hasbro.com/en-us/brands/monopoly*), except that children earn rewards/Mathopoly money by solving math problems. PAL Mathopoly was very successful with students in grades 2 and 3 because almost all of them displayed motivation and persistence in solving mental math problems.

Mental Math Competition

We held a competition and regrouped students into two teams based on their grade levels in the grades 4 and 5 class. Each game round was held for 5 minutes with 15 mixed math questions. After students put their hands on the table, each team decided the order of their players and sent one child to the front of the room at a time to play. The problem set was based roughly on the concepts emphasized in students' collected school homework, and the team that correctly answered the most questions won the competition.

To expose students to different mental math strategies, several online resources were used. One of the exemplary mental math worksheets used in the game was from the website *math-salamanders.com,* which provides free math worksheets, math games, and math help based on grade levels and math topics. The types of problems included addition, subtraction, place value concepts, properties of numbers (e.g., even and odd numbers), number patterns, and doubling or halving numbers. For example, second graders were asked questions like "300 + __ + 4 = 354," "5 feet = __ yards + __ feet," "How much is three dimes, two nickels, and one penny?" and "If the date is March 6, what date will it be in 3 months?" (*www.math-salamanders.com/year-3-mental-maths.html*). In the competition, students were forced to use mental math because of the time limit that we imposed. Under the pressure of competing, children started to challenge their abilities and began to use mental computation. For example, some students computed 4 + 7 + 6 by counting from left to right while completing their homework but demonstrated fluency in the facts of 10 by combining 4 and 6 to make a 10 first by saying, "It is much faster if I put 4 and 6 together to make a 10 first, and then add 7" in the context of competition.

One challenge the competition encountered was that students were not very confident in their mental computation when first using the mental math activities in the program. It took considerable time and practice for PAL Program students to transition from counting with physical objects (like fingers or cubes) to performing abstract operations with numbers. At the beginning, many of our younger students still relied on counting with fingers or writing their solutions out step-by-step, especially when they solved problems that called for operations with standard algorithms, such as addition, subtraction, and multiplication. Beckmann (2014) notes that the "commutative and associative properties [of addition and multiplication] underlie mental methods" (p. 100) and suggests multiple mental methods to enhance the flexibility of students' computations. Students needed an environment in which to practice using mental methods, rather than counting methods, to apply properties in mathematical operations, or to internalize learned number facts. In the PAL math enrichment, we found a fairly simple solution to this challenge: make students feel compelled to conduct mental computation under competitive pressure, but in the context of a game. The competitive environment allowed students to show progress in carrying out mental computation that they might not have shown otherwise.

Mental Number Line

The development of a *mental number line* reflects students' abilities to spatially represent number magnitude. Students with a good understanding of number magnitude can picture numbers along a mental number line (Schneider, Grabner, & Paetsch, 2009). Once the mental number line is established, it allows students to make quick judgments about number magnitude, such as quickly determining that 53 is larger than 43 (Dehaene, 2001). In the design of mental number line activities, Link, Huber, Nuerk, and Moeller (2014) suggested using two versions of the number line: a bounded one with a starting point and endpoint (e.g., 0 and 10) and an unbounded version with only the starting point and a fixed unit (e.g., the distance from 0 to 1), as shown in Figure 7.4. Based on this suggestion, we designed the Setting Up the Cones activities, in which students were asked to set up numbered cones in order according to their numbers on two versions of the number line.

Setting Up the Cones

In math enrichment, students conducted the Setting Up the Cones activities in the gym due to the limited space in the classroom and they were asked to accomplish tasks at four levels of difficulty—the entry, medium, advanced, and variation levels (not starting with 0)—within two versions of the number line (see Figure 7.5a and 7.5b).

With the bounded number line, the entry-level task is to locate the numbers 1 to 9 on a number line with a starting point of 0 and an endpoint of 10. Most students were able to locate the numbers in the correct order, but some of them set up the cones on the number line "unevenly." Perhaps they used tick marks to count instead of using the benchmarks (i.e., points of reference by which to compare two or more numbers numerically) when locating the numbers on the number line. The ability to relate given numbers to a benchmark (usually the midpoint on the number line) has proven crucial in developing a deeper understanding of number magnitude (Carpenter & Lindquist, 1989). Alternatively, perhaps they had gotten used to drawing number lines in their homework without attending to the need to have precisely equal intervals. For example, students commonly located the

FIGURE 7.4. Two versions of the number line.

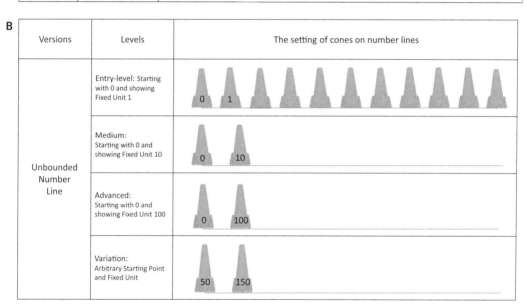

FIGURE 7.5. "Setting Up the Cones" activities.

number 5 between the numbers 4 and 6, but not in the precise middle of a number line starting with 0 and ending with 10, particularly if we did not provide standard tick marks on the number line.

Therefore, we initiated all the entry-level tasks with tick marks (without numbers) provided at the correct locations on the number line. After students developed the correct mental image of a number line (which should have equal intervals between any two successive numbers), we increased the complexity of the tasks. The next level involved students starting a series of number line estimation questions without using tick marks in each level of tasks. For example, students were assigned different sets of numbers, such as a set of even numbers, a set of odd numbers, and a set of arbitrary numbers when working on the two versions of the number line.

After sufficiently exposing students to these activities, it was exciting to hear students thinking aloud, saying "70 should be exactly in the middle of 50 and 90 [on the number line]," when the numbers "60" and "80" were both missing on the number line. This progression in students' development of their mental number lines demonstrated their ability to construct and modify knowledge to estimate number magnitude, which was initiated from counting by 1's (every increment on the entry-level number line is 1) and advanced to synchronizing three different place values on the number line. For example, locating 783 on the bounded number line 0–1,000 required higher cognitive ability because students needed to start by using 700 and 800 as two benchmarks, knowing that "seven-hundred something" should be located between 700 and 800. Then they zoomed in to the 780–790 interval according to the magnitude of the numbers (83), and ultimately estimated that 783 should be on the left of the midpoint (with 785 as a benchmark) of 780 and 790 on the number line.

Understanding of Place Value Knowledge

The base-ten system is a significant achievement of humankind; it enables us to express numbers by using only 10 distinct digits—0, 1, 2, 3, 4, 5, 6, 7, 8, and 9. The key innovation of the base-ten system is that we use place value to represent larger numbers (i.e., multidigit numbers) rather than creating new symbols (Beckmann, 2014). Elementary school students begin to develop an understanding of *place value knowledge* in kindergarten but continue to improve into fifth grade. With this in mind, it is important to determine the level of a student's comprehension of place value prior to making a decision about an activity.

To facilitate students' understanding of place value knowledge in the PAL Program, we assessed students' existing knowledge by checking their completed homework assignments, which effectively revealed what students knew about place value. We found that second graders began to perform addition and subtraction by using manipulatives or drawing figural blocks based on place value. In the PAL math enrichment program, we created an activity that integrated reading and math to facilitate students' understanding of place value knowledge. To achieve the goal of learning to add and subtract fluently within 10,000 using strategies based on place value, a story from a children's math book, *Sir Cumference and All the King's Tens: A Math Adventure* (Neuschwander, 2009), was selected to expose students to problem solving with place value. In the story, a large number of guests (9,999 in total) show up for King Arthur's birthday party, and the main character, Lady Di, is trying to find a method to count the total number of guests at the party. Lady Di starts with counting by ones, but this method is too slow and ineffective. Then she tries to count by tens, making all guests line up in rows of ten, but there still are too many rows. Finally, the guests are required to move into different-sized tents, which show new formations with groups of 1,000, 100, 10, and single individuals.

In the integrated lesson, the reading enrichment specialist led the partner reading activity for the first 20 minutes, in which students took turns reading pages aloud from the book. Then the math specialist led the addition-in-base-ten activity for the rest of the class period. The needed materials included a base-ten mat, 9 units/ones cubes, 9 tens rods, and 9 hundreds flats for each group (to support trading of smaller unit blocks for larger unit blocks, e.g., when getting the number 12, students had to represent it as 1 ten and 2 ones instead of 12 ones), as shown in Figure 7.6. The math specialist conducted this activity by verbally announcing a series of numbers in sequence and asking students to perform the addition by only manipulating the blocks on the mat, without writing down any numbers. The math specialist assigned three students with mixed-grade levels for each group. The designed problems involved several summation sets of 10 numbers, moving from single-digit numbers (e.g., 7 + 8 + 2 + 9 + 4 + 5 + 6 + 7 + 3 + 5) to mixed one-digit and two-digit numbers (e.g., 6 + 8 + 12 + 9 + 14 + 5 + 6 + 7 + 13 + 15); only one number was announced at a time.

While many students used the manipulatives, some students tried to do addition by counting when the numbers were called out but were incapable of handling

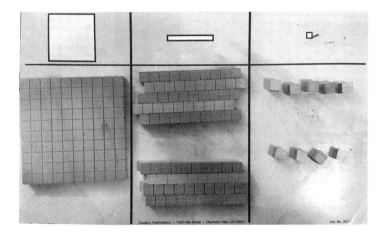

FIGURE 7.6. Blocks for the integrated addition-in-base-ten lesson on the mat.

the 10-number sequence in each problem. As a result, students were forced to regroup numbers in the base-ten system because they only had 9 blocks in each place value, so when the sum was more than 9 in the ones place students needed to regroup the numbers to the tens place. For example, when doing 8 + 9, a second grader complained that there were not enough ones blocks to use; a fourth grader on the same team replied, "We don't need more ones. We can trade 15 into a ten and 5 ones." This activity enabled students, especially the second graders, to visualize the composition of two single-digit numbers (when the sum was more than 10) in the base-ten system through manipulating blocks consistent with the number of items in each place of the base-ten system.

This integrated lesson also reinforced students' experience with decomposing numbers by recognizing their value in their base-ten representation, such as knowing that the 1 in "14" stands for 1 group of 10. Moreover, a student who was used to applying the counting strategy told the team members that "in the problem 8 + 11, it was easier to add a rod in the tens place and a cube in the ones place with the original 8." This strategy showed a grasp of place value and the ability to decompose and recompose numbers. Using a children's book story in math class provided a real-world scenario for engaging students in exploring abstract mathematical concepts. Appropriately manipulating blocks also can help students visualize the relationship among values in each place (e.g., 10 ones could be traded with 1 ten).

Understanding of Fractions

The concept of fractions, or rational numbers, is among the most difficult and important mathematical ideas children encounter during their school years, owing to the complex role fractions play in mathematics. For example, a fraction can be a ratio, an operator, a quotient, or a measure, depending on the context. To develop a conceptual understanding of fractions, two forms of interpretation about fraction knowledge are important: (1) understanding the part–whole aspect of fractions, such as a part of one entire object or a subset of a group of objects (the focus is on the relationship between parts and the whole) and (2) understanding the *measurement interpretation of fractions*—i.e., the fact that fractions (e.g., ¼, ⅓, ½, ⅔) can be ordered, and each fraction is treated as one number with its own magnitude (Fuchs et al., 2013; Hecht & Vagi, 2010).

In the PAL math enrichment program, the part–whole interpretation was initially introduced, and students practiced equally dividing a shape into several parts (up to 12). We asked students to identify or color different unit fractions on the same size of the whole (e.g., ⅓ and ⅕, respectively, on two identical circular pie charts) and improve their understanding of equivalent fractions through comparing the size of colored parts while maintaining the same size of the whole (as shown in Figure 7.7). To intensify students' grasp of part–whole concepts, we asked them to divide a circular pie chart into five equal pieces by drawing cutting marks in an advanced activity, and surprisingly they were intuitively drawing five cutting marks on the pie chart. After counting the number of partitioned pieces on the circular pie chart, they found that five cutting marks actually created six portions. In addition, some students were not able to draw precise figures to represent dividing a circular pie chart into equal pieces due to their limited drawing skills. Therefore, when students are introduced to the part–whole interpretation of fractions, we suggest the prolonged use of exemplary figures (e.g., templates like circular pie charts or rectangles bars) with precise cutting marks, especially for second and third graders.

Activities furthering the understanding of the part–whole interpretation of fractions were followed by activities that involved the measurement interpretation of fractions. Students were initially asked to place fractions on a 0-to-1 number line. We provided them with a segment of the 0-to-1 number line, with tick marks labeled ½, ⅓, ⅔, ¼, $\frac{2}{4}$, and ¾. To accomplish this task, students had to demonstrate their abilities in comparing fractions (e.g., knowing that ½ is larger than ⅓) and ordering fractions (e.g., placing all the given tick marks in the correct order of ¼, ⅓, ½ = $\frac{2}{4}$, ⅔, ¾ between 0 and 1 on the number line). In addition, we also required students to represent fractions through manipulating fraction tick marks, fraction tiles, and fraction circles. For example, in an advanced activity, students were given a set of fraction tiles including the segments of ½, ⅓, ¼, ⅕, ⅙, ⅛, $\frac{1}{10}$, and $\frac{1}{12}$; then, they were asked to solve addition and subtraction problems like ½ + ¼ or ½ – ⅓. This series of activities about the measurement interpretation of fractions was mostly given to fourth and fifth graders; but it was obvious that students had

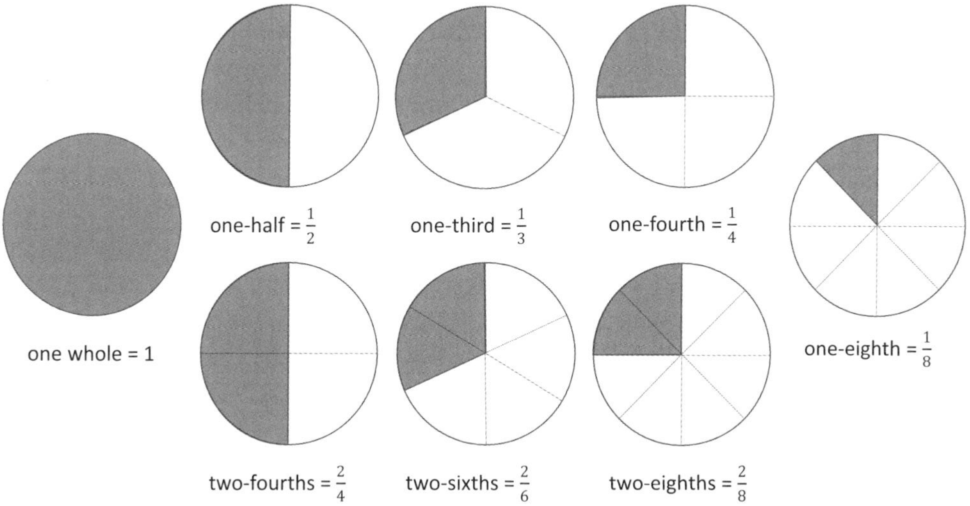

FIGURE 7.7. Unit fractions and equivalent fractions worksheet.

difficulties in dealing with the measurement interpretation of fractions because they did not comprehend unit fractions. We define a unit fraction as ⅟ₐ when we divide a whole into A equal parts and the amount formed by 1 of those parts is ⅟ₐ. In other words, A copies of the part compose the whole. For example, the unit fraction ½ means that we need 2 pieces of ½ to produce the 1 (as the whole), and the unit fraction ⅕ means the same: the whole consists of 5 pieces of ⅕. In the intervention, we found that students had difficulty comparing ½ and ⅕ because they were influenced by the fact that 5 is larger than 2 when learning whole numbers. Therefore, we reinforced the concept and application of the unit fractions, such as using a ⅕ segment as the unit to measure the length of objects in other intervention sessions.

Understanding of Equivalence

Students have trouble understanding that the equal sign means *equivalence* (Kieran, 1981). The equal sign is often viewed by elementary school students as an action like "to add up to," "to make," or "to get the answer," as noted in Chapter 6. As a result, many students are not able to read sentences that represent such relationships as $4 + 2 = 1 + 5$. It is crucial to expose students to activities that support an understanding of equivalence relations through appropriate examples.

As a suggested starting point for the understanding of equivalence, Kieran (1989) recommended that students begin with solving open sentences. In elementary school, there are two suggested forms of open sentences: the first one is called the "canonical" form, in which the operation is on the left of the equal sign (like $3 + 4 = \square$); the second one is the "noncanonical" form, with open sentences like $2 + \square = 5$ or $2 = 6 - \square$ (the box stands for the unknown number). In the PAL Program "Balance the Scale" activities were introduced to help students understand equivalence and to expose students to different forms of open sentences. Students in grades 2 and 3 were asked to manipulate blocks on one side of the balancing scale when the number was assigned on the other side. One exemplary task, $123 = \square \times 100 + \square \times 10 + \square \times 1$, is shown in Figure 7.8.

Students in grades 4 and 5 were asked to solve some "Balance the Scale" problems by giving a public oral presentation for their peers in class. For example, Figure 7.9 displays one student's solution to a problem in which there were nine flower-shaped symbols that represented the same unknown number on the left side of the scale, with the number 18 on the other side (a simple equation with one unknown). Students needed to figure out what number each symbol represented. One student's solution shows that her capacity to use algebraic symbols was immature because she was incapable of directly viewing all flower-shaped symbols as the same unknown number and drew "one flower-shaped symbol = one flower-shaped symbol + one flower-shaped symbol" (see the figural equation in Figure

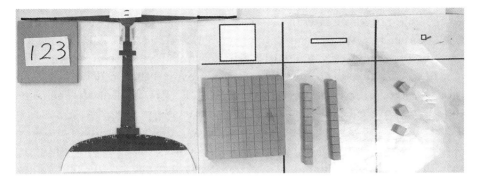

FIGURE 7.8. One student's demonstration in the balance the scale activities.

7.9). However, the student could balance the scale when putting 18 dots on the left side to maintain the equivalent quantity on the other side of the scale.

When the problem was changed to "18 = @ + @ + @ + @ + @ + @" (@ is a figure) on the scale, a fourth grader solved this problem by saying, "I have to find a number for the six symbols to balance the scale, so 6 times 3 is 18, the number on the right side. The @ is 3." Another fifth grader solved this problem by dividing 18 by 6 and commented, "This is the same problem with 6 × □ = 18." The students' solutions showed that they were able to figure out the concept of equivalence, even

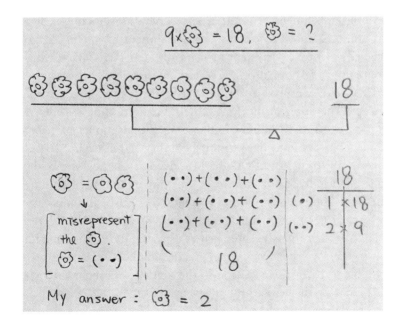

FIGURE 7.9. One student's solution to the 9 × __ = 18 balance the scale problem.

when they did not know how to use the correct algebraic symbols. However, the focus in this activity was to facilitate students' understanding of equivalence, so we did not require them to use standard algebraic symbols to solve problems.

In these "Balance the Scale" activities, we realized that students' misconception of the equal sign as a "do something signal" was challenged. Their ability to interpret equivalence relations of equality sentences improved as a function of carrying out these concrete activities. In addition, it is noteworthy that the "balance the scale with blocks" activity also supported developing an understanding of place value knowledge, and of equivalent fractions, as well, if whole numbers were replaced with fractions.

Program Effectiveness

To assess the effectiveness of math interventions, we conducted pretest and post-test measures three times a year in the PAL Program: at the beginning, the midpoint, and the end of the year. Students in grades 2 and 3 were combined into a single class as were students in grades 4 and 5. All students received either reading or math enrichment in the fall and then switched off at the midpoint so that they received both forms of enrichment by the end of the year. In one school, the younger group received math in fall, and in the other school the younger group received math in the spring. In every semester, grades 2 and 3 that received math enrichment at one site was the intervention group, and grades 2 and 3 class that received reading enrichment at another site served as the control group. At the same site, if grades 2 and 3 received math enrichment in the fall semester, grades 4 and 5 received reading enrichment in the same semester. This arrangement provided an opportunity to compare the cohorts' performance.

In the first year, we used an AIMSweb math test to assess students' mathematics concepts and application (M-CAP) and computation (M-COMP) fluency; the problems in the test included number sense, operations, patterns problems, measurement, geometry, and data and probability (AIMSweb, 2012). We did an analysis of the data for children who had received assessments in both winter and spring terms, essentially, prior to and at the end of the intervention during the spring term. We found that there was a statistically significant interaction between intervention (math versus reading) and assessment period (winter versus spring) ($p < .05$). That is, there was greater growth among children receiving the math intervention in their mathematics concepts and application and computation fluency attributable to their participation in the math enrichment than there was for children participating in the reading intervention.

In the second year, we focused instead on math fluency and executive functioning (Bull & Scerif, 2001), and assessed students' ability to locate numbers on the number lines, which our intervention had spent a good deal of time emphasizing.

For children who were present for pretest and posttest measures, analysis of data revealed a statistically significant improvement in the thousand number line test in the spring semester for the children receiving the mathematics enrichment compared to those receiving the reading enrichment ($p < .05$). That is, students who received math instruction were better than the control group at estimating the location of a number on the number line. The intervention group dropped from being an average of 177.50 integer points off from the targeted number on their estimations to 101.38, whereas the control group dropped only slightly from 145.60 to 135.24.

We note that in the fall of each year, there were no statistically significant improvements in children's skills. We think that this issue was attributable to personnel changes that required the newly hired instructors to become both proficient with PAL mathematics enrichment strategies and to learn how to manage classroom behavior while carrying out the strategies. However, once instructors acquired these skills, children started to benefit from the PAL mathematics enrichment program.

How Do the PAL Enrichment Activities Align with the CCSSM?

The PAL math enrichment activities were deliberately designed and appropriately arranged to align with the CCSSM and the eight SMP (Common Core State Standards Initiative, 2010a, 2010b). Under the guidance of the CCSSM and SMP, PAL math enrichment could efficiently facilitate students' mathematical development. Moreover, the PAL students' learning motivation in mathematics was enhanced through engaging activities, and their mathematics learning anxiety was reduced when they were evaluated using formative assessment in the activities.

Moreover, the daily lesson plan for math enrichment was based on monthly instructional goals and aligned with both CCSSM and SMP (Common Core State Standards Initiative, 2010a, 2010b). There were approximately 16 weeks in each semester of the PAL Program calendar, and every 4-week period was grouped as a 1-month unit with a particular set of monthly instructional goals. These goals targeted the content standards that were to be addressed in those 4 weeks and formed the basis for weekly and daily enrichment interventions. Table 7.1 presents the first-month lesson plan, containing the CCSSM our lesson plan rests on, the classroom activities designed for second and third graders, and corresponding SMP.

The first week's enrichment topic was "Exploring Numbers Surrounding Me with a Ruler," which included five daily activities involving the exploration of numbers that might be used in students' everyday lives (e.g., the length of the hand, foot, and arm; the dimensions of their book bags, and the dimensions of the classroom). In Week 1 activities, students were expected to "Use appropriate

TABLE 7.1. The First-Month Lesson Plan for Grades 2 and 3

Month 1

Instructional goal: To explore numbers in the base-ten system
(CCSSM: 2. NBT—Understanding place value)

	Classroom activities	SMP
Week 1	*Topic:* Exploring Numbers surrounding me with a ruler	5th SMP: Use appropriate tools strategically.
	Daily activities: Exploring numbers (e.g., length of hand, foot and arm; dimensions of book bags, and dimensions of classroom and recording all numbers in base-ten system)	
Week 2	*Topic:* Decomposing the counting numbers only through each number's place value	7th SMP: Look for and make use of structure.
	Daily activities: Sorting tens and ones, trading rods with cubes (an easier version of regrouping games), and coloring "hunting-numbers" math worksheets	
Week 3	*Topic:* Joining Problems with Regrouping	4th SMP: Model with mathematics.
	Daily activities: Interpreting problems like "result unknown, like 15 + 7 = __," "change unknown, like 15 + __ = 22," and "start unknown, like __ + 7 = 22"	
Week 4	A buffer to transition between Months 1 and 2	

Note. CCSSM, Common Core State Standards—Mathematics; NBT, numbers and operations in base-ten; SMP, Standards for Mathematical Practice.

tools strategically," which relates to the fifth standard for mathematical practice. In the second week, students reviewed how to break down numbers into their place values (e.g., $257 = 200 + 50 + 7$) by manipulating blocks. Similarly, five different daily games were conducted in Week 2, such as sorting tens and ones, trading rods with cubes (an easier version of the regrouping games), and a "hunting-numbers" coloring activity. In Week 2 activities, students were expected to "Look for and make use of structure," which relates to the seventh standard for mathematical practice.

The third week's enrichment topic was "Joining Problems with Regrouping," in which students were required to write an addition equation corresponding to a given situation and to solve the problem with base-ten blocks. Five daily activities were conducted according to the levels of difficulty of problems, such as interpreting problems, like "result unknown like $15 + 7 = \square$," "change unknown like $15 + \square = 22$," and "start unknown like $\square + 7 = 22$." In this week, students were expected to "Model with mathematics," which relates to the fourth standard for mathematical practice.

The last week acted as a buffer for the transition between the Month 1 and Month 2 topics. For instance, if students were not familiar with trading 10 ones to 1 ten, as in the week 2 activities, we played similar trading games as those in the previous week (such as a "making purchases and change" game), but in different contexts.

In addition, it is worth mentioning the importance of the diversity across daily lessons. After a long school day, students in the PAL Program would sometimes have trouble attending to the lesson. Therefore, introducing an array of diverse games on a daily basis effectively engaged students and enabled the math specialist to filter out unpopular games to inform future lessons.

Summary

The Chinese philosopher Confucius said, "I hear and I forget. I see and I remember. I do and I understand." In PAL math enrichment, most of the activities included hands-on manipulatives, board games, children's math books, and kinesthetic math games. Therefore, the participating students were learning through "doing math" in the daily math enrichment session. Our research on the PAL Program showed that a well-developed ASP is definitely able to create an enrichment environment in regular school systems to support students' mathematics learning. The PAL math activities not only focused on the cultivation of students' mathematical content knowledge but also sought to inspire greater interest in and a positive attitude toward learning math.

GLOSSARY

Derived fact strategies—Strategies in which students use a small set of known number facts to figure out the solution to another number sentence for which they do not know the answer.

Equivalence—In mathematics, understanding that both quantities on each side of the equals sign (=) should be identical.

Measurement interpretation of fractions—Fractions are viewed as cardinal numbers with which we can order and compare the value of the numbers.

Mental math—Doing math computations in one's mind without the aid of any calculating or recording devices.

Mental number line—A mental representation of number, usually represented as a straight line with numbers placed along it.

Place value knowledge—The numerical value that a digit has because of its position in a number under the base-ten system.

Unit fraction—A fraction in which when a whole is divided into equal parts, say A, the amount formed by one of those parts is $1/A$.

References

AIMSweb. (2012). *AIMSweb technical manual.* Bloomington, MN: NCS Pearson.

Beckmann, S. (2014). *Mathematics for elementary teachers with activities.* Upper Saddle River, NJ: Pearson Education.

Bull, R., & Scerif, G. (2001). Executive functioning as a predictor of children's mathematics ability: Inhibition, switching, and working memory. *Developmental Neuropsychology, 19*(3), 273–293.

Burns, M. (2007). Marilyn Burns: Mental math. *Instructor, 116*(6), 51–54.

Carpenter, T. P., Fennema, E., Franke, M. L., & Empson, S. B. (1999). *Children's mathematics: Cognitively guided instruction.* Portsmouth, NH: Heinemann.

Carpenter, T. P., & Lindquist, M. M. (1989). Summary and conclusions. In M. M. Lindquist (Ed.), *Results from the fourth NAEP mathematics assessment* (pp. 160–169). Reston, VA: National Council of Teachers of Mathematics.

Common Core State Standards Initiative. (2010a). *Common Core State Standards for Mathematics.* Washington, DC: National Governors Association Center for Best Practices & Council of Chief State School Officers. Retrieved from *www.corestandards.org.*

Common Core State Standards Initiative. (2010b). *Standards for Mathematical Practice.* Washington, DC: National Governors Association Center for Best Practices & Council of Chief State School Officers. Retrieved from *www.corestandards.org/Math/Practice.*

Cross, C. T., Woods, T. A., & Schweingruber, H. (2009). *Mathematics learning in early childhood.* Washington, DC: National Academies Press.

Dehaene, S. (2001). Précis of the number sense. *Mind and Language, 16*(1), 16–36.

Fuchs, L. S., Schumacher, R. F., Long, J., Namkung, J., Hamlett, C. L., Cirino, P. T., . . . & Changas, P. (2013). Improving at-risk learners' understanding of fractions. *Journal of Educational Psychology, 105*(3), 683–700.

Hecht, S. A., & Vagi, K. J. (2010). Sources of group and individual differences in emerging fraction skills. *Journal of Educational Psychology, 102*(4), 843–859.

Kieran, C. (1981). Concepts associated with the equality symbol. *Educational Studies in Mathematics, 12*(3), 317–326.

Kieran, C. (1989). The early learning of algebra: A structural perspective. In S. Wagner & C. Kieran (Eds.), *Research issues in the learning and teaching of algebra* (pp. 33–56). Reston, VA: NCTM.

Link, T., Huber, S., Nuerk, H. C., & Moeller, K. (2014). Unbounding the mental number line—New evidence on children's spatial representation of numbers. *Frontiers in Psychology, 4,* 1–12.

Neuschwander, C. (2009). *Sir Cumference and all the king's tens: A math adventure.* Watertown, MA: Charlesbridge.

Reys, B. J. (1985). Mental computation. *Arithmetic Teacher, 32*(6), 43–46.

Schneider, M., Grabner, R. H., & Paetsch, J. (2009). Mental number line, number line estimation, and mathematical achievement: Their interrelations in grades 5 and 6. *Journal of Educational Psychology, 101*(2), 359–372.

Sowder, J. T. (1990). Mental computation and number sense. *The Arithmetic Teacher, 37*(7), 18–20.

Online Instructional Resources

Football Multiplication Game: *www.teachercreated.com/products/football-multi-plication-game-7807.*
Mathopoly® board game: *www.mathopoly.ca/mathopoly-.html.*
Mental math competition activities: *www.math-salamanders.com.*
Mental math worksheet activities: *www.worksheetfun.com.*
Monopoly board game: *www.hasbro.com/en-us/brands/monopoly.*
tri-FACTa™ addition and subtraction game: *www.learningresources.com/product/tri-facta—8482-++addition+-+subtraction+game.do.*

8

Reading Fluency Practice as Reading Enrichment in After-School Literacy Programming

Paula J. Schwanenflugel

After-school programs (ASPs) are an ideal setting for improving reading skills in young readers. The extra hour in the ASP that elementary school children have after they complete their homework provides an excellent opportunity for after-school instructors to engage children in reading practice. Practice is the key to becoming a good reader, as it is in most of life's endeavors. Struggling readers generally do not enjoy reading practice for its own sake. They find it difficult— who likes to practice what they are not particularly good at? Children have often tallied up a great number of failure experiences related to reading by the time the after-school professionals see them. Left to their own devices, children might avoid reading practice, which is perfectly understandable. Structuring reading practice so that young readers have the supports they need to be successful is essential for obtaining meaningful improvements in children's developing skills. ASPs can help with this.

The purpose of this chapter is to provide a general account of the research necessary for understanding the development of reading, particularly the development of reading fluency. Having a basic understanding of how reading develops will help after-school professionals organize their own programs have so that they have a discernible impact on their own students' reading skills. This knowledge can guide them in making informed instructional decisions during a reading enrichment experience.

In high-poverty settings, such as the ones in which we work, one common problem is a lack of reading fluency skills, particularly in grades 2–5. (Hardly any child is particularly fluent prior to grade 2.) Becoming a fluent reader is an important academic goal for being able to read well, and most children will benefit from targeting this basic skill. So, implementing instructional strategies related to reading fluency is ideal for ASPs hoping to enrich and improve children's reading skills. But before discussing the research related to reading fluency, I briefly summarize the development of reading so that after-school instructors can better pinpoint the needs of individual children under their care. Then I discuss what reading fluency is and the research related to the importance of fluent reading. Finally, the practices that research shows are effective for promoting fluent reading among elementary school children are described.

Reading is developmentally organized. That is, some basic skills need to have a certain degree of proficiency before others can really take off. These basic skills form the foundation on which other skills depend.

Skills directly related to linguistic comprehension depend heavily on the characteristics of the linguistic environment in which children are raised. Linguistic skills accrue cumulatively from the moment of birth. The development of these skills tends to have a very long trajectory, essentially growing throughout a person's lifetime.

Other skills (generally those related to recognizing written words) depend more heavily on direct instruction from teachers and adults. These skills tend to require consistent practice to be mastered well. Most children receive these lessons from their teachers during formal reading instruction in school. In what follows, we provide a brief, albeit simplified, version of the developmental skills that need to be established for learning to read well.

Emergent Literacy

Emergent literacy is the term that educators give to the knowledge and set of skills that young children bring with them about reading and writing when they first enter school. We like to think of these emergent literacy skills as being analogous to the way a bridge is constructed. Emergent literacy skills serve as the bedrock into which most bridges (i.e., reading skills) are built. If the bridge's abutments are placed on shifting sand instead of bedrock, the bridge might not be strong enough to support heavy traffic over the long haul (i.e., complex reading) and may collapse. We can add cantilevers and trusses (i.e., phonics, reading strategies), but ultimately the bridge will not work well enough to do the difficult job it needs to do (comprehension) without the bedrock.

Print Knowledge

The availability of and exposure to print materials prior to starting school is one of the environmentally-based issues that affect children's early learning about literacy. Some children come from homes rich in books, magazines, and newspapers. Other children, often from low-income families, come from homes where the preponderance of text they see is the *environmental print* found on cereal boxes, item labels, shopping lists, and so forth, not books. These forms of the printed word can be important sources of emergent literacy learning if adults point out the relevance of it for literacy (Purcell-Gates, 1996). An example of environmental print is shown in Figure 8.1. An alert after-school instructor (or parent) can point out how the C, a, and o can be seen in these two stylized Coca-Cola and Cheerios labels.

Approximately two-thirds of low-income families do not own a single children's book (Binkley & Williams, 1996). In poorer neighborhoods, few stores carry children's books, and they are often sold in counterintuitive places, such as drugstores, grocery stores, and Dollar-type stores where families might not think to look for them (Neuman & Celano, 2001). As a result, some children in these families might have limited experience with reading materials, compared to those children who have a vast array of experiences with children's books. The result is that some children may start school not yet understanding such emergent literacy basics, such as where the cover of the book is, what an author is, how to hold a book the right way, or how we move our fingers from left to right while reading (Clay, 1979).

A cynic might ask, "Why don't these families just take their children to the library?" Public libraries are not a direct replacement for having a home library filled with books. Library branches in low-income neighborhoods generally contain fewer titles overall, and often have less working-family friendly hours compared to those in more affluent neighborhoods (Krashen, 1995). Fines levied for

FIGURE 8.1. Adults can point out how the words *Coca-Cola* and *Cheerios* each have the letters *C* and *o*.

late book returns are discouraging for young parents, too, who fear that their pre-schooler might mangle or lose the library books. Replacement library-bound copies cost more than twice that of regular paperback versions, so these fears are real.

ASPs in high-poverty neighborhoods can help with this print accessibility issue by participating in book give-away programs, such as the Dolly Parton Imagination Library (Ridzi, Sylvia, & Singh, 2014). Every children's book that can be sent home makes a difference, and ASPs also can help parents recognize the need for bedtime reading by participating in book giveaway programs and sending home notes encouraging parents to read to their children (Reardon, Waldfogel, & Bassock, 2016).

Linguistic Skills

Children's oral language skills are very foundational for reading. These language skills arise from the opportunities to participate in conversations with the adults and others around them. You can predict how many words young children know by tracking the quality and quantity of language directed at the children (Hart & Risley, 2003). Some children hear their parents describe the world around them in an extensive color commentary. Others mainly hear adults issuing orders (e.g., "Please eat your dinner"; "Don't interrupt"; "Stop running through the house"). Some children have great parents who generally do not talk much.

The resulting variation in the language that children hear is astounding. By the time they are just barely preschoolers, some children have heard massive amounts of language compared to others, and their resulting language growth differences are extensive (Mayor & Plunkett, 2011). Both in-school programs and ASPs can provide verbal stimulation that helps children catch up (Biemiller & Slonim, 2001) and can encourage children to describe their thoughts, actions, and feelings in language.

Language skills are vital because they help children comprehend what they read (Ouellette, 2006). Struggling readers often have problems with vocabulary and will stumble upon words they do not know. After-school instructors can observe many young readers sound a word out right, only to shrug their shoulders because they believed that they had misread it. If children do not know the meaning of several words on a page, they will have trouble understanding the text in its entirety. Instructors can help when the situation arises by providing a quick definition for the word using words the children are likely to know—for example, "*Jig?* Oh, that's a dance where you dance with your hands on your waist and kick your feet." They can use what we like to call dime words rather than nickel words. Table 8.1 features some examples of what we mean. Children's vocabularies grow in measurable ways when they have teachers who linguistically recast simple sentences into complex ones (Ruston & Schwanenflugel, 2010).

As educators, we are always asked about whether there is a particular set of words that children should learn. This is not the best way to think about the problem. Instead, it is better to let vocabulary learning occur spontaneously as a natural part of conversation or as children encounter words they do not know.

Furthermore, the more words children know, the more likely they are to have developed precise phonological (language sound) information (Metsala, 1997) that they can use to help them learn to read. For example, children who know the words *fin, tin,* and *bin* need to mentally distinguish the initial sounds of these words. Being able to distinguish and manipulate these language sounds in your head is called *phonological awareness,* a key skill for learning to read.

Alphabet and Phoneme Knowledge

Most children come are able to recite the alphabet before starting school (i.e., "ABC Song"). Fewer preschoolers are able to visually recognize and name letters presented randomly to them. Children who know the names of even 10 letters by the end of preschool are less likely to have reading issues later (Piasta, Petscher, & Justice, 2012).

Luckily most letter names in English have the letter sounds somewhere in their names (except for the uncooperative letters *h, w,* and *y*), so knowing letter names supports the learning of letter sounds, too, for example, B (the letter) → *bee* (the letter name) → /b/ (the letter phoneme "buh"). Knowing letter sounds is essential to learning how to read, and most children will have learned most of their letter sounds by the end of kindergarten.

Most ASPs serving older children will not have to engage in direct instruction of these basics. Struggling readers will still need extra help learning to identify the

TABLE 8.1. Examples of How After–School Staff Can Expand on Children's Vocabulary by Using Dime Words Rather Than Nickel Words

Child says (nickel word) . . .	After-school instructor responds (dime word) . . .
"Larger!"	"Shall I make it more *gigantic*, even more *humungous*?"
"It go away!"	"It *floated* away! It just *drifted* away!"
"No more."	"Is that *sufficient* for you?"
"I want some!"	"You want some *sprinkles*? How about putting these chocolate *jimmies* on your ice cream?"
"Gimme some sparkles, please!"	"Oh, you want some *sequins*? Some *glitter*? Do you like the way they *shimmer* in the light?"
"I want a pear!"	"Do you have a *hankering* for a *Bartlett* pear right now?"
"I dress in Halloween."	"Oh, you put on a Halloween *costume*? Is it a special *occasion*?"

phonemes of language, particularly if they have been identified as needing special services in reading. All after-school personnel from the "snack lady" to the physical activity director can practice recasting children's simpler language into more complex forms to improve children's vocabulary and oral language skills.

Learning to Read Words

Reading words requires that a child to be able to map the spellings of a word onto its sounds (using what colloquially is often called *phonics*). In total, there are around 44 basic sounds in English, called *phonemes,* but there are often many different spellings for a particular phoneme (Denes, 1963). Sometimes individual sounds are represented by groups of letters such as *ch, ck, ng, ea, ee,* and *wh.* The /i/ sound (as well as many other sounds) as in *beat* has a number of ways it can be spelled, and can be represented by not only a single *–e,* as in *he* and *be,* but also by groups of letters, such as *-ee* as in *meet, -ea* as in *seat, -ei* as in *weird, -ie* as in *piece, -e__e* as in *here,* and *-y* as in *lovely.* When children can figure out how to map these groups of letters onto sounds, they can try to match the sounds to a word in their vocabulary that fits. Children have to learn to recognize words that are exceptions to basic phonics rules, too, such as the words *said, are,* and *listen.* Luckily, about half the words in English are spelled in a regular manner and another third are just a single phoneme off from being regular (Hanna, Hanna, Hodges, & Rudolph, 1966). That means children are likely to come up with a good guess as to what a word is likely to be by translating the spelling of most words into a series of sounds.

Ehri (1991) has described the general phases children appear to go through while learning to read words. First, early in reading, children may read words using a *prealphabetic* strategy because they do not yet have full command of the alphabet and might use some highly distinctive letters in a word to make a guess. For example, they might recognize the tall double-*l,* and guess the written names *Billy* or *Molly.*

When they have better command of the alphabet, they can begin to distinguish more links between letters and sounds, and may use just a few of a word's letters (and maybe a picture too) to make a guess at the word. Ehri calls this phase the *partial alphabetic phase.* In our experience, struggling readers can be stuck in this phase for quite a while.

In the next phase, which Ehri calls the *full alphabetic phase,* children recognize the need to learn all the rules that connect letters and groups of letters to particular sounds and syllable pronunciations. Reading is slow and plodding during this phase because there are a lot of rules to learn. In the last phase, in the *consolidated alphabetic phase,* children start to read using units constructed of larger groups of letters that occur together often, such as *-ed, -ing, -tion,* and *-ly*. With practice, this helps them read words more quickly and accurately.

In after-school reading enrichment instruction for second- and third-grade children, it is not unusual to have children in all four of the latter stages of learning to read words. After-school personnel can structure opportunities to practice these skills by having children read aloud. During these read-alouds, they can assist children as needed in recognizing common spelling patterns and phonics rules. Once an instructor recognizes the patterns present in a young child's oral reading, he or she can consider the special kinds of supports that a particular child may need in reading words. Some children might still need to learn some phonics rules, while others might just need the supported reading practice typical of the next phase.

Reading Fluency

Fluent reading is generally defined as the reading of real text that is quick, accurate, and expressive. Fluent reading supports good comprehension, although it does not guarantee it. Dysfluent reading, or reading that is choppy, monotone, slow, and inaccurate, appears to outright interfere with good comprehension. Children may be able to read grade-appropriate texts fluently, but not read difficult, complex, or advanced texts. If children cannot read grade-appropriate texts fluently, which is not uncommon in many after-school settings, then reading fluency practice is necessary.

What happens cognitively as children begin to read fluently? First, they read by recognizing larger units within words. That is, instead of reading words sequentially, letter by letter, specific common patterns and even whole words are recognized as a single unit. For example, count the number of *t*'s in the following bit of text as quickly as you can.

> When Wesley was a child just learning to read, he became an avid reader by reading the *Magic Treehouse* (Osborne, 2001) books. He really enjoyed traveling mentally to places like the Arctic or Africa to see all the animals that didn't exist in his neighborhood.

How many *t*'s were there in this short sequence? There were 15 of them. If you missed a few, you probably missed the *t*'s in the words *the, that, to,* and perhaps *just*. That is because a fluent reader does not read these words by reading letters from left to right, but instead sees them more-or-less as a single unit (Cunningham, Healy, Kanengiser, Chizzick, & Willits, 1988).

Fluent readers pronounce words quickly and accurately (Adams, 1990), rather than hesitantly and slowly. The speed with which words are read distinguishes good from poor readers pretty much throughout life, but there is considerable progress in how quickly children can read words during the early elementary school years. The after-school instructor can readily discern whether children are fluent by listening to them read aloud. If there are lots of hesitations, slow reading of words, misread or reread words, or words read with emphasis on the wrong syllable (e.g., _a_bility), even when reading texts at a child's grade level, then the literacy professional can conclude that the child needs some fluency practice.

Another aspect of reading fluency is _word reading autonomy._ That is, when text is presented, fluent children cannot help but read print even when they would rather not. For example, it is impossible for you as a fluent reader to follow this command:

Do not read this message!

As children become fluent readers, they too cannot help but read print. This word reading autonomy begins fairly early in the process of learning to read fluently, as soon as children begin to understand how speech sounds relate to letter patterns (Schwanenflugel, Morris, Kuhn, Strauss, & Sieczko, 2008). If after-school instructors see children voluntarily pointing at and reading the text all around them as they walk through the school hallways, it is likely that they have developed some degree of word reading autonomy.

Finally, and most important, fluent readers are _expressive_ when they read. That is, fluent readers generally use intonation that largely conveys the message of the text. Let's consider this short passage below. You might want to read this aloud to yourself.

> Every day Frog and Toad played together in the forest. Eventually, the increase in the distance they wandered led them far away from their homes. One day, they became quite lost and ran into two trailheads that began right next to each other. Not knowing what to do, they considered both. Toad asked, "Do you think we should follow one of these trails?" Pointing downhill, Frog answered, "Let's try that," and ran ahead.
>
> Toad reasonably feared they might really get lost, so he worriedly asked Frog to come back. But Frog paid no attention. Toad repeated, "Please come back!" Again, there was no response, so Toad began to follow him. To increase his speed to catch up, Toad hopped after him with his biggest hops.

Expressive readers reading this aloud might pause briefly, but changes in pitch would mark the end of every sentence. Certainly, unnatural pauses occurring randomly in midsentence would be very rare. Expressive readers might or might not pause at all at commas, but if they did, that is where they would do it. They might read everything within quotation marks with a raised pitch compared to the rest of the passage. There would be a distinction in loudness and pitch between the first instance of _come back_ and the one two sentences later. When reading the question, their voice would raise in pitch at the end. When focusing on a particular item (as in . . . *Let's try that*), they might emphasize *that*. Finally, children who read with expression would read all words with stress placed on the correct syllable. For example, they would emphasize the first syllable of the noun *increase,* while placing stress on the second syllable of the verb *increase* several sentences later.

Over the past few years, we have done a lot of research on the development of *reading prosody,* or reading expression. We have examined the oral reading of children by studying a spectrogram of their readings. A *spectrogram* is a visual representation of speech, an audio map of sorts that depicts some basic features of children's speech. These spectrograms show us visually whether the child has raised his or her pitch, whether or not he or she has gotten louder, and whether he or she has paused anywhere during the reading. We often look at spectrograms of children's oral readings of the same types of texts that teachers use to examine their oral reading fluency. Figure 8.2 shows an example of a spectrogram of a fluent reader reading the sentence, "Would you like to see my garden?"

Note that the content words *you, like, see,* and *garden* are all read more loudly than the function words *to* and *my.* The first syllable of the word *garden* is spoken more loudly than the second syllable, indicating that the child has emphasized the correct syllable. The child's pitch is raised at the end of this yes–no question, as it should be.

From our research, we have learned a great deal about the oral reading prosody of less fluent readers: Children who are less fluent tend to pause a lot while reading. They make unnaturally long pauses between sentences. They pause mid-sentence, often before difficult words, and even where there is no punctuation at all. These pauses are long and intermittent, varying in ways that do not match the text. They give their reading an unevenness that makes it difficult for the listener, let alone the reader, to understand what is being read. This type of pausing

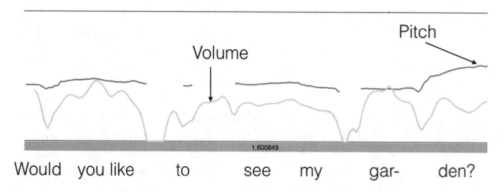

FIGURE 8.2. Example of pitch and volume tracks of a fluent third-grader reading "Would you like to see my garden?"

is sometimes called *pausal intrusion* by reading educators because these pauses intrude on our ability to comprehend the sentence.

The reading of less-fluent readers can sound rather monotonous and flat. In particular, the pitch changes at the ends of basic sentences mark an important reading prosody boundary. Flattened pitch there sounds odd. Indeed, when we measured pitch changes from our spectrograms, we too could see the monotone pattern. The pitch declines at the ends of sentences for less-fluent readers were not as steep as those of fluent readers (Schwanenflugel, Hamilton, Kuhn, Wisenbaker, & Stahl, 2004). Fluent readers read with pitch patterns much like the adults around them, but less fluent readers did not. Less-fluent readers also showed generally less variation in pitch across a segment of text than fluent readers did (Benjamin & Schwanenflugel, 2010).

We have found that less-fluent readers' pitch changes often do not match the message of the sentence (Schwanenflugel, Westmoreland, & Benjamin, 2016). We usually raise our pitch when we are directly quoting someone or when we are drawing people's attention to something, as in "Look at this!" A less-fluent reader might say all the words in this short sentence in an equally loud way. Less-fluent readers also make less distinction between the syllables in a word in both pitch change and loudness (Schwanenflugel & Benjamin, 2016). Think of how the word *activities* might sound when read robotically, and you can understand what is meant here.

To summarize, the reading prosody of fluent readers should sound fairly similar to ordinary speech in terms of changes in pitch, loudness, and pauses within the text. Of course, only professionals, such as newscasters or actors, can read in a way that really disguises the fact that they are reading, so we do not wish to overexaggerate the similarity of fluent reading to spontaneous speech. But, after-school instructions should be able to identify children who have issues with reading expression by determining that the children's reading sounds unusually awkward, flat, and choppy.

Reading Fluency for Good Comprehension

The main reason that after-school literacy instructors should care about whether children are reading fluently is that lack of fluency hinders children's ability to understand what they are reading. Particularly in early elementary school, the correlation between reading fluency and reading comprehension is incredibly high, as much as .85 in some studies (Reschly, Busch, Betts, Deno, & Long, 2009). This correlation means that most children of this age who are able to read grade-level texts fluently generally understand what they have read. Most children who do not read fluently are experiencing comprehension difficulties. The after-school staff can measure reading fluency by measuring children's reading rate, which can serve as a pretty good indicator of children's reading comprehension skills. But if they also listen for children's reading prosody, they get an even better estimate of children's ability to understand what they are reading (Schwanenflugel & Benjamin, 2016).

Fluency alone becomes a somewhat weaker indicator of reading skills as children approach the end of elementary school (Schwanenflugel & Kuhn, 2016). This occurs primarily because the difficulty of texts that children are being asked to read as they graduate into middle school require skills other than fluency, such as a strong vocabulary, good inference skills, and a substantial prior knowledge base from which to draw on.

There will be a subset of older elementary school children (approximately 10–15%) who can read fluently but not have much reading comprehension (Meisinger, Bradley, Schwanenflugel, & Kuhn, 2009). This type of reading is sometimes called *word calling*, a trend that is very noticeable among some English learners. Approximately half of English learners will be able to read a text with the appropriate degree of fluency, yet not really understand it (Quirk & Beem, 2012). After-school literacy instructors need to be alert for this possible pattern among this subgroup of children, in particular.

The reduced relationship between fluency and comprehension as children finish elementary school does not mean that fluency practice is no longer relevant. Fluency is thought to be a fundamental bridge to comprehension. Indeed, disfluent reading is a barrier to comprehension for many adolescent struggling readers, and even for some adult readers (Brasseur-Hock, Hock, Kieffer, Biancarosa & Deshler, 2011). Reading fluency skills remain a strong proxy for the general status of a child's reading skills. Thus, after-school staff can make a pretty good guess as to children's general reading skills merely by listening to them read aloud.

Transitioning from Oral Reading to Silent Reading

So far, we have emphasized the importance of *oral* reading fluency during elementary school. At some point, however, children will be fluent enough to prefer silent reading over oral reading. Indeed, the reliance on oral reading is a transitional period until children become fluent enough to prefer silent reading.

There are many theories as to why children need this transitional period of reading aloud prior to reading silently. From a sociocultural perspective (Prior et al., 2011), children transition to reading silently in the following way: First, they learn about books by being read to on their guardians' laps as infants and toddlers. Then, when they begin the process of learning to read, they read aloud to those same guardians who can provide word recognition and comprehension assistance. Then children go through a period where they find it more comfortable to read aloud to themselves. Finally, they move to reading silently to themselves, as reading itself becomes internalized.

From a cognitive-processing perspective, the reason that children seem to perform better with oral reading than silent reading is that they rely on the auditory feedback that they get from listening to themselves read. Indeed, even adults have been shown to use this auditory feedback even when listening to themselves speaking. It helps them realize that they said the wrong word, for instance. Basically, this feedback helps to specify the message of the text (Lind, Hall, Breidegard, Balkenius, & Johansson, 2014). This auditory feedback may also amplify the little voice in their heads that can be heard when reflecting on the process of reading something difficult silently to oneself. Further, this auditory feedback that children get from listening to themselves read keeps the information in their working memories until they have had a chance to fully process the message of the text. It helps them to attend better, so that they read all the words in a text and fully consider its meaning.

Comprehension is superior from reading aloud than from silent reading from first through fifth grades, although this trend diminishes by seventh grade (Prior et al., 2011). The issues we have raised here might help to account for the fact that the practice of including 10–20 minutes of sustained silent reading present in so many programs has been shown to have limited effectiveness (National Reading Panel & National Institute of Child Health and Human Development, 2000). Young children may simply need concerted time to read aloud with appropriate supports.

Certainly, older readers attending ASPs who already have excellent reading skills might not need the focused attention on oral reading that their peers need. Their comprehension following silent reading might even be superior to that following oral reading. For these high-performing children, it might be just as beneficial to set them up in a quiet corner in the after-school area where they can read to themselves. Making sure that they are held accountable for the reading through activities such as journaling or answering comprehension questions will keep them honest about reading books for meaning.

Evidence-Based Instruction of Reading Fluency

Most effective fluency instruction is structured to find ways to ensure that children receive enough scaffolded reading practice to obtain automaticity and fluent oral reading. The word *scaffolding* in education refers to the various ways that teachers help children to reach an educational goal by providing just the right level of assistance, but not too much. This assistance is gradually removed as children's skill level increases so they can complete the task by themselves. For our purposes, the goal of these practices is for the children to be able to read a passage fluently and expressively. The practices described in the next sections are classroom strategies that have been identified by researchers as being effective for improving reading fluency in young children.

Fluency-Oriented Reading Instruction

The most common instructional practice used to improve reading fluency is *repeated reading* (Kuhn & Woo, 2008). Repeated reading is the centerpiece of Fluency-Oriented Reading Instruction (FORI). In FORI, children are given a particular text to practice reading aloud each week. They will be asked to read this text over and over again, anywhere from 3 to 15 times in a single week. For example, Stahl and Heubach (2005) conducted a study using FORI in which a weekly lesson plan used repeated reading to promote fluency in settings where the majority of children were not reading on grade level. In the FORI strategy, children read the same grade-level basal reader text aloud every single day in various ways and again at home for homework. For many children, grade-level texts are fairly out of reach, and they struggle mightily with them. In the current context of the Common Core State Standards, there is an emphasis on increasing the text complexity that children are exposed to within the curriculum, so fluency practice is essential. FORI requires using complex texts that are somewhat out of reach for the children, so it is in line with these current standards.

The FORI lesson plan varies throughout the week. At the beginning of the week, repeated reading practice is carried out with the teacher reading a text aloud and expressively and the children following along silently in their books. Teachers circulate around the room to ensure that the children are on the right page and perhaps pointing to words as they are read.

The next day, teachers carry out an echo reading of the same text, as they read a few sentences aloud, while the children echo these segments back until the text is completed. Ideally, teachers will read enough text, generally two or three sentences, to ensure that the children will have to follow along in the text rather than just retrieve the segment from working memory.

The following day, teachers will conduct a whole-classroom choral reading of the same text, in which the teacher and children read the text aloud together in unison. To keep the lesson interesting, teachers can mix it up by having the girls, and then the boys, read aloud together. Or they could do a highly expressive reading followed by a not-so-expressive one. Or they could divide children into teams, having the red team read a segment aloud, followed by a blue team read-aloud, and so forth. Again, throughout, the teacher would be circulating around the room to ensure that there are no social loafers who are merely sitting around, not reading.

On the third day teachers will carry out partner reading. This is a strategy in which children work in pairs such that they take turns reading pages of the text, usually with one taking the left page and the other taking the right. It is also ideal if children can help their partners read the text, making small corrections from time to time, so generally a teacher might pair a child with better skills with one that has poorer skills. It is also ideal if the children that are paired get along together personally, so that they will be courteous while providing reading feedback.

The last day of the week, teachers will conclude with an activity involving the book that requires children to refer back to the book to enrich their understanding or memory of it. The activity could be as simple as drawing a picture of the book's main characters or solving some sort of puzzle related to the book. Or it could be something as complex as addressing a writing prompt or project related to the topic of the book. It can be a jeopardy type of game, as well.

Fundamentally then, the main strategy behind FORI is to have children engage in many repeated readings of the passage. The goal of repeated reading practice is the development of automaticity for words in the practiced texts, along with the belief that these repeated readings will eventually transfer to the reading of unpracticed materials over time. Several studies have found FORI to be effective in promoting general reading fluency among struggling second-grade readers (Stahl & Heubach, 2005; Morrow, Kuhn, & Schwanenflugel, 2006).

Wide Fluency-Oriented Reading Practice

Wide FORI is a variant of basic FORI, in that it features some repeated reading practice, but it provides a greater variety of experiences with text. In the Wide FORI approach, the number of texts that children read each week is expanded from one to two or three, depending on their length (Kuhn, 2005). This type of program is sometimes just called *wide reading*.

The rationale in Wide FORI for using a variety of texts is based on three facts. First, most text we read is highly repetitive, so fluency with a particular text can be accrued more quickly than we originally thought for most kids. We now know that practicing a given word for a few times is probably enough for most children to begin to recognize the word automatically. We also know that approximately 100 words comprise about half of the running words in elementary school texts (Adams, 1990). So, practice on one text is much like practice on another. Second, repeatedly reading the same text over and over can be rather boring, potentially damaging reading motivation. If there is no particular need for the repetition, then it probably should be avoided. Finally, children can benefit from learning about a greater variety of ideas and develop a more diverse vocabulary if they are flooded with different books. Ultimately, this wider exposure might be as important to future comprehension as fluency is.

The Wide FORI approach follows the same basic fluency practices of Stahl and Heubach's (2005) basic FORI (echo, choral, and partner reading), but children read three passages in a week rather than the same one over and over again. Children receive new texts on Mondays, Wednesdays, and Fridays, in a typical week.

Whether they are fully fluent with the text or not, they move on to the next one. This means that children might complete from one to four readings of any particular passage. Full mastery of the text is not emphasized.

Several studies comparing basic FORI and Wide FORI approaches have found a slight advantage for Wide FORI over basic FORI on fluency development (Kuhn, 2005; Kuhn et al., 2006; Schwanenflugel et al., 2009). There also may be an advantage for reading comprehension and reading motivation developed as an outgrowth of Wide FORI practice (Schwanenflugel et al., 2009). This makes sense given the broader vocabulary and variety of ideas that the children have been exposed to with the Wide FORI approach. For this reason, the Wide FORI approach was used in our own ASP as outlined in Chapter 10.

Readers' Theater

Like basic and Wide FORI, Readers' Theater (Martinez, Roser, & Strecker, 1999) is another fluency-oriented program that promotes fluency through oral reading practice and repetition. In Readers' Theater, students read plays created for the program that emphasize text written at various reading levels. Teachers choose a script to use in their classroom that will be enacted for the week. Children are assigned parts, and the scripts are read repeatedly until children are fluent with them.

One advantage of Readers' Theater is that it provides a reason for all the repeated reading that goes on in the classroom. Because children are engaging in a performance of sorts, they perform while reading their books. Expressive reading is encouraged. Thus, this program has many of the same elements of basic and Wide FORI in that it emphasizes development of automaticity, accuracy, and good reading expression.

Many of the plays used in the program are adapted from popular children's books. Performances with fancy costumes and line memorization are not necessary or, perhaps, even desirable. (Lots of attention to these ancillary features can take away from the overall goal of increasing reading practice.) However, the plays can be carried out as elaborately or as simply as the teacher or children might want. In fact, often teachers using this approach will have their students give performances for other classes in the school. More simply, groups of children will perform for their peers within the classroom. This program can be adapted by giving older children writing activities that involve creating original plays from their favorite books. In the after-school setting, instructors might set up the goal of using the end of the day on Fridays as time to have family engagement activities, where families can come and watch children read in pared-down mini-performances.

Although most studies of Readers' Theater lack control groups, second-grade children in one study made more progress in reading fluency over the course of the school year than might be expected for typical second graders (Young & Rasinski, 2009). Another study of older elementary school children found improvements in fluency mainly in reading expression (Clark, Morrison, & Wilcox, 2009). Our best guess is that the program is likely to be effective in improving at least some aspects of children's fluency because it shares many features of the other programs previously described.

Choosing a Fluency Program That Works for You

Regardless of the reading fluency approach that is chosen, the most important aspect of fluency practice is scaffolded oral reading practice, that is, practice that ensures that children receive the assistance they need to read the text correctly and that promotes expressive reading. Improvements in reading fluency using scaffolded practice take time. Some research estimates that a minimum of 20 minutes of oral reading, and preferably as many as 30 minutes, per day is needed to make meaningful gains (Kuhn & Woo, 2008). My belief is that basic FORI and Readers' Theater strategies may not incorporate enough practice, generally. In basic FORI, especially if the texts are not long enough, by the end of the week children can read the texts very quickly (usually in 5 minutes or so), and the teachers, not seeing a need for the additional practice, move on to other lessons (Schwanenflugel et al., 2009). The drawback of Readers' Theater is that children spend only 5–10 minutes on concerted oral reading practice according to estimates obtained from available studies. Even then, only part of that time is spent reading aloud by a given child, who only reads his or her part.

None of these problems are insurmountable, however, and all can be dealt with by making some minor changes. Both basic FORI and Readers' Theater can use more complex and longer texts as one solution. In the case of Readers' Theater, reassigning parts as children become fluent with the texts seems to be in order. Teachers can choose scripts that contain a substantial amount of oral reading for each child. However, because of the issues with these fluency approaches, we opted to use the Wide FORI approach for which children are given ample time for oral reading practice extended over a wide variety of complex texts.

We have not discussed reading comprehension in this chapter very much, other than to discuss how fluency provides a bridge to good comprehension. Clearly, a reading lesson that does not also focus on comprehension is missing the key point of reading. Comprehension practices can and should be intermingled with fluency-oriented practices. In Chapter 9, we describe how we have integrated content-oriented reading comprehension instruction within fluency instructions in the PAL reading enrichment program (see also K. Stahl, 2008).

The truth is that American children do not spend nearly enough time reading during the school day. Oddly, on average, only 18 minutes out of the standard 90-minute literacy block is spent in the actual reading of text (Brenner, Hiebert, & Thompkins, 2009). Most likely, only a few of these 18 minutes are actually spent on the oral reading practice. Regardless, good ASPs can do much to increase the amount of time that children spend engaged active oral reading of text.

Determining Whether Reading Fluency Practice Is Making a Difference

How can after-school literacy instructors determine whether their literacy practices are making a difference in accelerating young children's reading fluency? After-school staff generally do not have the resources or assessment skill levels to conduct a formal assessment of children's reading skills. So, all assessments should be considered informal and might be used mainly for determining whether there is a subset of children who do not seem to be benefitting from the program or to serve as feedback with regard to the general effectiveness of the program. Box 8.1 outlines a set of procedures that after-school staff can use to basically determine whether children are making progress in reading fluency.

After-school staff should assess children's reading fluency at least three times a year, at the beginning of the program, in the winter, and then again at the end of the program. If there is money available, the after-school coordinator can sign up for services such as AIMSweb (*https://aimsweb.pearson.com*), which provides fluency assessments designed for children at various grade levels. Alternatively, he or she can use the results of assessments provided by the school with permission from the child's parent. Or assessments of fluency can be conducted by selecting a grade-level text from informal inventories, such as ones from the *Qualitative Reading Inventory* (Caldwell & Leslie, 2009) or *Developmental Literacy Inventory* (Temple, Crawford, & Gillet, 2008). At its most basic, assessments should involve the staff having the children read the passage aloud, while they make note of reading errors and time the oral reading. Box 8.1 describes how errors and words correct per minute are determined. Recordings of these oral readings can be helpful for going back later to count reading errors and measuring changes in children's reading expression over time. Expression can be measured using the scale presented in Box 8.1.

There are also informal approaches the after-school staff can use for making teaching decisions in the moment:

1. *Listen to the basic fluency that children exhibit while they are reading aloud.* Instructors can ask themselves: Are the children able to read all the words in the text? Are they reading relatively quickly and accurately? If so, instructors

BOX 8.1. INFORMAL ASSESSMENT OF READING FLUENCY

Words Correct per Minute

Determining words correct per minute (WCPM) is a basic assessment of reading fluency. The tester should follow directions provided by the inventory for calculating WCPM or select the first minute of the reading and subtract reading errors from the number of words in the passage up to that point. *Reading errors* include inserting or omitting a word, reversing two words, skipping a line, mispronouncing or being unable to read a word in 3 seconds. The table below presents the 50th percentile (average) for each grade for WCPM as described by Hasbrouck and Tindal (2006).

Grade	Fall	Winter	Spring
2	51	72	89
3	71	92	107
4	94	112	123
5	110	127	139

Oral Reading Expression

The tester can also evaluate *oral reading expression*. We prefer the *Comprehensive Oral Reading Fluency Scale* (Benjamin et al., 2013, p. 13) because its descriptors were derived from the spectrographic information obtained from the readings of fluent and less-fluent children. The scale has two 4-point subscales, *intonation* and *natural pausing*. The endpoints of the subscales are included below.

Intonation Subscale

4 Rating (i.e., fluent)—Makes noticeable pitch variations throughout to communicate meaning; makes appropriate and consistent end of sentence pitch changes. One or two exceptions may exist.

1 Rating (i.e., disfluent)—Reads with flat or unnatural intonation throughout; does not make sentence boundaries with distinct pitch changes except occasionally.

Natural Pausing Subscale

4 Rating (i.e., fluent)—Pauses may be used to convey meaning; between-sentence pauses are short, but natural. Unexpected pauses occur < 1 per sentence on average.

1 Rating (i.e., disfluent)—Reading is broken and effortful with numerous pauses throughout. Reads primarily in groups of one or two words without pausing.

might consider upping the challenge somewhat by using more difficult or longer texts. Are children slow and plodding? Then children probably will benefit from further reading practice on texts of this type.

2. *Listen to the expressiveness that children display while reading aloud.* Ideally, children will read texts expressively. Instructors can ask themselves: Do children use expression that matches the meaning of the text? Do they emphasize the right words as they read? Do they emphasize the right syllables? If the reading sounds relatively natural, then children probably have enough fluency with that particular passage. If not, then the instructor can carry out his/her own reading with particular attention to appropriate expression. Instructors can have children practice reading aloud with expression.

3. *Try to determine whether the children have a basic understanding of what they are reading.* One goal of reading fluency is that children can read text well enough to develop a good basic understanding of the text. Instructors can ask themselves: Can children summarize the passage? Can they draw conclusions from it? If so (and the reading is relatively fluent), children might benefit from more difficult texts. If not, then staff members can discuss difficult vocabulary and they can read complex sentences with expression to help children understand how a fluent reading might sound. Children will probably need extra fluency practice on that level of text.

GLOSSARY

Autonomy—The speed, accuracy, and effortlessness of skills that come with practice.

Emergent literacy—The set of knowledge and skills that young children develop about reading and writing.

Environmental print—The print that is all around us and that is shared by persons living in a similar environment such as cereal boxes, labels, street signs, store signs, company logos, and restaurant menus.

Expressive reading—Intonation and expression that match the message of the text.

Fluent reading—Reading that is quick, accurate, and expressive, and that generally supports good comprehension.

Pausal intrusion—Unnecessary pauses that occur while reading aloud that interferes with the interpretation of the message.

Phonemes—The basic, distinguishable sounds of a language that distinguish one word from another.

Phonics—A method of reading by teaching children how to match letters or groups of letters onto the phonemes, or basic sounds, of the language.

Reading prosody—The expression and intonation with which children and adults read text aloud. It includes pitch changes, volume changes, pause patterns, and rhythmic quality of the oral reading.

Repeated reading—An instructional strategy for promoting reading fluency where children repeatedly read a text over a number of days.

Scaffolding—An educational technique wherein teachers or parents provide various levels of assistance depending on the skill level of the child so that the child can complete an educational goal.

Spectrogram—A visual representation of the pause, pitch, and loudness features of speech, as well as some others.

Wide reading—An instructional strategy for promoting reading fluency by having children read a wide variety of texts.

Word calling—The tendency of some children to have difficulty understanding a text despite reading with grade-level fluency.

References

Adams, M. J. (1990). *Beginning to read: Thinking and learning about print.* Cambridge, MA: MIT Press.

Benjamin, R. G., & Schwanenflugel, P. J. (2010). Text complexity and oral reading prosody in young readers. *Reading Research Quarterly, 45*(4), 388–404.

Benjamin, R. G., Schwanenflugel, P. J., Meisinger, E. B., Groff, C., Kuhn, M. R., & Steiner, L. (2013). A spectrographically grounded scale for evaluating reading expressiveness. *Reading Research Quarterly, 48*(2), 105–133.

Biemiller, A., & Slonim, N. (2001). Estimating root word vocabulary growth in normative and advantaged populations: Evidence for a common sequence of vocabulary acquisition. *Journal of Educational Psychology, 93*(3), 498–520.

Binkley, M., & Williams, T. (1996). *Reading literacy in the United States: Findings from the IEA Reading Literacy Study.* Washington, DC: U.S. Government Printing Office.

Brasseur-Hock, I. F., Hock, M. F., Kieffer, M. J., Biancarosa, G., & Deshler, D. D. (2011). Adolescent struggling readers in urban schools: Results of a latent class analysis. *Learning and Individual Differences, 21*, 438–452.

Brenner, D., Hiebert, E. H., & Tompkins, R. (2009). How much and what are third graders reading?: Reading in core programs. In E. H. Hiebert (Ed.), *Reading more, reading better* (pp. 118–140). New York: Guilford Press.

Caldwell, J., & Leslie, L. (2009). *Qualitative reading inventory.* Boston: Allyn & Bacon.

Clark, R., Morrison, T. G., & Wilcox, B. (2009). Readers' Theater: A process of developing fourth-graders' reading fluency. *Reading Psychology, 30*(4), 359–385.

Clay, M. M. (1979). *Early detection of reading difficulties.* Portsmouth, NH: Heinemann.

Cunningham, T. F., Healy, A. F., Kanengiser, N., Chizzick, L., & Willitts, R. L. (1988). Investigating the boundaries of reading units across ages and reading levels. *Journal of Experimental Child Psychology, 45*(2), 175–208.

Denes, P. B. (1963). On the statistics of spoken English. *Journal of the Acoustic Society of America, 35*(6), 892–904.

Ehri, L. C. (1991). Phases in learning to read words by sight. *Journal of Research in Reading, 18*(2), 116–125.

Hanna, P. R., Hanna, J. S., Hodges, R. E., & Rudorf, E. H. (1966). *Phoneme–grapheme correspondences as cues to spelling improvement.* Washington, DC: U.S. Department of Health, Education, and Welfare.

Hart, B., & Risley, T. R. (2003). The early catastrophe: The 30-million word gap by age 3. *American Educator, 27,* 4–9.

Hasbrouck, J., & Tindal, G. A. (2006). Oral reading fluency norms: A valuable assessment tool for reading teachers. *The Reading Teacher, 59*(7), 636–644.

Krashen, S. (1995). School libraries, public libraries and the NAEP scores. *School Library Media Quarterly, 23,* 234–237.

Kuhn, M. R. (2005). A comparative study of small group fluency instruction. *Reading Psychology, 26,* 127–146.

Kuhn, M. R., Schwanenflugel, P. J., Morris, R. D., Morrow, L. M., Bradley, B. A., Meisinger, E., Woo, D., & Stahl, S. A. (2006). Teaching children to become fluent and automatic readers. *Journal of Literacy Research, 38,* 357–387.

Kuhn, M. R., & Woo, D. G. (2008). Fluency-oriented reading: Two whole-class approaches. In M. R. Kuhn & P. J. Schwanenflugel (Eds.), *Fluency in the classroom* (pp. 17–35). New York: Guilford Press.

Lind, A., Hall, L., Breidegard, B., Balkenius, C., & Johansson, P. (2014). Speakers' acceptance of real-time speech exchange indicates that we use auditory feedback to specify the meaning of what we say. *Psychological Science, 25*(6), 1198–1205.

Martinez, M., Roser, N. L., & Strecker, S. (1999). "I never thought I could be a star": A Readers Theatre ticket to fluency. *The Reading Teacher, 52*(4), 326–334.

Mayor, J., & Plunkett, K. (2011). A statistical estimate of infant and toddler vocabulary size from CDI analysis. *Developmental Science, 14*(4), 769–785.

Meisinger, E. B., Bradley, B. A., Schwanenflugel, P. J., & Kuhn, M. R. (2009). Myth and reality of the word caller: The relationship between teacher nominations and prevalence among elementary school children. *School Psychology Quarterly, 24,* 147–159.

Metsala, J. L. (1997). An examination of word frequency and neighborhood density in the development of spoken-word recognition. *Memory and Cognition, 25*(1), 47–56.

Morrow, L. M., Kuhn, M., & Schwanenflugel, P. J. (2006). The family and fluency instruction. *The Reading Teacher, 60,* 322–333.

National Reading Panel & National Institute of Child Health and Human Development. (2000). *Report of the National Reading Panel: Teaching children to read: An evidence-based assessment of the scientific research literature on reading and its implications for reading instruction: Reports of the subgroups.* Washington, DC: Author.

Neuman, S. B., & Celano, D. (2001). Access to print in low-income and middle-income communities: An ecological study of four neighborhoods. *Reading Research Quarterly, 36*(1), 8–26.

Osborne, M. P. (2001). *Magic tree house boxed set, books 1–4: Dinosaurs before dark, the knight at dawn, mummies in the morning, and pirates past noon.* New York: Random House.

Ouellette, G. P. (2006). What's meaning go to do with it?: The role of vocabulary in word reading and reading comprehension. *Journal of Educational Psychology, 98*(3), 554–566.

Piasta, S. B., Petscher, U., & Justice, L. M. (2012). How many letters should pre-schoolers in public programs know?: The diagnostic efficiency of various preschool letter-naming benchmarks for predicting first-grade literacy achievement. *Journal of Educational Psychology, 104*(4), 945–958.

Prior, S. M., Fenwick, K. D., Saunders, K. S., Ouellette, R., O'Quinn, C., & Harvey, S. (2011). Comprehension after oral and silent reading: Does grade level matter? *Literacy Research and Instruction, 50,* 183–194.

Purcell-Gates, V. (1996). Stories, coupons, and the TV guide: Relationships between home literacy experiences and emergent literacy knowledge. *Reading Research Quarterly, 31*(4), 406–428.

Quirk, M., & Beem, S. (2012). Examining the relations between reading fluency and reading comprehension for English Language learners. *Psychology in the Schools, 49*(6), 539–553.

Reardon, S. F., Waldfogel, J., & Bassock, D. (August 26, 2016). The good news about educational inequality. *The New York Times.* Retrieved from *http://nyti.ms/2bMURct.*

Reschly, A. L., Busch, T. W., Betts, J., Deno, S. L., & Long, J. D. (2009). Curriculum-based measurement oral reading as an indicator of reading achievement: A meta-analysis of the correlational evidence. *Journal of School Psychology, 47,* 427–469.

Ridszi, F., Sylvia, M. R., & Singh, S. (2014). The Imagination Library program: Increasing parental reading through book distribution. *Reading Psychology, 25*(6), 548–576.

Ruston, H. P., & Schwanenflugel, P. J. (2010). Effects of a conversation intervention on the expressive vocabulary development of prekindergarten children. *Language, Speech, and Hearing Services in Schools, 41*(3), 303–313.

Schwanenflugel, P. J., & Benjamin, R. G. (2016). The development of reading prosody and its assessment. In J. Thomson & L. Jarmulowicz, (Eds.), *Linguistic rhythm and literacy* (pp. 187–213). Amsterdam: John Benjamins.

Schwanenflugel, P. J., Hamilton, A. M., Kuhn, M. R., Wisenbaker, J., & Stahl, S. A. (2004). Becoming a fluent reader: Reading skill and prosodic features in the oral reading of young readers. *Journal of Educational Psychology, 96,* 119–129.

Schwanenflugel, P. J., & Kuhn, M. R. (2016). Reading fluency. In P. Afflerbach (Ed.), *Handbook of individual differences in reading: Reader, text, and context* (pp. 107–119). New York: Routledge.

Schwanenflugel, P. J., Kuhn, M. R., Morris, R. D., Morrow, L. M., Meisinger, E. B., Woo, D. G., & Quirk, M. (2009). Insights into fluency instruction: Short- and long-term effects of two reading programs. *Literacy Research and Instruction, 48,* 318–336.

Schwanenflugel, P. J., Morris, R. D., Kuhn, M. R., Strauss, G. P., & Sieczko, J. M. (2008). The influence of reading unit size on the development of Stroop interference in early word decoding. *Reading and Writing, 21*(3), 177–203.

Stahl, K. A. D. (2008). Creating opportunities for comprehension with fluency-oriented reading. In M. R. Kuhn & P. J. Schwanenflugel (Eds.), *Fluency in the classroom* (pp. 55–74). New York: Guilford Press.

Stahl, S. A., & Heubach, K. M. (2005). Fluency-oriented reading instruction. *Journal of Literacy Research, 37*(1), 25–60.

Temple, C. A., Crawford, A. N., & Gillet, J. W. (2009). *Developmental Literacy Inventory.* New York: Pearson.

Young, C., & Rasinski, T. (2009). Implementing readers theatre as an approach to classroom fluency instruction. *The Reading Teacher, 63*(1), 4–13.

9

Improving Informational Text Literacy

Using Social Studies Education Theory to Promote Social Studies Literacy After School

Justin T. Dooly

Development of good literacy in students is important for promoting academic achievement, maintaining good health, decreasing incarceration rates due to lower levels of literacy, and participating fully in social and civic life. Until recently, most instructional practices related to reading have viewed reading as simply a basic set of skills that could be adapted to any text structure (Shanahan & Shanahan, 2008). While this may or may not be true for some aspects of reading (e.g., phonics, letter recognition, phonological awareness, sight word reading), students may struggle while interacting with some types of texts while having little difficulty with others. For example, children may have little difficulty in comprehending stories or narratives, but more difficulty in comprehending informational texts. Further, they may struggle more with informational texts related to certain academic topics, such as social studies texts, than others. However, good literacy skills require that children learn to adapt their understanding of reading to comprehend the full variety of text types that they encounter.

The purpose of this chapter is to discuss some of the issues associated with the reading and instruction of informational texts in the after-school setting. I focus primarily on social studies texts as a case study, although many of the issues associated with social studies texts also apply to science and other academic types of texts.

Distinguishing Informational from Narrative Texts

Narrative texts and informational texts have been understood to accomplish different literary goals. The distinction between narrative texts (also referred to as stories) and informational texts (also referred to as *expository* texts) is one of text *genre*. Fang (2008) described narrative texts as helpful for learning to read, while informational texts were contingent on developing an additional set of skills that could be used for reading to learn. In many cases, students struggle with the transition to informational texts.

It is important to understand what distinguishes narratives from informational texts. Narrative texts generally consist of repetitive structures (e.g., character, setting, problem, solution, and outcome) (Hall-Kenyon & Black, 2010). Usually stories begin by the author introducing characters and settings. Then, often a protagonist is faced with some sort of problem or issue that must be overcome. Then the protagonist and supporting characters attempt various solutions, until the problem is resolved and (most typically in children's texts) a positive outcome is found. This pattern can be seen over and over again, particularly in stories written for young children, so much so that the pattern has been referred to as a *story grammar* (Stein & Nezworski, 1978). The term *story grammar* refers to the typical information that is characteristic of most stories judged to be good. Most notably, narrative texts rely on the reader's prior knowledge to convey a message. Although the story itself might be novel, the ideas within them are usually just derived from existing knowledge, and the overall purpose is to entertain (Brewer & Lichtenstein, 1982). Over time, with increased exposure, students become familiar with common narrative text structures and become more proficient in terms of their literacy and comprehension abilities.

Informational texts, on the other hand, deliver informational and factual knowledge based on content-specific information (e.g., vocabulary, themes, questions, and reflections). Unlike the repetitiveness of narrative structures, informational texts have a variety of typical structures. These structures can be expressed in various ways, such as chronological order, description, compare and contrast, cause and effect, and problem and solution (see Brock and Schwanenflugel, Chapter 10, this volume, for further discussion of these structures). Such texts provide the reader with explicit and new information from numerous academic disciplines. In a basic way, informational texts are designed to teach.

For most students, the transition to an increased exposure to informational texts begins around the fourth grade. Results from high-stakes testing indicate that "many preadolescents struggle with reading, especially when facing expository content area text" (Miller & Veatch, 2010, p. 154). Further, "69% of eighth-grade students in the United States are below proficient in their ability to comprehend text written at their grade level, regardless of text type" (p. 154). Although these statistics are abysmal by themselves, one can only imagine the comprehension issues facing children raised in poverty or having learning disabilities. According to Halvorsen et al. (2012) those in the lowest socioeconomic groups are "less likely to be provided with opportunities to develop content area literacy and social studies knowledge in the primary grades" (p. 199). For students who have learning disabilities, O'Connor, Beach, Sanchez, Bocian, and Flynn (2015) assert that this lack of exposure to informational texts could prevent them from achieving the goals set out by the Common Core State Standards. Importantly, in today's knowledge economy, lacking facility with informational texts might impede children from achieving the positive life outcomes associated with obtaining satisfying employment and participating in civic matters. In all, poor literacy and reading comprehension abilities, particularly in reading informational text, have fundamentally important consequences.

What makes the transition from comprehension of narratives to comprehension of informational texts so difficult? Hall-Kenyon and Black (2010) outline three potential reasons for such difficulties. First, the numerous informational text structures (i.e. chronological, descriptive, compare–contrast, cause–effect, and problem–solution) conflict with the reader's schema for the structures presented through narrative text (e.g., character, setting, problem, solution, and outcome). These difficulties stem, in part, from of a lack of experience working with informational texts and, in part, because these different text structures increase the cognitive demands on the reader. Second, informational texts require students to retain information new to the reader. Recall that factual texts expose the reader to new information, whereas narrative text relies on retrieving existing knowledge to support comprehension. Acquiring new information by nature then, makes comprehension more difficult because it requires updating and integrating new knowledge with one's prior knowledge (Kintsch, 2004). Third, Hall-Kenyon and Black point out that there needs to be a pedagogical distinction between narrative text instruction and informational text instruction. As a result, informational texts require teachers to attend to nuanced comprehension strategies not needed for narrative literacy instruction.

Unfortunately, teachers are not generally attending to the differences in text types. Fang (2008) stated that "despite this shift in reading materials, little discrimination is made in the type of reading instruction that students receive between primary and intermediate grades" (p. 476), which is presumably the period in which more informational texts are introduced. This pedagogical mismatch between the materials that children typically receive in literacy instruction and the basic reading instruction methods that are used is a major limitation of our current approaches to literacy education. Thus, a focus on informational texts in after-school programs (ASPs) using appropriate instructional techniques can have enduring benefits for children that work across the curriculum.

Instructional Approaches from Literacy Education

Research from the field of literacy education has produced four instructional approaches to informational text that target student comprehension and can be used in after-school literacy programming. The first of such approaches is the content-oriented approach, the second has been termed the strategies approach, and the strategies approach, the critical literacy approach, and the fourth is known as the disciplinary approach. Each of these is described in the next sections.

The Content-Oriented Approach

Vaughn and colleagues (2013) describe the *content-oriented approach* (COA) as rooted "within a text-processing view of comprehension" (p. 78). This view is rooted also in Kintsch's (1998) construction-integration model, which requires the reader to link new knowledge to prior knowledge. Successful comprehension is said to occur when such connections are created between the text and existing knowledge. This comprehension approach focuses "on what readers do with text information to represent it and integrate it into a coherent whole" (McKeown, Beck, & Blake, 2009, p. 220).

   McKeown et al. (2009) suggest that strengthened comprehension might be derived "from a focus on continually striving for meaning" (p. 220). To facilitate this aim, McKeown et al. advise educators to approach informational texts using collaborative discussion, summarization, instructional conversation, collaborative reasoning, and dialogic instruction with the explicit purpose of using talk to generate meaning from the text. In this sense, the content-oriented approach can be reduced to a non-domain-specific (e.g., social studies, science, and business) thought process that promotes text comprehension through the reader's ability to create meaning out of new information *after* reading.

The Strategies Approach

A second approach to literacy instruction, sometimes called the *strategies approach* (SA), is rooted in a model of thinking that results in problem-solving routines for dealing with text *during* the reading process. McKeown et al. (2009) describe the strategies approach within this model of thinking as one that considers "when and how to call up specific routines to deal with new information" (p. 220). In general, students with strong comprehension abilities have been thought to implement various strategies (e.g., identifying their goal, evaluating their progress, considering evidence, underlining, monitoring, cooperative learning) linked to enhanced comprehension. Collin (2014) noted, too, that alternate procedures associated with this approach are: (1) "to carry out cognitive processes such as anticipating, acquiring, evaluating, reflecting on, synthesizing, and recalling information; (2) to monitor, evaluate, and repair these processes (see also McKeown et al., 2009); and (3) to negotiate learning with others" (p. 309).

With this in mind, the strategies approach differs from the content approach in two ways. The first deals with the sequence in which the strategies are implemented in the reading comprehension process. The COA to comprehension typically occurs in the form of discussion following the reading; however, the SA enlists the use of strategies during the reading itself. In a second sense, the two approaches differ pedagogically, as each attempt to facilitate comprehension in vastly different ways. Whereas the COA represents nonspecific methods for comprehension—usually through discussion—the SA represents more specific methods to promote comprehension. Given this distinction, the following example of an informational text illustrates how the strategies approach was implemented into the PAL ASP.

America's Landscape, by Lynn M. Stone (2002), is one text that we used that seemed to call for the use of the strategies approach. This predominantly geography-based text is written at a second-grade reading level and is designed to teach this age group about geography.

Recall that the strategies approach emphasizes enlisting general thought processes during reading. As such, when we used *America's Landscape*, students were directed to call attention to boldfaced headings (e.g., *The Appalachians, The Rockies,* and *America's Forests*) at the top of each page as a cue signaling a change in content. Students were taught that bold printed words (e.g., *tundra, landscape, continental,* etc.) were more significant to the text. They also became aware that these words could usually be found in the glossary.

In our experience with the ASP, this approach to comprehension development worked well for students. They routinely understood and differentiated vocabulary words from normal text, and they consulted the glossary for the meanings of vocabulary words, such as *alpine* and *landforms*. Further, students demonstrated an understanding that section headings and the table of contents provide context clues when consulting the text for answers by routinely checking the headings when asked questions such as where a tundra could be found or what a landscape is.

The Critical Literacy Perspective to Social Studies

The critical literacy perspective (CLP) for teaching literacy using social studies texts is a "a pedagogical approach to reading that focuses on the political, sociocultural, historical, and economic forces that shape young students' lives" while also increasing students' "responsiveness toward societal problems in their world" (Soares & Wood, 2010, p. 487). Its primary objective then, is to create readers who understand their values, as well as their responsibility to confront issues within society.

The CLP details five themes to accomplish these goals. The themes include examining multiple perspectives, finding an authentic voice, recognizing social barriers, finding one's identity, and a call to service. Let's take each of these in turn.

The first and second themes reflect similar ideas. The first theme, examining multiple perspectives, requires students to understand that people interpret their experiences from numerous perspectives. It is with this in mind that students question the author's intent, values, and perspectives to "explore the nature of the events in which they take part" (Soares & Wood, 2010, p. 489). The second theme, finding the one's authentic voice, requires the reader to analyze the text to see how the author's language promotes certain perspectives. This theme mirrors one aspect of examining multiple perspectives, as it hinges on questioning how the use of language benefits dominant voices and excludes others. Such an approach encourages students to speak out against the ways in which dominant perspectives are represented in comparison to alternative viewpoints. As a result, both themes allow students to unburden themselves from over-represented perspectives.

One text we used in the PAL Program addressed the combined components. The book *It's a Fair Swap!* (Miller, 2008) is a primarily second- and third-grade reading-level text that highlights concepts of economics (e.g., trade, rational decision-making processes, and issues of fairness) in the context of early European and Native American relations. Some students may or may not have encountered accurate information surrounding Native American injustice yet. In this sense, the text could be adopted for late elementary, middle, and/or even high school environments as a tool to allow students to develop more nuanced understandings of this topic.

From the CLP perspective, students and teachers can begin a discussion of this book by noting the title and questioning the extent to which fairness can be attributed to the Native American experience. Further conversations regarding the title could reflect interpretations about how the text reflects the dominant culture (i.e., European) and dominant racial perspectives (i.e., white), and European attempts to silence minority voices. With even a little background information about Native American experiences with European cultures, one would be hard-pressed to accept a narrative asserting that fairness and equality existed between the native and European groups. In fact, this idea wholly contradicts a historical analysis about the relationships between Native Americans and Europeans and shows how this title, text, author, and publisher attempted to downplay the events in a way that benefitted dominant culture voices. As such, teachers and students alike can work to spot misrepresentations such as these in textbooks; by doing so, these comprehension activities would promote an analysis of text using multiple perspectives. Students can further their understanding of how the use of language can inhibit minority voices.

The third theme of the CLP aims to increase students' recognition of social barriers (e.g., stereotyping and assumptions) in an effort to bridge the gap between social groups (e.g., racial, gender, ethnic, age, political). Two books, *After the Attack* (Fifer, 2005), which discusses the attacks on the World Trade Centers on 9/11/2001, and *Islamic Culture* (Toor, 2006) pair in a way that might undermine negative stereotypes of persons of Middle Eastern descent and of Islamic religion. Figure 9.1 provides a weekly plan for comprehension activities based on these three themes from the CLP that PAL Program instructors used to approach this divisive issue. This approach encouraged students to reevaluate their understanding of the relationship among the American, global, and Islamic communities. These comprehension activities were put into practice within the context of the Wide FORI approach discussed in Chapter 10.

The fourth theme of critical literacy encourages students to find one's identity as represented *positively* within the text. Soares and Wood (2010) assert that "when young learners relate to characters and situations found in books that are reflective of their own diversity, they are better able to make connections to their everyday lives" (p. 491). Unfortunately, current classroom textbooks, particularly the smaller-leveled books that we used in the ASP, have done a poor job of capturing a wide range of perspectives and identities. The lack of such textbooks poses significant obstacles for teachers who want to assist children in connecting literacy to their everyday lives and emerging identities as an aspect of literacy learning.

We were, however, able to find and use some texts that met this objective. Our student population was predominantly African American, so it seemed appropriate to enlist the text, *African American Culture* (Nichols, 2006), a book written approximately at a fourth- to fifth-grade readability level. The book discusses the issue of culture as manifested through its artistic expression (e.g., writings, portraits) and artists (e.g., Phyllis Wheatley, Eugene Warburg, and Zora Neale Hurston). In contrast to many books that view African American culture through the historical lens of slavery, the book dealt with culture through overwhelmingly positive references to the arts. This allows the instructor to expand the context by which the African American experience is perceived not only by children of color, but also by the children in the classroom as a whole. The text counteracts entrenched approaches and affords African American children a positive and expanded understanding of their culture.

The fifth theme critical literacy theme involves a call to service, which potentially strengthens democratic and civic participation and encourages cooperation from children of diverse backgrounds. This component was emphasized to a lesser degree in our program.

In the PAL Program, students seemed to enjoy lessons that were reflective of

DAY	MONDAY	TUESDAY	WEDNESDAY	THURSDAY	FRIDAY
Text	*After the Attack*	*After the Attack*	*Islamic Culture*	*Islamic Culture*	*After the Attack/ Islamic Culture*
Comprehension Activity	**Examining Multiple Perspectives:** • Activate prior knowledge (i.e., short video displaying media reactions and coverage). **Finding Authentic Voice:** • Introduce vocabulary words (e.g., *terrorist, hijack*) to gain an understanding of how such terms were then associated with Islamic people.	**Recognizing Social Barriers:** • Analyze the negative shift in perception toward Islamic people and Middle Eastern backgrounds after 9/11 (e.g., YouTube videos, primary documents, firsthand accounts from such people).	**Finding Authentic Voice/Examining Multiple Perspectives:** • Activate prior knowledge (e.g., ask students to identify common attitudes toward and themes related to the Islamic community). Such comments should sound negative given the previous content.	**Finding One's Identity:** • Vocabulary in cultural context, wherein students select culturally/religiously specific words represented in the glossary (e.g., *hadith, hajj, madrassa, mihrab*) gather an understanding of the definition(s), and apply the third concept of the CLP as a way to address negative stereotypes.	**Examining Multiple Perspectives:** • Compare and contrast the ideas, perceptions, and connotations associated with both texts. **Recognizing Social Barriers:** • Line of contention requires students to choose which perspective most accurately reflects the Islamic culture and its people. Discussion follows to understand student rationale for their decisions.

FIGURE 9.1. Example of a CLP weekly plan.

the critical literacy approach to social studies. The students critically examined issues of social progress, civic participation, and social injustice—all key ideas when considering the goals for critical literacy and social studies education. For perspective, after reading *The Gettysburg Address* (Armentrout & Armentrout, 2005), students were asked to consider whether slavery existed in altered forms following Lincoln's address and the close of the Civil War. Students involved in the discussion wrestled with this abstract question and concluded that—from their parents' perspectives— having a job in some ways related to a modern-day continuation of slavery. Students mentioned the rigorous work schedule(s) their parents kept, as well as their unfair wages, as evidence for making this assertion. Obviously, the fact that work is actually paid and that persons have an option to quit were also brought up as real differences from actual slavery Answers were no doubt influenced by the students' experiences, political figures at the time, as well as parental influence. Students, by and large, seemed highly engaged in these critical and thought-provoking discussions. Many were surprised but grateful to have been able to be a part of such discussions, as further questioning into the matter indicated that such discussions were, to a large extent, absent from their educational experiences.

The Disciplinary Approach

The third approach is the *disciplinary approach*, in which literacy is taught through the discipline itself and draws on the disciplinary literacies seen in academia (Collin, 2014). Gee (2010) explains that literacy is not an isolated component. Rather, literacy should be taught through the context of specific disciplines (e.g., history, mathematics, geography). In this approach, students model the experts, and in doing so, confront "the particular challenges of reading, writing, speaking, listening, and language" through the context of a specific field of study (Collin, 2014, p. 310). Fang (2012) suggested that the disciplinary approach must focus on strategies within cognitive aspects (e.g., understanding a text, writing an essay, or solving a problem), must emphasize specific content-centered language patterns, must use students' lived experiences to guide learning, and must engage in discussion surrounding certain elements of critical literacy (e.g., multiple perspectives, finding authentic voice, reorganizing social barriers, and separation across borders). Overall, disciplinary literacy has been viewed in a positive light within the academic community because it puts children on the path to understanding the reasoning and evidence patterns used in each discipline.

One set of texts, *Heroes of the American Revolution*, was aligned with the disciplinary approach to comprehension instruction. PAL instructors used two texts, *Crispus Attucks* (McLeese, 2005) and *Phillis Wheatley* (McLeese, 2005), to implement a disciplinary approach. These texts seemed to be inherently characteristic, as both incorporated several elements typically found in historical studies.

For example, both texts included timelines and items from historical archives, techniques common to historical study, as well as provocative illustrations (such as illustrations of slaves being sold at auction or reproductions of paintings showing George Washington with his slaves in the background) that could lead to discussion of historical contexts. In this sense, it appears that certain texts may lend themselves more to the disciplinary approach, depending on the content of the text.

Addressing the Four Literacy Strategies

The reading enrichment curriculum in the PAL Program emphasized informational texts of two kinds. In the first year, we emphasized science materials, and in the second we emphasized social studies texts. Although the main focus of this chapter is on strategies for social studies texts, our goal in the ASP was not only to improve children's developing comprehension skills for content-area texts, but also to build their knowledge of science and social studies in general. By teaching children to comprehend informational texts using the content-oriented or strategies approaches, they should be able to transfer their knowledge about reading content area texts from one type of content to another. However, for many social studies texts in particular, our ASP also emphasized a critical literacy and disciplinary approach to comprehending informational texts to better ground children in strategies and viewpoints related to social studies reasoning.

Although we have up to this point emphasized instructional approaches from literacy education, there are alternative approaches to understanding informational texts that emanate from the disciplines themselves. In the next section, we provide examples of approaches from social studies education that might be used to inform instruction of informational text.

Social Studies Education Approaches to Informational Text Literacy

In this section, we discuss three social studies education theories as examples of how after-school professionals can model social studies education approaches in an instructional setting. The first is the traditional social studies instruction (TSSI) approach. The second theory advocates using social studies texts as a platform for democratic citizenship. The third theory takes the form of a discipline-based approach to social studies education. In what follows, each of the three theoretical approaches will be explored and connected to the PAL literacy program for elementary school students. A weekly plan based on the text, *The Bill of Rights*, by David and Patricia Armentrout (2005), is also presented to illustrate each approach.

Leming: The TSSI

The TSSI approach is described by Leming (1994) as "text-oriented, whole group, teacher-centered instruction with an emphasis on memorization of factual information" (p. 18). In TSSI, teachers are seen as knowledge gatekeepers, and students view educators as experts in a particular field or subject. The task of educators, as experts, is to help students master the content—more commonly referred to in today's educational climate as standards. This teaching method not only reaffirms standardized testing practices, but also promotes acquisition of knowledge or cultural transmission as education's primary focus. This point of view, as a whole, emphasizes historical facts, dates, and chronological ordering as paramount to the social studies experience. Figure 9.2 provides an example of a PAL weekly plan consistent with the TSSI approach.

Leming's approach to social studies instruction, in some ways, mirrors standards-based teaching. It has been viewed by some as a "stick to the facts" and "maintain neutrality" approach to social studies education (Ross, 2000, p. 43). Ross has a negative view of TSSI and suggests that the approach maintains the guise of control through replicating a solitary reality or construction of knowledge. In terms of informational text literacy development, Leming's approach promotes the idea that students must first understand, develop, and fine-tune knowledge for effective informational text literacy. From this point of view, to ask students to think critically in any context prior to such mastery of basic facts would be not only inappropriate in relation to the sequence in which students learn material, but would also be a disservice and a hindrance to a students' literacy education.

Ross: The Democratic Citizenship Approach

Unlike Leming, Ross (2000) promotes an approach to social studies education known as the *democratic citizenship approach* (DCA). In this view, citizenship education is the ultimate goal of social studies instruction; that is, students should not be taught in a way that makes them merely parts of a global capitalist economy. The emphasis is not on vocabulary terms or factual information. Instead, this pedagogy attempts to motivate students to "question, understand, and test the reality of the social world we inhabit," which are essential skills for full participation in a democracy (Ross, 2000, p. 59). This echoes Karp (2007), who notes:

> If we recognize that effective education requires students to bring their real lives into the classrooms and to take what they learn back to their homes and neighborhoods in the form of new understandings and new behavior, how can we not do the same? Critical teaching should not be merely an abstraction or academic formula for classroom "experimentation." It should be a strategy for educational organizing that changes lives, including our own. (p. 189)

DAY	MONDAY	TUESDAY	WEDNESDAY	THURSDAY	FRIDAY
Text	*The Bill of Rights*	*The Bill of Rights*	*The Gettysburg Address*	*The Gettysburg Address*	*The Bill of Rights/ The Gettysburg Address*
Comprehension Activity	**Activation of Prior Knowledge:** • Use book cover to engage in conversation to access students' prior knowledge surrounding topic. **Teacher Talk:** • Emphasize importance of dates (e.g., 1776, 1777, 1781, 1791).	**Informational Text Understanding:** • Determine text structure and develop understanding for quick reference cues to determine structure. **Information Building:** • Understand important information (e.g., civil liberties, American revolution, the Articles of Confederation).	**Prior Knowledge Activation:** • Use book cover to engage in conversation to access student prior knowledge surrounding topic. **Timeline Analysis:** • Read and identify significant dates associated with The Bill of Rights and other movements.	**Hands-On Activity:** • Recreate timeline represented in book to reinforce important events and information.	**Team Vocabulary/ Comprehension Game:** • Teachers create questions related to dates, specific vocabulary, people and what they did, etc., to assess student comprehension.

FIGURE 9.2. Example of a TSSI weekly plan.

These statements promote a social studies education directed toward "outcomes and consequences that matter"—not merely standardized test results (Ross, p. 59).

The DCA and the TSSI approaches offer students similar learning opportunities, but the DCA includes citizenship education related to race and equality issues. Two sections of *The Bill of Rights* book, "Other Important Amendments" and "Civil Liberties for All," allow for teacher-directed and student-involved discussions surrounding the issue of *equality*. Students can potentially discuss for whom equality was initially meant (i.e., white, land-owning males of age), based on information presented in the text. They eventually understand how the concept of *equality* has changed to encompass ever-expanding groups of people. Given the students' ages and/or backgrounds, some may have explored such topics before. Their existing knowledge can be used to lead a discussion that tackles how various minority groups (e.g., Native Americans, African Americans, females, and immigrants) might have been affected by equality issues in the United States. Other notable discussions stemming from the DCA approach in the PAL Program included the gender–wage gap, Native American forced migration, slavery, voting rights, and segregation. The point, here, is that history education and informational text literacy are transformed into areas of study based on student-driven discussion, interaction, and contemplation about societal issues.

In our PAL classroom, one discussion led students to question whether segregation still persists in American society. Students made value judgments about such questions based on what they already knew and what they gleaned from the text. Equally important, they learned how to pursue a respectful discussion in the face of opposing opinions, a positive feature of the DCA, as it promotes habits of respect amid diversity. In fact, the opposing views expressed prompted some students to apply this classroom question to their communities; days later, students could still be heard discussing their arguments based on their observations made outside of school. At this point, students have taken a topic about a past issue (that is, segregation being taught as a past problem that had been resolved) and applied it actively to their own lives.

While prior knowledge and content are necessary to the DCA approach, as it is to the TSSI approach, student-driven discussion is one of the DCA's primary learning platforms. Children learn to discuss points of view by adhering to information presented in the text and integrating this information into their prior knowledge and experiences.

Figure 9.3 outlines a lesson plan emulating the goals associated with the DCA to social studies education. Note that this lesson plan does not completely conform to our use of the variant of the Wide FORI approach that emphasized reading multiple texts around a theme each week. Instead of this multiple-text approach, because the book was long we divided it into two to four sections and read part of the book each day using the fluency-oriented activities, but oriented the discussions

DAY	MONDAY	TUESDAY	WEDNESDAY	THURSDAY	FRIDAY
Text Sections	*The Bill of Rights:* Declaring Independence, The Articles of Confederation, The Constitutional Convention	*The Bill of Rights:* Human Rights, A New Constitution, No Bill of Rights?, Ratification of the Constitution	*The Bill of Rights:* The Bill of Rights Is Approved, The Preamble to the Bill of Rights	*The Bill of Rights:* The First Ten Amendments, Other Important Amendments, Timeline	*The Bill of Rights:* Civil Liberties for All, Preserving the Document
Comprehension Activity	**Activation of Prior Knowledge:** • Conversation about what the Bill of Rights means in connection with modern movements (e.g., women's rights, civil rights).	**Group Discussion:** • Analyze and discuss portion titled "Human Rights." • Guide discussion to address extent to which The Bill of Rights is reflective of ideals about human rights.	**Group Discussion:** • Analyze and discuss portion titled "The Bill of Rights Is Approved." Use section one of The Bill of Rights to question the statement "That all men are by nature equally free and independent." • Address students' prior knowledge to evaluate this claim.	**Group Activity:** • Students work in groups of two and are assigned two to three amendments to analyze and describe instances when their rights have been dismissed. A group discussion will follow to address all 10 amendments in detail.	**Group Discussion:** • Discuss and analyze portion titled "Civil Liberties for All." Consider the progression in which The Bill of Rights became more inclusive but not all-encompassing. • Discussion questioning in what ways segregation and racial injustice exist today.

FIGURE 9.3. Example of a DCA lesson plan.

and activities around the DCA. Breaking up the text in this way gave the students increased time for the extensive discussions and other required DCA activities designed for student-derived meaning making.

Bain: The Discipline Approach

Like the TSSI approach, this approach also requires students to learn facts and vocabulary related to a discipline. However, Bain (2008) asserts that, "historians work to give meaning to historical facts, while students must work to give meaning to their historical experiences" (p. 332). Bain's approach to social studies education mirrors the disciplinary approach to literacy in that it, too, emphasizes disciplinary strategies used to analyze the texts. According to Bain, the disciplinary approach to history is one that includes determining problems, working with evidence, and creating evidence-based claims within the discipline (see also, Wineburg, 1994). In the disciplinary approach to literacy, persons use their understanding of how such work is carried out to understand the significance of informational texts.

From a discipline perspective, the text *The Bill of Rights* is ideal for replicating a historian's approach to text. In general, historians incorporate firsthand sources into history construction, and this text provides ample opportunities for readers to interact with a few of these primary resources. For example, the authors included an excerpt from the Bill of Rights, portraits of influential leaders, and photographs of events from several minority civil rights movements. From an educational perspective, these historical documents not only promote an understanding of how historians use sources to construct history, but also reduce the potential for significant bias and inaccurate historical arguments. Figure 9.4 outlines a lesson plan from the PAL Program that can be used to support comprehension using the discipline approach.

An important strategy related to the discipline approach is the *history events chart*. Shanahan and Shanahan (2008) described this as a strategy in which students "write down answers to the questions of who, what, where, when, (how), and why in order to summarize the key narrative events" (p. 55). At its core, this strategy requires students to model the general questions historians ask when interpreting history. The first four questions are straightforward and relatively simple to answer, but the last question, "why," requires higher-order thinking and a deeper understanding of the relationships between multiple events. In the discipline approach, the importance to history usually requires students to show the connection between one historical event (i.e., the Bill of Rights) and another (i.e., the Civil Rights Movement). Historical figures, on the other hand, are typically considered important for their accomplishments for the greater good or within certain movements. The history events chart from *The Bill of Rights* text is an example of this strategy.

DAY	MONDAY	TUESDAY	WEDNESDAY	THURSDAY	FRIDAY
Text	*The Bill of Rights*	*The Bill of Rights*	*The Bill of Rights*	*The Gettysburg Address*	*The Gettysburg Address*
Comprehension Activity	**Activation of Prior Knowledge:** • Address questions relevant to whom The Bill of Rights applied to across time and what it meant to those individuals.	**History Events Chart:** • Select one or two key events, people, or documents to answer the six questions: who, what, when, where, why, and importance to history. **Vocabulary Development:** • Students work in groups and write vocabulary words (e.g., *militia, parchment, parliament, ratified*) on a large sticky note. For each word, students write the definition found in the glossary, write a sentence from the text where the word is found, and create a new sentence modeling appropriate use of the word.	**Applied History Events Chart:** • Students generate formal written responses specifically for the term The Bill of Rights.	**Vocabulary Development:** • Students work in groups and write vocabulary words (e.g., *abolished, census, Emancipation Proclamation, orator*) on a large sticky note. For each word, students write the definition found in the glossary, write a sentence from the text where the word is found, and create a new sentence modeling appropriate use of the word.	**Timeline Analysis:** • Students re-create timeline depicted in text, selecting certain events most important to The Gettysburg Address and proceeding effects. Under each event, students answer the six questions: who, what, when, where, why, and importance to history.

FIGURE 9.4. Example of a discipline approach weekly plan.

History Events Chart for the Bill of Rights

Who: American citizens (p. 4), white land-owning males of age, women, minorities
   (p. 26)
What: Basic rights guaranteed to all American citizens (p. 4)
Where: America (p. 6)
When: 1700s, 18th century and forward (pp. 8, 10, and 14)
Significance to history (why?): This written document established the precedent that all
      men were equal, which led to the 13th, 14th, and 15th amendments, as well as the
      women's rights and civil rights movements.

First, students answer the five questions shown above. Note the emphasis on citing specific page numbers. This chart not only emulates the positive practices from the field of history, but it also serves as a quick reference guide for addressing further questions. Then students are asked to connect their answers to each of the questions in written paragraph form as shown in the following example.

History Events Chart for the Bill of Rights: Formal Academic Writing

The Bill of Rights is an American document written in the 18th century that guaranteed basic rights to all American citizens. Citizens, at this point, were white, land-owning males; however, women, African Americans, and other minorities were given those rights later on. This document remains important to American history, as it established the precedent that all men are created equal. Such a precedent was used to create the 13th, 14th, and 15th amendments, which abolished slavery, and extended citizenship and voting rights to African Americans. Further significance can be found in later movements, like the Women's Rights Movement and the Civil Rights Movement.

Students in the PAL Program emulated this process effectively and had no serious problems. They seemed to have little difficulty in deriving the information based on the explicit questions of who, what, where, when), but had tremendous difficulty evaluating and attributing historical significance posed by the "why" question. After-school instructors will need to walk elementary school children carefully through the process of evaluating social studies texts for their historical significance using this disciplinary approach.

Using a Combination of Social Studies Approaches in ASPs

In the PAL Program, we used elements of each of these three approaches to varying degrees depending on the nature of the books and topics we were covering that week. If the books provided original documents, the discipline approach was used. If the books covered topics that required critical analysis, the DCA was used. For other topics that were less controversial and perhaps less thought provoking, such as landscape forms, an approach closer to the TSSI was used. At the elementary school level, providing children with a variety of social studies approaches to understanding social studies texts is reasonable and appropriate.

Connecting Social Studies to Content Literacy Instruction

There are clear similarities between the literacy approaches and the social studies education approaches to informational text comprehension. Therefore, the following sections discuss several studies that have connected social studies approaches with informational text literacy instruction.

The CLP and Ross

In many ways, the CLP and the Ross (2000) DCA have similar goals. As mentioned earlier in brief detail, the CLP "curriculum allows students to develop necessary dispositions to think as social scientists, develop abilities to take a critical posture toward content, and develop their capacities to transfer social studies concepts to their own lives (Soares & Woods, 2010, p. 487). In much the same sense, Ross (2000) asserts that teaching through the DCA requires inquiry into the issues facing people in their day-to-day lives. Both present alternative ways to model social studies instruction as a curriculum that places issues such as racial prejudice, inequality, and racism at the forefront of education.

Disciplinary Literacy Instruction and Bain

The disciplinary literacy instruction approach asserts that each discipline encompasses unique practices in how the "disciplines create, disseminate, and evaluate knowledge" (Shanahan & Shanahan, 2008, p. 48). Shanahan and Shanahan distinguish between three levels of informational text literacy: basic literacy, intermediate literacy, and disciplinary literacy. *Basic literacy* is defined as "literacy skills such as decoding and knowledge of high-frequency words that underlie virtually all reading tasks" (e.g., the, have, because, of) (p. 44). *Intermediate literacy* is defined as "literacy skills common to many tasks, including generic comprehension strategies, common word meanings, and basic fluency" (p. 44). *Disciplinary literacy* on the other hand, is defined as "literacy skills specialized to history, science, mathematics, literature, or other subject matter" (e.g., derivative, natural selection) (p. 44). It is at the level of disciplinary literacy that students fail to master the skills needed in order to succeed with informational and content-specific literacy.

　　Achieving disciplinary literacy requires understanding that each discipline has its own specific literacy and vocabulary patterns, as well as universal patterns that can be found in any text. *The Bill of Rights*, for example, highlights the importance of vocabulary primarily found in history (e.g., Bill of Rights, Parliament, American Revolution, and Articles of Confederation). In other areas of study, discipline-specific vocabulary might include *supply* and *demand* (economics), *alternator* and *carburetor* (mechanics), *amortization* and *depreciation* (business), and *mountain* and *canyon* (geography). As such, texts from each discipline can be approached from the viewpoint of a professional in the field (e.g., as a historian, economist, or geographer, depending on the topic of the text).

In terms of comprehension strategies, Shanahan and Shanahan suggest several instructional approaches that might have some utility for both educators and students from both a social studies and disciplinary literacy perspective. One strategy is having students develop the *history events chart*, such as the one we described earlier. Another is the *multiple-gist strategy*, which requires students to read and summarize one text on a particular topic. Next, students read another text on the same topic and, then incorporate the summary of the first text into a summary of the second text. This process is repeated for a third text. This multiple-gist strategy allows students to compare and contrast and to synthesize information from among many texts. We did not use this strategy during the ASP because of the age of the children and the length of the after-school sessions. Besides, social studies text comprehension was only one of several goals that we had for the reading enrichment program, one of which was an intensive focus on improving children's general reading fluency as well.

The Decline of Social Studies
Instruction in Elementary School Classrooms

The purpose of this chapter has been to emphasize reading comprehension through the use of social studies informational text; however, a second purpose is to call attention to the seriously declining importance of social studies instruction at the elementary school level. In a study conducted by Perie (1997), elementary teachers spent 50% (2 hours per day) on English, reading, and other language arts curriculum, while social studies instruction received 13% (35 minutes per day). As a result of No Child Left Behind and subsequent Common Core and Race to the Top education initiatives, a fast-paced, standards approach to education has resulted in elementary school teachers emphasizing math and literacy instruction at the expense of social studies, among other subjects (e.g., science and arts) (Heafner & Fitchett, 2012).

Moreover, Heafner and Fitchett (2012) present national findings that suggest social studies instruction has decreased on average of 17 minutes per week, while reading instruction has increased by 40 minutes per week. Other reports indicate more substantial decreases in social studies instruction. Between 1993 and 2008, third- through fifth-grade social studies instruction decreased by 56 minutes per week. This trend continued in the early and mid-2000s, with a further decrease of 19 minutes spent on social studies instruction per week (see Heafner & Fitchet, 2012). In more current contexts, Fitchett, Heafner, and VanFossen (2014) reported that first- through fifth-grade teachers spend only 30 minutes per week on social studies in states that require social studies standardized testing. In those states without testing on the subject, teachers spend 18 hours less per year on social studies instruction.

Despite being viewed as one of the four core content areas (e.g., English, math, social studies, and science) in education, there has been a dramatic decrease in instructional time devoted to social studies as a result of testing and the emphasis placed on math and reading, in particular. At its most basic, this lack of instructional attention does not allow students to learn important social studies content. To a greater extent, though, this emphasis on math and reading diminishes the role and importance of social studies in the lives of young people. If at a young age, students are not discussing the issues of racism, equality, and violence, and this trend continues into middle and high school, students may be unable to critically engage with the world they inhabit as adults. This chapter, in general, has attempted to demonstrate the ways in which the PAL ASP attempted to combine social studies and reading in order to counteract these regressively negative trends in education.

Implications for ASPs

The focus of this chapter has been on social studies literacy. We have shown how various instructional strategies can be incorporated in ASPs that include content-area literacy. However, it is important to recognize that many of the strategies described would apply to other types of informational text literacy, including comprehension of science texts and other forms of informational text literacy. More important, we found that a continued focus on informational text literacy has promoted the PAL Program's literacy goals in a way that not only emphasized the students' basic skills for general reading fluency, but also improved their comprehension of informational texts. ASPs related to reading enrichment can and probably should approach their task as a multifaceted one.

GLOSSARY

Critical literacy—An approach to reading instruction that focuses on the political, cultural, historical, and economic impacts on text.

Democratic citizens approach—An approach to teaching children how to interpret social studies texts by questioning, understanding, and evaluating them so that they become better participants in a democracy.

Discipline(ary) approach—An approach to teaching the discipline and understanding associated informational texts that takes into account the disciplinary practices and understandings used to create them.

History events chart—An approach in which students write down answers to the questions of who, what, where, when, how, and why in order to summarize the key narrative events.

Story grammar—Typical information present in most stories judged to be good stories, such as characters, location, initiating events, protagonists' responses and plans, goal attempts, outcomes, and reactions. Readers use this schema to understand and recall story information.

Traditional social studies instruction approach—An approach to understanding informational text that focuses on having students master the content of the text, not evaluating it.

References

Bain, R. B. (2008). Into the breach: Using research and theory to shape history instruction. *Journal of Education, 189,* 159–167.

Beck, I. L., & McKeown, M. G. (2006). *Improving comprehension with questioning the author.* New York: Scholastic.

Brewer, W. F., & Lichtenstein, E. H. (1982). Stories are to entertain: A structural-affect theory of stories. *Journal of Pragmatics, 6*(5), 473–486.

Collin, R. (2014). A Bersteinian analysis of content area literacy. *Journal of Literacy Research, 46*(3), 306–329.

Fang, Z. (2008). Going beyond the fab five: Helping students cope with the unique linguistic challenges of expository reading in intermediate grades. *Journal of Adolescent and Adult Literacy, 6,* 476.

Fang, Z. (2012). Approaches to developing content area literacies: A synthesis and a critique. *Journal of Adolescent and Adult Literacy, 56,* 103–108.

Fitchett, P. G., Heafner, T. L., & VanFossen, P. (2014). An analysis of time prioritization for social studies in elementary school classrooms. *Journal of Curriculum and Instruction, 8*(2), 7–35.

Gee, J. P. (2010). A situated-sociocultural approach to literacy and technology. In E. A. Baker (Ed.), *The new literacies: Multiple perspectives on research and practice* (pp. 165–193). New York: Guilford Press.

Hall-Kenyon, K. M., & Black, S. (2010). Learning from expository texts: Classroom-based strategies for promoting comprehension and content knowledge in the elementary grades. *Topics in Language Disorders, 30*(4), 339–349.

Halvorsen, A. L., Duke, N. K., Brugar, K. A., Block, M. K., Strachan, S. L., Berka, M. B., & Brown, J. M. (2012). Narrowing the achievement gap in second-grade social studies and content area literacy: The promise of a project-based approach. *Theory and Research in Social Studies Education, 40,* 198–229.

Heafner, T. L., & Fitchett, P. G. (2012). National trends in elementary instruction: Exploring the role of social studies curricula. *Social Studies, 103*(2), 67–72.

Karp, S. (2007). Why we need to go beyond the classroom. In W. Au, B. Bigelow,

& S. Karp (Eds.), *Rethinking our classrooms: Teaching for equity and justice* (pp. 188–191). Milwaukee, WI: Rethinking Schools.

Kintsch, W. (1998). *Comprehension: A paradigm for cognition.* New York: Cambridge University Press.

Kintsch, W. (2004). The construction-integration model of text comprehension and its implications for instruction. In N. Onrau & R. B. Ruddell (Eds.), *Theoretical model and process of reading* (Vol. 5, pp. 1270–1328). Newark, DE: International Reading Association.

Leming, J. S. (1994). Past as prologue: A defense of traditional patterns of social studies construction. In M. Nelson (Ed.), *The future of social studies* (pp. 35–41). Boulder, CO: Social Science Education Consortium.

McKeown, M., Beck, I., & Blake, R. (2009). Rethinking reading comprehension instruction: A comparison of instruction for strategies and content approaches. *Reading Research Quarterly, 44*(3), 218–253.

Miller, M., & Veatch, N. (2010). Teaching literacy in context: Choosing and using instructional strategies. *The Reading Teacher, 64*(3), 154–165.

O'Connor, R. E., Beach, K. D., Sanchez, V. M., Bocian, K. M., & Flynn, L. J. (2015). Building BRIDGES: A design experiment to improve reading and United States history knowledge of poor readers in eighth grade. *Exceptional Children, 81*(4), 399–425.

Perie, M. (1997). *Time spent teaching core academic subjects in elementary schools: Comparisons across community, school, teacher, and student characteristics.* Washington, DC: U.S. Government Printing Office.

Ross, E. W. (2000). Redrawing the lines: The case against traditional social studies instruction. In D. Hursch & E. W. Ross (Eds.), *Democratic social education: Social studies for social change* (pp. 43–63). New York: Falmer Press.

Shanahan, T., & Shanahan, C. (2008). Teaching disciplinary literacy to adolescents: Rethinking content-area literacy. *Harvard Educational Review, 78*(1), 40–59.

Soares, L. B., & Wood, K. (2010). A critical literacy perspective for teaching and learning social studies. *The Reading Teacher, 63*(6), 486–494.

Stein, N. L., & Nezworski, T. (1978). The effects of organization and instructional set on story memory. *Discourse Processes, 1*(2), 177–193.

Vaughn, S., Swanson, E. A., Roberts, G., Wanzek, J., Stillman-Spisak, S. J., Solis, M. & Simmons, D. (2013). Improving Reading Comprehension and Social Studies Knowledge in Middle School. *Reading research Quarterly, 48*(1), 77–93.

Wineburg, S. S. (1994). The cognitive representation of historical texts. In G. Leinhardt, I. L. Beck, & C. Stainton (Eds.), *Teaching and learning in history* (pp. 85–135). Hillsdale, NJ: Erlbaum.

Social Studies Resources Cited

Armentrout, D., & Armentrout, P. (2005). *The Bill of Rights.* Marlborough, MA: Newbridge Educational.

Armentrout, D., & Armentrout, P. (2005). *The Gettysburg Address.* Marlborough, MA: Newbridge Educational.

Fifer, B. (2005). *After the attack.* Glenview, IL: Scott Foresman.

McLeese, D. (2005). *Phyllis Wheatley.* Marlborough, MA: Newbridge Educational.

McLeese, D. (2005). *Crispus Attucks.* Marlborough, MA: Newbridge Educational.

Miller, M. (2008). *It's a fair swap!* Glenview, IL: Scott Foresman.

Nichols, C. (2006). *African American culture.* New York: Newbridge Educational.

Stone, L. (2002). *America's landscape.* Vero Beach, FL: Rourke Educational Media.

Toor, A. (2006). *Islamic culture.* New York: Newbridge Educational.

10

The PAL Reading Enrichment Program in an Experimental After-School Setting

Megan P. Brock
Paula J. Schwanenflugel

The intention of the Physical Activity and Learning (PAL) Program was to address the academic, social, and physical needs of students. It was designed for the purpose of providing optimal socialization and learning experiences in a safe, supportive environment. Academically, the program's directors and staff worked to improve students' performance in reading and mathematics. In this chapter we describe the reading enrichment intervention conducted as part of the PAL Program and evaluate its success.

Reading well is an important contributor to academic success. Many children who participated in the program were identified by their schools as not meeting curricular goals for achieving the necessary minimum standard score on the English language arts assessment of the state-mandated assessment in the prior year, called the criterion-referenced competency test (CRCT). In addition, reading fluency assessments administered by the PAL reading enrichment specialists at the beginning of the program revealed that 75% of students referred to the PAL Program scored within the bottom quartile of the oral-reading fluency norms reported by Hasbrouck and Tindal (2006). Fluency is considered an essential element of reading proficiency (Rasinski, 2014). The decision was made in the after-school reading enrichment program to focus on children's oral reading fluency as the major skill target and on comprehension of informational text as the secondary target skill.

What Research Says about Improving
Reading in Middle-to-Late Elementary School

The PAL Program's literacy enrichment intervention was grounded in prior research that took place in second-grade classrooms that showed improvements in reading fluency and comprehension through the use of instructional strategies emphasizing both repeated readings and a variety of texts (Kuhn et al., 2006; Schwanenflugel et al., 2009). Accurate reading, automatic word reading, and good oral reading expression are three elements that together characterize fluent reading. Ultimately, to be a fluent reader is to engage in effortless, accurate reading with adequate expression during oral reading that conveys an understanding of the text being read. The Common Core State Standards Initiative (2016) identifies reading fluency as a foundational reading skill. Fluency is acknowledged as the bridge between word recognition and comprehension of the text, as indicated by the high correlation between the two skills in elementary school. Because of this high correlation, oral reading fluency is a major indicator of reading proficiency during elementary school and beyond (Schwanenflugel & Kuhn, 2016).

According to Rasinski (2014), early elementary school children who have issues with reading fluency may continue to struggle with literacy in general in upper elementary, middle, and secondary grades. Rasinski, Rupley, Paige, and Nichols (2016) suggest that students in the primary grades who are disfluent readers should engage in meaningful, authentic instruction activities specifically crafted to improve their fluency. *Wide reading* and repeated readings are important tools for teaching fluency—both of which are implemented in the PAL reading enrichment program. Wide reading refers to the reading of a great number of texts. *Repeated reading* refers to the rereading of a text to improve the fluency with which the child can read it. Often, children do not have enough oral reading practice with given texts in the classroom to achieve fluency (Rasinski, 2012; Kuhn, Rasinski, & Zimmerman, 2014). Further, typical oral reading routines in classrooms consist of a scant few minutes a day of practice. Thus, children often move from text to text, never having the opportunity to learn how to read fluently.

The weekly plan for the PAL Program models that of previous large-scale interventions for improving classroom fluency instruction, while also supporting children's comprehension skills through various oral reading strategies (Kuhn et al., 2006; Schwanenflugel et al., 2009). The Wide Fluency Oriented Reading Instruction (FORI) approach combines elements of repeated reading, wide reading, and comprehension activities. Kuhn et al. (2006) and Schwanenflugel et al. (2009) found that the Wide FORI approach was more consistently effective for improving fluency and comprehension compared to approaches that leaned more heavily on repeated reading practice (and control practices). This approach assisted students in developing textual fluency, prosody, and comprehension by employing instructional principles such as modeling, scaffolding, and repetition.

The Wide FORI Approach

The Wide FORI approach was developed and evaluated by Kuhn and her colleagues (Kuhn et al., 2006; Schwanenflugel et al., 2009), and is designed as a whole-class program, although the approach can also be used with small groups of children (see Kuhn, 2005). Teachers implemented evaluation studies in second-grade classrooms where many children experienced difficulties in learning to read well. There was reason to believe, however, that it might be a reasonable strategy for use in the after-school setting because the program had a clear structure and a consistent lesson plan that was amenable to a routine. The fluency strategies also were relatively simple to implement.

Despite the fact that the Wide FORI approach had been evaluated with younger elementary school children only, we decided to experiment with using the approach in the PAL Program with older elementary school children in grades three through five. Children typically transition from choppy, inaccurate, slow reading to fluent oral reading of grade-level texts during the second and third grades. However, as noted earlier, fluency issues often persist well beyond third grade, and we reasoned that the Wide FORI approach might be appropriate for older children as well, particularly the kind of struggling readers that we were trying to reach in the after-school program (ASP). These children tended to have basic reading skills but lacked fluency and comprehension, the two skills for which the Wide FORI approach had proved to be effective.

In the Wide FORI, students engage in repeated oral reading of various texts and engage in related activities at least once each week. At the beginning of the week, the adult who is leading the readings provides a high degree of support. As the week progresses, guidance is slowly relinquished so that, as students become more skilled, they gain more autonomy in reading the text.

The approach requires that each child have his or her own copy of the text being read or, at minimum, one that can be shared with another student as they sit reading it side by side. Ensuring enough copies necessitates a materials budget for books. The approach also requires that children are reading books at their grade level, even if it is beyond individual children's current skills. To ensure that grade-level books were being used, Kuhn and her colleagues supplied them (with input from the teacher).

The Wide FORI uses various strategies to engage in repeated oral readings of text. Teacher-led read-alouds, echo reading, choral reading, and partner reading are four oral reading activities in particular that are used interchangeably throughout the week (Kuhn et al., 2006; Schwanenflugel et al., 2009). These strategies are described in next sections.

Teacher–Led Read–Alouds

During a teacher-led read-aloud, the students are instructed to listen to the teacher read the selected text aloud while they follow along in their own text. Sometimes pointers, such as popsicle sticks, are used to emphasize following along in the text. While reading aloud, the teachers roam the room actively determining that the children are, indeed, following along, moving children's hands to the correct location in the text if they have lost their place.

Echo Reading

In echo reading, a teacher reads two to three sentences from the text aloud before asking the students to read, or *echo*, the same passage of text aloud. The teacher's resonating voice models the volume and pace in which the text should be read by students. The children then repeat aloud what the teacher has just read, while the teacher reads along with them. Echo reading requires teachers to read just enough text so that children cannot simply parrot back the text without looking at it. The amount of text in each echoed segment needs to exceed working memory so that children have to focus on the text when it is their turn to read.

Choral Reading

As in echo reading, the teachers and students both read the same passage aloud, together in unison. The teacher's voice guides the pace and volume of the reading. Teachers canvas the room to prevent social loafing, listening to the children to ensure that all are, indeed, reading along with the class.

Partner Reading

For partner reading, the teacher pairs students according to reading proficiency and behavior. Ideally, a student with somewhat higher reading proficiency is paired with one having lower proficiency so that at least one in the pair has the skills to support the other in reading challenging passages. Children alternate reading pages aloud, usually with the child on the left reading the left-hand page of the open book and the child on the right reading the right-hand side. Teachers monitor that children are either reading aloud or helping each other when they get stuck on a word.

The Wide FORI approach follows a weekly plan. On the first day of the week, the text is read aloud *to* the students *by* the teacher, who stops once in a while to point out various features of the text for comprehension. The teacher might pause to identify vocabulary words, ask questions for comprehension, or point out genre-specific features such as headings, boldfaced words, and so forth.

On the second day of the week, children echo read the text after the teacher first models the segment. Children are allowed to partner read if time permits. Again, the teacher can query for comprehension.

On the third day of the week, a second book is introduced. The teacher leads the students in a discussion of the newly introduced text. They then engage in a choral reading of the book. The fourth day of the week consists of partner reading this second text. The students are also able to participate in a hands-on activity that relates to the overarching theme (if there is one) that connects the various texts for the week. Having an overarching theme allows for some commonality and repetition among the words and ideas expressed in the texts, that work toward developing a knowledge base and related vocabulary concepts. This repetition may help with later comprehension.

On the last day, the third and final book for the week is introduced and echo read by students and the teacher. They then discuss the text. Each day the book can be read aloud again as homework.

Prior Evaluations of Wide FORI Effectiveness

In the initial exploration of the effectiveness of the Wide FORI approach, Kuhn et al. (2006) randomly assigned second-grade classrooms to one of three literacy instruction approaches: a Wide FORI approach, a basic FORI approach in which one text was read repeatedly during the week, or a business-as-usual approach in which no particular fluency instruction method was emphasized. The basic FORI and the Wide FORI approaches were identical in that daily fluency activities took place (choral, echo, and/or partner reading), but only on a single text each week. The approaches differed only in the number of texts children read aloud each week (three versus one). The teachers in the Wide FORI condition focused on a blended approach of repeated reading using fluency-oriented strategies but they were applied to a variety of texts each week. Teachers assigned to the basic FORI and Wide FORI conditions received professional development to implement the condition's respective fluency activities in whole-class reading. Those assigned to the control group (the business-as-usual group) used whatever literacy strategies they normally chose for fluency, generally round-robin reading and reading work-shops (Kuhn et al., 2006).

The study reported that teachers who received professional development on the fluency-oriented instruction interventions spent a greater part of their class-room reading instruction using fluency activities compared to teachers not receiv-ing the professional development. Furthermore, the basic FORI and Wide FORI approaches were both effective in improving the reading skills of second-grade students (Kuhn et al., 2006). Second graders in both the basic FORI and Wide FORI conditions showed significant growth in word reading efficiency and reading comprehension compared to the control group, but only the Wide FORI approach improved reading fluency as well.

Schwanenflugel et al. (2009) extended the inquiry to evaluate both short- and long-term effects of the programs on the development of reading skills. They found that, at the end of second grade, children in the Wide FORI group had developed better reading fluency. They also had improved reading motivation in that they had developed a better reading self-concept compared to control children. By the end of third grade, they also showed better reading comprehension skills.

The findings of these two studies demonstrated the effectiveness of Wide FORI. It seemed to be beneficial for achieving a range of important reading skills: word reading efficiency, reading comprehension, and fluency. The decision was then made to adopt the Wide FORI approach in the PAL Program.

Wide FORI in the PAL Program: A Focus on Informational Texts

In the PAL Program, the weekly plan reflected that of the Wide FORI program, except that the target of the oral readings was informational text. Each week children read two-to-three informational texts related to a particular topic, while engaging in the core fluency-oriented practices (i.e., echo reading, choral reading, and partner reading). The decision to work with informational texts was made because, in the primary grades, little emphasis is placed on content-area literacy in subjects such as social studies and science, despite the fact that integration of content literacy is integral to academic achievement as children advance in their schooling (Halvorsen et al., 2012; Vitale & Romance, 2011). Students spend much of their early reading time on narrative texts, which follow a very different schema. Informational texts are designed to be learned from—they convey factual information, often contain much new vocabulary, and introduce new concepts. Students are left at a disadvantage once they enter fourth grade, because they are expected to smoothly transition to informational texts, which are now used more heavily than before (Hall, Sabey, & McClellan, 2005). The new requirements of the Common Core State standards should ameliorate this issue somewhat. These standards require children to transition toward having half of their total reading materials be informational texts by the end of elementary school. Duke (2000) stated that many students struggle with texts that are organized in unfamiliar informational text schemas because the knowledge of and familiarity with these schemas are integral to comprehension of the text content. This claim is corroborated by reports of the decline in reading achievement after third grade, which has been termed the *fourth-grade slump* (Chall, Jacobs, & Baldwin, 1990). Students are likely to struggle in the fourth grade when comprehension requires the ability to learn from text content in informational texts (Chall & Jacobs, 1983).

Research has shown that effective incorporation of informational texts in the primary grades can lead to success with reading and comprehending informational texts (Hall, Sabey, & McClellan, 2005; Halvorsen et al., 2012; Williams et al., 2007). Williams et al. (2007) and Hall et al. (2005) argue that the emphasis on content and informational text features helps students acquire background knowledge of respective disciplines and familiarity with features of the genres. Because a familiarity with informational text is crucial in future schooling, the PAL staff decided to incorporate explicit instruction of informational text features within lessons to build students' informational text literacy skills. Planning included attention to vocabulary, text structures, and text features—all of which are seen as necessary in understanding informational texts (Hoffman, Collins, & Shickedanz, 2015). Instructors used various instructional methods, such as incorporating disciplinary and critical analysis strategies, as explained in Chapter 9. These strategies were carried out, where relevant, within the context of Wide FORI fluency programming as a way of improving children's understanding of informational text. Each week, however, our instruction included some elements related to strategies for comprehension of informational text.

Emphasis on Vocabulary

Instructors chose no more than ten vocabulary words from each book to address throughout the week. The instructors explicitly emphasized and defined those words while reading the texts with the students so that they understood the meaning of those words as represented within the context of the book. This was typically done by pausing during the oral reading activity and either explaining or querying the meaning of the terms for the students or encouraging students to infer the meaning of new words from context. Often, the teacher encouraged students to use informational text features, such as the glossary, to both determine the meaning of the text and also to become familiar with how to use a glossary. The teacher sometimes provided examples of how the word related to other subjects with which children were more familiar. At other times, particularly for the second and third grade students, the instructor encouraged students to engage in a word hunt, which allowed children to volunteer words from the text whose meaning was unfamiliar.

If affixes (prefixes or suffixes) were present, the instructor identified and explained the concept of affixes to the students. White, Sowell, and Yanagihara (1989) suggest that learning how to use affixes to infer potential meanings of words is a necessary vocabulary skill. Students should be able to identify a group of letters in a vocabulary word as an affix, "remove" the affix from the word to find the root word, and interpret how the affix changes the meaning of the word. A working knowledge of affixes is particularly important for understanding scientific words, and they are ubiquitous in science texts written for the fourth and fifth grades, we observed. By contrast, we found that such affixes were less common in social studies books and in other books designed for second- and third-grade children. In general, we found that affixes were difficult for children to identify, comprehend, and remember; so we gave explicit instruction addressing affixes when they appeared in text.

Emphasis on Structure

Informational texts often use a variety of text structures to present information (Meyer & Poon, 2001; Price, Bradley, & Smith, 2012). Text structures determine how information is organized within the text, and they consist of the following forms.

Sequence Structure

In sequence texts, text content is organized in a manner in which the order of the content is salient to understanding. For example, when explaining a process that occurs in a science text, authors might discuss the steps taken to achieve a particular result. For example, an author might discuss the processes of transpiration, evaporation, condensation, and precipitation in the order that they occur when explaining the water cycle.

Description Structure

In a description text, authors provide details about a single subject. For example, in a text about butterflies the author may entitle the text "Butterflies" before subsequently providing information about the classification of the insect, its habits, and its reproduction ability, among other details.

Compare–Contrast Structure

In a compare–contrast text, authors discuss similarities and differences between subjects. For example, in a text about adaptive behaviors, the author may discuss how animals, such as the brown bear and the polar bear, adapt to environments with adverse climates. Within the text, the author may discuss similarities and differences between the bears' fur coats, hunting behaviors, and hibernation patterns.

Problem–Solution Structure

In a problem–solution text, authors may discuss a particular issue before providing information regarding the manner in which the problems are resolved. For example, in texts about sustainability, authors may discuss how the increase in development, or construction, projects that urbanize our communities leads to the loss of land, among other implications. Authors may then discuss some solutions that people have devised to address community problems caused by increasing construction, such as the emergence of land trusts and national/state parks to protect the land and its animal inhabitants.

Cause–Effect Structure

In a cause–effect text, authors reveal causal relationships. For example, when discussing the greenhouse effects an author may discuss how the rising amount of carbon dioxide released in the atmosphere may affect the earth's temperature.

Emphasis on Text Features

In contrast to narrative texts, informational texts often have features unique to the genre such as headings; bolded, highlighted, or otherwise formatted vocabulary words; glossaries containing significant words; an index; charts; graphs; maps; and other related elements (Meyer & Poon, 2001; Price et al., 2012). Just as the teacher identifies particular vocabulary words and text structures, he or she also can identify these text features in a meaningful way. For example, when the class is reading aloud and stumbles across a boldfaced vocabulary word, the teacher might ask the students why the font of the word is formatted in that manner and point to another text feature, the glossary, to find the meaning. To familiarize students with tables or charts, the instructor typically explicitly explains the subject of the graphic organizer before explaining how the content is organized. Once students become competent in recognizing text features, the instructor can transition to obtaining feedback from students about how they interpret features. In other words, once the teacher has explained the purpose of a table or chart in the initial reading of the text, he or she might ask the students questions that necessitate the use of the table or chart to answer them. The instructor might encourage the use of the table of contents by asking students about the type of information that might be found on a particular page of text.

The Wide FORI approach that was developed and adopted for the PAL intervention incorporated informational text strategies as sources of comprehensive support in developing reading skills related to informational texts. We emphasized instruction in vocabulary, explicit text structure, and explicit text features as a means of familiarizing students with informational texts and encouraging successful exploration of the texts. We wanted the children to understand content while building fluency skills through repeated, deep readings of the texts over the course of a week.

A Week in PAL Literacy Enrichment

Preparation for the PAL Literacy Enrichment began each week with selecting two or three books, depending on their length, around a topic or general theme. By combining information from these books, we enabled the children to develop a general knowledge base around the selected topic.

Fluency and comprehension activities were planned and organized in a manner in which autonomy was slowly relinquished to the students. Early in the week, the instructor would bear responsibility for reading and supporting comprehension of the text; by the end of the week, the children would be able to read aloud and comprehend the texts themselves. Fluency activities (teacher read-alouds, choral reading, echo reading, and partner reading) were strategically ordered to gradually increase autonomy around fluent oral reading; therefore, although the week began with the teacher reading the text aloud to the students, it ended with the students reading *with* the teacher during choral read-alouds or with another student in partner reading. While reading each book, the instructor created appropriate comprehension questions that emphasized key elements of the topic; selected topic vocabulary, features, and structures he or she would like to emphasize; and planned the hands-on related activity for enhancing student understanding of the selected topic. By the end of the week, students should develop sufficient understanding of basic concepts and vocabulary skills related to the topic to enable them to comprehend on their own a new text on the topic. They should be able to read grade-level books on that topic with some degree of fluency.

The goal in formulating comprehension questions was to create questions of various levels of abstractness around the acronym CAR (concrete, abstract, relate). *Concrete questions* are those whose answers can be found directly in the book and for which the information is explicitly represented in the text. *Abstract questions* ask children to make predictions, draw inferences, solve problems, and evaluate the information in the book. These are often questions that begin with *why* and *how. Relate questions* ask children to relate the information in the book to their own personal experiences and prior knowledge. For each book, the instructor created two inference-level, or abstract, questions, two concrete-level questions, and two questions to elicit students' prior knowledge. By including questions at these three levels of complexity, we encouraged children to comprehend deeply and to demonstrate what they have learned (see Hamilton & Schwanenflugel, 2011). The range in the level of abstractness of questions encouraged complex discourse about the text, but allowed all children to participate in the discussion (Zucker, Justice, Piasta, & Kaderavek, 2010). Questions of varying difficulty engaged students' cognition processes and produced richer dialogue.

In the instructor's copy of the text, instructors either wrote questions directly in the text or placed a sticky note where they believed it was most appropriate to ask the question. Similarly, instructors also made note of particular text features (bolded words, graphs, headings, etc.) and text structures (sequence, compare–contrast, etc.) that they explicitly addressed during the reading. They placed a sticky note near vocabulary words they wished to focus on.

These planning activities were completed ahead of time so that comprehension could be optimally addressed in the classroom. For example, in preparation for reading a text about predators of the ocean, the instructors placed a note to themselves on the page containing a table that compared and contrasted sharks. The note served as a reminder to explain why the book's text structure could be classified as compare–contrast. The instructor might also pose a question that required students to use the text's compare–contrast content in the graphic organizer, such as "How are hammerhead sharks and goblin shark similar and different?"

The PAL Program weekly plan also featured an enrichment activity that extended children's understanding of the weekly topic in some way. This activity usually followed the reading of the second book in the weekly plan and occurred generally on the fourth day. Having read a few books on the topic, students were able to maximally benefit from an activity that ideally allowed them to integrate information from the books and perhaps extend their knowledge of the topic even further. The activity planned for that week was typically inexpensive and took approximately 10–15 minutes to complete. For example, if the topic of the week was *the human body*, the instructor might look for age-appropriate videos explaining the various systems of the body discussed in the text. The instructor might use the various teacher-generated lessons available online that contained age-appropriate hands-on activities or games requiring minimal materials.

With only approximately 50 minutes available to incorporate all these activities, the instructor carefully planned the time allotted for each activity. For example, on days in which the teacher wished to conduct both choral and echo reading, he or she scheduled a transition approximately midway through the lesson time. The weekly plan presented in Figure 10.1 is a general example of the comprehension activities of a typical week in the ASP; Appendix 10.1 provides a specific example of one week's plan.

We elaborate on the plan in the following sections.

Day 1

On the first day of the week, the after-school instructor begins by activating students' prior knowledge of the topic of the books that will be read that week. This can be done by simply asking students to volunteer what they know about a particular subject. For example, if the topic of the week is *nutrition*, the after-school instructor might ask what students discussed regarding nutrition during the school day with their classroom teacher. Having gauged the level of students' knowledge of the subject, the teacher moves forward with a fluency activity. If he or she is working with second- and third-grade students, the session can begin with a teacher-led read-aloud of the text. (If the students are fundamentally more fluent and do not need this, the instructor can begin with echo or choral reading.) The students silently read along as the instructor reads the text aloud to them. Throughout this reading, the instructor may pause the teacher read-aloud to ask questions to gauge listening comprehension. For example, if the text discusses the significance of nutrition

DAY	MONDAY	TUESDAY	WEDNESDAY	THURSDAY	FRIDAY
Theme-related texts	Text 1	Text 1	Text 2	Text 2	Text 3
Fluency activities	• Teacher read-aloud • Echo reading	• Choral reading • Partner reading	• Echo reading • Choral reading • Partner reading*	• Choral reading • Partner reading	• Choral reading
Comprehension activities	• Discuss the theme • Activate prior knowledge • Introduce selected vocabulary • Comprehension questions • Word hunt	• Expository strategy—comprehension • Vocabulary query • Comprehension questions • Partner questioning	• Introduce new vocabulary • Word hunt • Comprehension questions • Partner questioning*	• Vocabulary query • Comprehension questions • Partner questioning • Hands-on activity	• Comprehension game

FIGURE 10.1. PAL reading enrichment weekly plan. The asterisk indicates that the particular activity is only performed if time permits. Also note that fluency and comprehension activities can be performed interchangeably throughout the reading enrichment session.

labels on food items and it provides an example of a nutrition label, the instructor may want to ask questions prompting students to dissect the example while also connecting the text to their own experiences: "How many calories per serving are in this item? Are there more or less calories in this item compared to the milk that you drank for snack?" (Note that the first of these questions would be considered a concrete question, whereas the second would be an abstract one.)

Once the read-aloud is complete, the instructor can then lead the students in echo reading. She or he may decide if they are fluent enough to transition to choral reading for the last few minutes of the reading enrichment lesson. Again, fluency activities can be paused at good stopping points during the reading to deal with comprehension.

Day 2

On the second day of the plan, fluency is emphasized again when the same text is read again as a choral reading. The instructor can pause to ask comprehension questions and address text structure/feature concerns as the text is read. Approximately halfway through the session, the instructor will transition students to partner reading. By this time, having read the text approximately four times, students should be fluent enough in their reading of it to be able to read with some minimal assistance from their partner. Students are encouraged to ask each other questions about the text when they finish reading it.

Day 3

The second text of the week is introduced on the third day. Once again, the instructor begins the lesson by asking two prior knowledge questions of the students. Then the instructor and students engage in an echo reading of the text. If they complete the reading of the text, the instructor can lead the students in choral reading to close out the session. As mentioned earlier, the instructor will have already placed or noted preconceived questions and activities within their own copy of the text to address during the readings.

Day 4

On the fourth day, the second book is read again, but this time using choral reading. The instructor still addresses comprehension questions and deals with issues of vocabulary, text features, text structures, and content, with notes strategically placed in the text as a reminder. After choral reading, students can be asked to partner read the text. Typically partner reading commences about halfway through the reading session to ensure that students are able to engage in all fluency activities. Then, the day ends by having students engage in the hands-on activity for the last 15–20 minutes of the session.

Day 5

On the last and final day, the instructor begins with a choral reading of the third text of the week. Mindful of the need to address the prepared questions placed in the text, the instructor should make sure to end the choral reading 20 minutes before the session ends. At this point, the students transition to play a comprehension "jeopardy" or "topic bee" comprehension-type game.

The comprehension bee serves as a way to assess what children have learned about the week's topic, review what they have learned, and help them integrate the knowledge they have learned from the assigned books. Students are organized into two teams; each child has the opportunity to answer a question about the topic from the week's readings. The game is played by having one member of each team move to the front of the classroom to answer a question. These students are instructed to raise their hand or use a bell or buzzer to indicate that they know the answer to the question the instructor poses. If the student responds incorrectly, the representative of the other team has an opportunity to answer. If no one answers correctly, the instructor reveals the correct answer. The comprehension game is an opportunity for friendly competition and assessment of students' understanding of the topic.

If students have access to personal laptops, the Kahoot game app (*https://kahoot.it/#*) can serve as an entertaining alternative. In this variant, students engage in the comprehension bee from their own seats. The instructor projects a multiple-choice question on the board while students answer the question from their own laptop. The number of students getting the item correct then appears on the screen. Troublesome questions can then be discussed as a class.

For the most part, we have used this lesson plan as a skeleton that guides our activities during the reading enrichment portion of the ASP. At times, we chose to extend the hands-on activity, add additional partner reading, or otherwise appropriately change the plan. Moreover, as children become fundamentally more fluent, it makes sense to skip the teacher read-aloud, and perhaps the echo reading as well, and just focus on choral and partner reading. In fact, this is what we did for fourth- and fifth-grade students during the second half of the year. If students seem to be able to execute a basic reading, albeit not 100% fluent, of the text, then it makes sense not to offer the heavy scaffolding the teacher read-aloud and echo reading provide. The important thing is to conduct fluency and comprehension activities every day. At a minimum, students should read 25–30 minutes during the reading enrichment period, apart from any discussion, questioning, or other activities that take place. This program ensures that children receive this type of reading practice every day.

In the PAL Program, we provided this intensive reading enrichment program for an hour each day for half the school year. In our program, second and third graders were placed in one group, and fourth and fifth graders were placed in another. When one group was participating in a reading enrichment, the other was participating in a math enrichment, as described in Chapter 7. In midyear, the children switched from one type of enrichment activity to the other. Our goal was to have sufficient intensity on a given set of skills to make a meaningful difference.

Program Effectiveness

We did a basic evaluation of the program's effectiveness each year of the program by measuring children's fluency in words correct per minute (WCPM), which is standard practice. Because some of the children in the program were receiving a math enrichment when the others were receiving a reading enrichment, this method of implementing the intervention in phases allowed us to use the group receiving the math enrichment as a control for evaluating the effectiveness of the reading enrichment. This helped control for the self-selection effects that plague the research evaluating ASPs. That is, children whose parents enroll them in ASPs might not be all that similar to children whose parents elect not to enroll them. In this case, the children being compared were all attending the PAL Program; the only difference was that all children were not currently receiving the reading enrichment. This allowed us to discern the value added by having a reading enrichment program such as this one.

The First Year

In the first year of the program, the reading enrichment focused on science texts. We hoped that concentrating on grade-level informational texts using the fluency-oriented practices as shown in Figure 10.1 would give children the instructional supports needed to improve their reading fluency. We evaluated the effectiveness of the program using fluency assessments collected prior to their participation in the intervention and then again at the end of the school year when the intervention was stopped. Both math-enrichment control children and reading-enrichment children were tested. Passages from the AIMSweb curriculum-based measurement (R-CBM; AIMSweb Technical Manual, 2012) were read aloud by each student. This assessment requires students to read three grade-level passages aloud for 1 minute, while the tester marks reading errors on her own copy of the assessment. WCPM for each of the passages is calculated, and the median score is used to reflect that child's reading fluency. This assessment was chosen because it is a widely used measure of fluency that has strong reliability and validity. There was a statistically significant assessment (pretest vs. posttest) × intervention type (reading intervention enrichment vs. mathematics enrichment control) interaction, $p <$ .05. Children who received the Wide FORI reading enrichment made greater progress on reading fluency than children who received the mathematics enrichment, as might be expected. (You can find the effectiveness of the mathematics enrichment on fluency skills in Chapter 7.) Improved fluency resulting from reading enrichment after 1 year can be seen in Figure 10.2.

Thus, the intervention was successful at improving the reading skill at which this intervention was heavily targeted: general reading fluency. Unfortunately, the AIMSweb assessment of fluency only included narrative passages. So, although our findings show that children were more generally fluent after the intervention than before, it did not show that we accomplished our goal of increasing children's fluency in reading informational text.

However, we did track children's performance as a class during the weekly Jeopardy!-type game on Fridays to discern whether their comprehension and recall of science texts improved over the course of the program. For children who attended regularly, this is exactly what happened ($p < .05$). There was a substantial

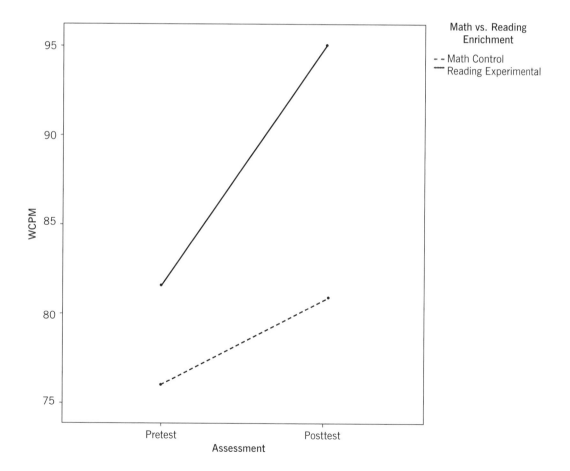

FIGURE 10.2. Improvements in reading fluency as a function of the PAL reading enrichment program in the first year.

24% improvement in their ability to answer questions about the texts they had read during the week (Dooly, 2015). Thus, we feel that the strategies we used we had moved children toward the goals we had set out for the program.

The Second Year

Our goal in the second year was to determine whether providing a social-studies literacy intervention improved children's reading of social studies texts. Research has shown that children and adults generally read informational texts less fluently than narratives (Barth, Tolar, Fletcher, & Francis, 2014). Thus, it was necessary to establish that the interventions had the effect of improving children's oral reading fluency for those types of texts.

The assessment used to track improvement during the second year of our program was a grade-level social studies passage selected from the *Developmental Literacy Inventory* (DLI; Temple, Crawford, & Gillet, 2009). The DLI is a tool educators can use to informally assess oral reading fluency, comprehension, and word recognition using narrative and informational (science or social studies) text passages. Because informational text was the focus of this intervention, we were particularly interested in effecting changes in children's ability to fluently read this material.

Children were initially tested in the beginning of September and then once again at the end of the intervention. The recordings of the reading were used to determine the WCPM as a measure of fluency. First, we wanted to ensure that there was no a priori difference between the reading-intervention and math-control children in terms of the overall number of days that they attended (i.e., see the discussion on dosage in Chapter 3). In fact, the mean number of days, 51, children attended was the same for both groups. We performed a 2 time (September, December) intervention (reading, mathematics) analysis of variance to determine whether growth in reading fluency was larger for the intervention group over this time period compared to the control group. Indeed, we found this statistically significant effect ($p < .05$). Thus, because of the intensive focus on fluency, children who received the intervention were able to read social studies texts with greater fluency than before and made more progress in fluency than children who did not receive the intervention. Improved fluency resulting from reading enrichment after 2 years can be seen in Figure 10.3.

Although we used different assessments each year of the program, we note that both assessments contained grade-level passages that had been carefully vetted and deemed suitable for use in determining children's oral reading fluency as measured by WCPM. We think that this type of assessment is the most basic measure of reading fluency, although other skills such as changes in reading expression and reading accuracy can also be evaluated. In Box 10.1, we provide suggestions for how to select texts to use in evaluations, how to administer the assessment, how to score children's oral reading, and finally how to determine how well children are reading compared to national averages, using the Hasbrouck and Tindal (2006) reading fluency norms.

To summarize, our statistical analyses showed that, regardless of whether we used science or social studies texts, our program appeared to enhance the reading fluency of children. This improvement was accomplished by having an intensive focus on fluency for informational text in the ASP for only half the school year.

As noted in Chapter 3 on process evaluation, staff members' adherence to the program as designed makes a big difference. Fidelity should be evaluated as part of determining whether a program was or was not successful. To ascertain that the

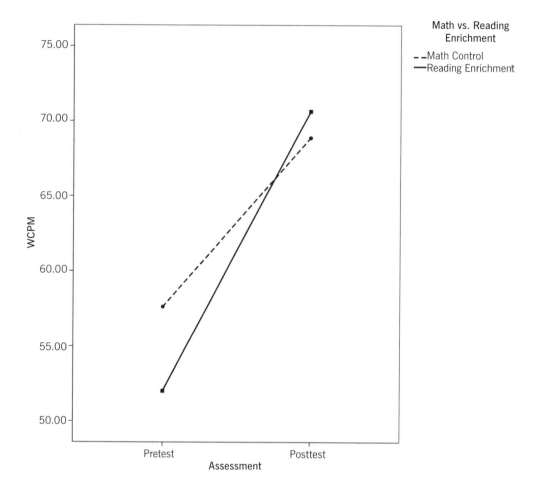

FIGURE 10.3. Improvements in reading fluency as a function of the PAL reading enrichment program in the second year.

BOX 10.1.　HOW TO MEASURE BASIC READING FLUENCY

Select text passage and materials to use in the assessment:

1. Decide whether you wish to assess general fluency or genre-specific fluency.
2. Select a carefully vetted grade-level text that matches your goals.
    a. Examples of general fluency assessments include Dynamic Indicators of Basic Early Literacy Skills (DIBELS-ORF), AIMSweb Oral Reading Fluency (R-CBM), Gray Oral Reading Test (GORT-5), among others.
    b. Genre-specific fluency: Passages available from Developmental Literacy Inventory, Qualitative Reading Inventory, among others.
3. Materials needed include a basic recording device, child assessment copy, tester assessment copy, pencil, and timer.

Instructions:

1. Instruct the student to read the text aloud with comprehension (or use instructions from your assessment package).
2. Start recorder and timer (or simply determine the time later). Mark the following as errors (or mark the errors described in the manual of your assessment package):
    a. **Inserting** a word
    b. **Omitting** a word
    c. **Reversing** words (switching the order of two words)
    d. **Skipping** a line (and student should be directed back to read the line)
    e. **Mispronunciation** counts each time the word is mispronounced, **except in the case of proper nouns**—if a student consistently uses the same wrong pronunciation of a proper noun, it only counts as a single error.
    f. **Pausing** for more than 3 seconds. Then say, "Skip it" and do not provide the word.

Determine basic reading fluency:

If the student reads for less than or longer than 1 minute, simply subtract the number of errors from the number of words read, then divide that number by the number of seconds the child read. Multiply by 60. The result is WCPM.

Example: 75 words read – 3 errors = 72 correct words

72 words correct / 42 seconds = 1.714

1.714 × 60 = **103 WCPM**

Alternative: Count the number of words read in the first minute of reading only and subtract errors.

To determine how fundamentally fluent each child is compared to his or her peers, compare the child's WCPM for that child's grade and time of year (see Hasbrouck & Tindal, 2006).

weekly plan was being followed for this reading enrichment program, the program director (P. J. S.) observed each instructor in the classroom approximately once per month and discussed the instructor's plan for that week. The Reading Enrichment Observational Checklist that was used during the observation can be found in Figure 10.4. The instructors of this program rigorously followed the weekly plan shown in Figure 10.1, which might not be found in every after-school setting. In every case, the instructors displayed complete adherence (100%) to the basic elements of the Wide FORI weekly plan.

Conclusion

We feel that the reading enrichment program that we developed for the ASP was an effective way of improving children's reading skills. We recognize that the general improvement of students' reading fluency was likely not solely attributable to the reading enrichment program itself. Naturally, the children are actively receiving literacy instruction during the school day as well. The improvements shown for the control children in Figures 10.2 and 10.3 indicate that the instruction that took place during the school day was successful, too. However, our findings suggest that even children who attend schools with effective teaching practices can experience additional benefits from a reading enrichment program like the one we have implemented. The fact that we were able to observe accelerated improvement over the period assessed means that children's attendance in this reading-enrichment program likely had a positive value-added impact on their skills.

The PAL Program reading-enrichment curriculum is the first of its kind that we know of that directly incorporates an informational text focus within a Wide FORI program. It is also the first in an after-school setting and the first to work with children beyond second grade. The practices used in the Wide FORI program appear to be general enough to positively affect the reading skills of struggling elementary school children. In fairness, we should also point out that program merely ameliorated our students' fluency issues and that they will need to continue to improve their fluency further to catch up to their peers.

Over time, as children become more fundamentally fluent, instructors may decide to modify the fluency practices used in the program. They may wish to dispense with the more basic and highly scaffolded fluency practices, such as teacher read-aloud and echo reading as children become more fluent, and emphasize choral and partner reading instead. Eventually, attention might be given to transitioning children to silent reading practice. This type of transition will likely entail an additional set of instructional practices, which are beyond the scope of the current chapter.

Nevertheless, all students within our program, regardless of the reason for

❑ Instructor has weekly plan that includes two to three related grade-level texts (or segments of larger text if text is long). List texts:

❑ Instructor has weekly plan that relates to a topic or essential question. List topic or essential question:

❑ Weekly plan includes one enrichment activity related to topic. List enrichment activity:

❑ Instructor has used at least one of the core fluency-oriented practices during the hour. Check all that were seen:
  ❑ Teacher read-aloud
  ❑ Echo reading
  ❑ Choral reading
  ❑ Partner reading

❑ Instructor spent a minimum of 15 minutes on fluency-oriented practices.

❑ Instructor has used *at least* one of the following comprehension-related practices during the hour. Check all that were seen:
  ❑ Instructor activated prior knowledge (provide examples):
  ❑ Instructor emphasized vocabulary words (note some words):
  ❑ Instructor pointed out meanings of word affixes (for older grades only). List affixes:

❑ Instructor identified informational text comprehension features such as subgenre, key words; cause–effect; timeline; map; compare-contrast. List informational text feature:

❑ Instructor engaged in critical literacy or disciplinary literacy strategy. List informational text strategies:

❑ Instructor asked comprehension questions at various levels of abstractness (concrete, abstract, relate) or had children ask their own questions. List some questions:

FIGURE 10.4. Reading Enrichment Observation Checklist.

which they were admitted, were able to spend an additional hour each day receiving explicit instruction on the content and structure of informational texts while participating in fluency activities. We were able to successfully provide an important literacy support for improving literacy skills of some our schools' most struggling young readers.

GLOSSARY

Cause–effect structure—A structure found in informational texts in which causal relationships between ideas are discussed.

Compare–contrast structure—A structure found in informational texts in which the authors discuss similarities and differences between subjects.

Description structure—A structure found in informational texts in which a number of details are provided about a single subject.

Fourth-grade slump—Hypothetical slump in reading achievement that occurs in fourth grade as a function of the switch to more difficult reading materials, particularly informational texts.

Problem–solution structure—A structure found in informational texts in which authors may discuss a particular issue before providing information regarding the manner in which the problem or problems are resolved.

Sequence structure—A structure found in informational texts wherein text content is organized in a manner in which order is salient to understanding.

Wide reading—An instructional strategy that focuses on reading a great number and variety of texts (i.e., stories, informational texts, poetry, plays) to improve skills.

References

AIMSweb Technical Manual. (2012). Bloomington, MN: NCS Pearson. Available at *www.aimsweb.com/wp-content/uploads/aimsweb-Technical-Manual.pdf.*

Barth, A. E., Tolar, T. D., Fletcher, J. M., & Francis, D. (2014). The effects of student and text characteristics on the oral reading fluency of middle-grade students. *Journal of Educational Psychology, 106*(1), 162.

Chall, J. S., & Jacobs, V. A. (1983). Writing and reading in the elementary grades: Developmental trends among low-SES children. *Language Arts, 60*(5), 617–626.

Chall, J. S., Jacobs, V. A., & Baldwin, L. E. (1990). *The reading crisis: Why poor children fall behind.* Cambridge, MA: Harvard University Press.

Common Core State Standards Initiative. (2016). *Common Core State Standards for English language arts and literacy in history/social studies, science, and technical subjects.* Washington, DC: National Governors Association for Best Practices and Council of Chief State School Officers. Retrieved October, 26, 2016, from *www.corestandards.org/wp-content/uploads/ELA_Standards1.pdf.*

Dooly, J. T. (2015). *An after-school program to improve science literacy among elementary school children*. Poster presented to Center for Undergraduate Research Opportunities Symposium, University of Georgia, Athens, GA.

Duke, N. K. (2000). 3.6 minutes per day: The scarcity of informational texts in first grade. *Reading Research Quarterly, 35*(2), 202–224.

Hall, K. M., Sabey, B. L., & McClellan, M. (2005). Expository text comprehension: Helping primary-grade teachers use expository texts to full advantage. *Reading Psychology, 26*(3), 211–234.

Halvorsen, A. L., Duke, N. K., Brugar, K. A., Block, M. K., Strachan, S. L., Berka, M. B., & Brown, J. M. (2012). Narrowing the achievement gap in second-grade social studies and content area literacy: The promise of a project-based approach. *Theory and Research in Social Education, 40*(3), 198–229.

Hamilton, C. E., & Schwanenflugel, P. J. (2011). *PAVEd for Success: Building vocabulary and language development in young learners*. Baltimore: Brookes.

Hasbrouck, J., & Tindal, G. A. (2006) Oral reading fluency norms: A valuable assessment tool for reading teachers. *The Reading Teacher, 59*(7), 636–644.

Hoffman, J. L., Collins, M. F., & Schickedanz, J. A. (2015). Instructional challenges in developing young children's science concepts. *The Reading Teacher, 68*(5), 363–372.

Kuhn, M. R. (2005). A comparative study of small group fluency instruction. *Reading Psychology, 26*(2), 127–146.

Kuhn, M., Rasinski, T., & Zimmerman, B. (2014). Integrated fluency instruction: Three approaches for working with struggling readers. *International Electronic Journal of Elementary Education, 7*(1), 71.

Kuhn, M. R., Schwanenflugel, P. J., Morris, R. D., Morrow, L. M., Bradley, B. A., Meisinger, E., . . . Stahl, S. A. (2006). Teaching children to become fluent and automatic readers. *Journal of Literacy Research, 38*, 357–387.

Meyer, B. J., & Poon, L. W. (2001). Effects of structure strategy training and signaling on recall of text. *Journal of Educational Psychology, 93*(1), 141.

Price, L. H., Bradley, B. A., & Smith, J. M. (2012). A comparison of preschool teachers' talk during storybook and information book read-alouds. *Early Childhood Research Quarterly, 27*(3), 426–440.

Rasinski, T. V. (2012). Why reading fluency should be hot! *The Reading Teacher, 65*(8), 516–522.

Rasinski, T. (2014). Fluency matters. *International Electronic Journal of Elementary Education, 7*(1), 3–12.

Rasinski, T. V., Rupley, W. H., Paige, D. D., & Nichols, W. D. (2016). Alternative text types to improve reading fluency for competent to struggling readers. *International Journal of Instruction, 9*(1), 163–178.

Schwanenflugel, P. J., & Kuhn, M. R. (2016). Reading fluency. In P. Afflerbach (Ed.), *Handbook of individual differences in reading: Reader, text, and context* (pp. 107–119). New York: Routledge.

Schwanenflugel, P. J., Kuhn, M. R., Morris, R. D., Morrow, L. M., Meisinger, E. B., Woo, D. G., & Quirk, M. (2009). Insights into fluency instruction: Short- and long-term effects of two reading programs. *Literacy Research and Instruction, 48*, 318–336.

Temple, C. A., Crawford, A. N., & Gillet, J. W. (2009). *Developmental Literacy Inventory*. Boston: Pearson.

Vitale, M. R., & Romance, N. R. (2011). Adaptation of a knowledge-based instructional intervention to accelerate student learning in science and early literacy in grades 1 and 2. *Journal of Curriculum and Instruction, 5*(2), 79–93.

White, T. G., Sowell, J., & Yanagihara, A. (1989). Teaching elementary students to use word-part clues. *The Reading Teacher, 42*(4), 302–308.

Williams, J. P., Nubla-Kung, A. M., Pollini, S., Stafford, K. B., Garcia, A., & Snyder, A. E. (2007). Teaching cause—effect text structure through social studies content to at-risk second graders. *Journal of Learning Disabilities, 40*(2), 111–120.

Zucker, T. A., Justice, L. M., Piasta, S. B., & Kaderavek, J. N. (2010). Preschool teachers' literal and inferential questions and children's responses during whole-class shared reading. *Early Childhood Research Quarterly, 25*(1), 65–83.

Appendix 10.1. Reading Enrichment Lesson Plan Example

<table>
<tr>
<td colspan="2" align="center">Theme: Food Week
Day 1
 Book: Food
Vocabulary: carnivorous, vegetation, omnivores, regurgitated </td>
</tr>
<tr>
<td>Comprehension Activity</td>
<td>Activate Prior Knowledge
"Have you learned about nutrition in school? What did you learn during those lessons?"

Questions to ask throughout the book and/or after reading:
"Can you compare and contrast omnivores, herbivores, and carnivores?"<br>"Which of these are considered humans?"<br>"What are some ways we process food to preserve it?"<br>"If the tide is red in California, is shellfish safe to eat? Why or why not?"<br>"Why does drying or freezing food help preserve it?"</td>
</tr>
<tr>
<td>Fluency Activities</td>
<td>Teacher Read-Aloud
During this time, the book is read aloud by the teacher while students follow along silently in their own text. Throughout this reading, the teacher also introduces preselected vocabulary.

Echo Reading
The teacher reads two to three sentences from the text aloud before asking the students to read, or echo, the same passage of text aloud with the teacher. The teacher's voice models the volume and pace in which the text should be read aloud by students.</td>
</tr>
<tr>
<td>Comprehension Activity</td>
<td>Vocabulary
carnivorous, vegetation, omnivores, regurgitated
Have students find definitions in the glossary to volunteer to read aloud for the class.

Affix(es) to Emphasize
Re- means to return, to cycle, to recover, to do again
Give additional examples to students, such as recycle and repopulate.

Word Hunt
Students have the opportunity to share words that they are unfamiliar with or do not know.</td>
</tr>
<tr>
<td colspan="2" align="center">Theme: Food Week
Day 2
 Book: Food
Vocabulary: carnivorous, vegetation, omnivores, regurgitated </td>
</tr>
<tr>
<td>Fluency Activities</td>
<td>Choral Reading
The teachers and students read simultaneously at the same volume level and pace. The teacher's voice is slightly louder to act as a guiding tone. The teacher monitors for on-task behavior by perusing the room, leaning toward children to listen for oral reading, redirecting students who have lost their place, and removing disruptive children who need to read with the volunteer.</td>
</tr>
</table>

(continued)

Partner Reading	The teacher uses a preselected list of pairs of students who will read together. Each pair consists of students with higher and lower reading skills. The students alternate reading pages.
Partner Questioning	Once students have partner-read, they may "quiz" each other using the author-provided questions or questions the teacher provides.
	Once all partners have completed the activity, the teacher discusses the questions with the entire group to ensure comprehension and to clarify.
Comprehension Activity	**Discussion of Text Structure** Ask students if the text is a sequence, description, compare–contrast, problem–solution, or cause–effect text. Ask them to provide evidence from the text. *Note.* If students are unfamiliar with these terms, allot time when a new text structure is introduced for explicit instruction and provide additional examples. As students retain this knowledge, transition by querying the structure of the text, as above. **Vocabulary** Reemphasize the same vocabulary from first 2 days while the text is read together. **Affix(es) to Emphasize** Reemphasize same affixes from first 2 days. **Questions** Review comprehension questions from the day before to check for assessment of comprehension. To make this more exciting, the instructor may turn this into a game by dividing the class into two or more teams to have them work as small groups to answer questions.

Theme: Food Week
Day 3

Book: *Food Machines*
Vocabulary: *hydroponics, efficient, composition, experimental*

Comprehension Activity	**Activation of Prior Knowledge** "Flip through the book. Do you believe this book contains information that you have already learned about? For example, have you ever heard of the term *greenhouse effect*? If so, how might that term relate to food choice?"
Fluency Activities	**Echo Reading** The teacher reads two to three sentences from the text aloud before asking the students to read, or *echo*, the same passage of text aloud with the teacher. The teacher's voice models the volume and pace in which the text should be read aloud by students. **Choral Reading** The teachers and students read simultaneously at the same volume level and pace. The teacher's voice is slightly louder to act as a guiding tone. The teacher monitors for on-task behavior by perusing the room, leaning toward children to listen for oral reading, redirecting students who have lost their place, and removing disruptive children who need to read with the volunteer. If time permits, students partner-read.

(continued)

Comprehension Activity	**Discussion of Text Structure** Ask students if the text is a sequence, description, compare–contrast, problem–solution, or cause–effect text. Ask them to provide evidence in the text. *Note.* If students are unfamiliar with these terms, allot time when a new text structure is introduced for explicit instruction and provide additional examples. As students retain this knowledge, transition by querying the structure of the text, as above. **Vocabulary** Throughout the reading, emphasize the vocabulary words that are selected in the text. If the word contains an affix, explicitly address and explain the affix. *hydroponics, efficient, composition, experimental* Have students find definitions in the glossary to volunteer to read aloud for the class. **Affix(es) to Emphasize** *Hydro-* refers to water in some way. Provide additional examples, such as *hydrometer* or *hydroelectric*. **Questions after partner reading:** "How do greenhouses work?" "Can we apply what we learned earlier in the semester to what we are learning about now?" "Why is carbon dioxide an important gas?" "Can you describe one of the several types of greenhouses we've read about?" **Word Hunt** Students share words from the reading that they are unfamiliar with or do not know.

Theme: Food Week
Day 4

Book: *Food Machines*
Vocabulary: *hydroponics, efficient, composition, experimental*

Fluency Activities	**Choral Reading** The teachers and students read simultaneously at the same volume level and pace. The teacher's voice is slightly louder to act as a guiding tone. The teacher monitors for on-task behavior by perusing the room, leaning toward children to listen for oral reading, redirecting students who have lost their place, and removing disruptive children who need to read with the volunteer. **Partner Reading** The teacher uses preselected list of pairs of students who will read together. Each pair consists of students with higher and lower reading skills. The students alternate reading pages. **Partner Questioning** Once students have partner-read, the students may "quiz" each other using the author-provided questions or questions the teacher provides. Once all partners have completed the activity, the teacher discusses the questions as a group to ensure comprehension and to clarify.

(continued)

Comprehension Activity	**Vocabulary** Throughout the reading, emphasize the vocabulary words that are selected in the text. If the word contains an affix, explicitly address and explain the affix. *hydroponics, efficient, composition, experimental* **Affix(es) to Emphasize** *Hydro-* refers to water in some way. Provide additional examples such as *hydrometer* or *hydroelectric*. **Questions** Address questions from previous day. **Hands-On Activity** Engage in the Activity or Experiment. *Complete a food chain activity.* Step 1. Students go to the nearest playground with a notebook and pencil. Instruct students to write plants and animals that they see in 5–10 minutes. Return to the classroom. Step 2. Use the board to create a list of plants and animals observed. Step 3. Instructor and children jointly map a food chain similar to one provided in *Foods*.
	Theme: Food Week **Day 5** **Book:** *Healthy Food Choices*
Fluency Activities	**Choral Reading** The teachers and students read simultaneously at the same volume level and pace. The teacher's voice is slightly louder to act as a guiding tone. The teacher monitors for on-task behavior by perusing the room, leaning toward children to listen for oral reading, redirecting students who have lost their place, and removing disruptive children who need to read with the volunteer.
Comprehension Activity	**Vocabulary** Less emphasis is placed on vocabulary and text structure due to the limited time students have with the text. However, a quick definition can be provided for new vocabulary words as they are encountered in the text during the choral reading. Ideally, the final text for the week reinforces prior vocabulary and concepts, rather than introduces new ones. **PAL *Jeopardy!* Game** This game consists of questions about the vocabulary and concepts encountered while reading the three books related to the topic. The class is split into two teams. Each team chooses a representative to come to the front of the classroom to pick a question written on strips of paper and thrown into a hat or bowl. If the selected question is answered correctly, their team will earn the points the question is worth (indicated on the back of the question). This process is reiterated until all the children have had a turn.

Index

Note. *f, t,* or *b* following a page number indicates a figure, a table, or a box.